The
Kitchen
Diva's
Diabetic Cookbook

The Kitchen Diva's
Diabetic Cookbook

150 HEALTHY, DELICIOUS RECIPES FOR
DIABETICS AND THOSE WHO DINE WITH THEM

Angela Shelf Medearis

JACKIE MILLS, MS, RD,
NUTRITION CONSULTANT

PHOTOGRAPHY BY PENNY DE LOS SANTOS

**Andrews McMeel
Publishing, LLC**
Kansas City · Sydney · London

Andrews McMeel Publishing, LLC
an Andrews McMeel Universal company
1130 Walnut Street, Kansas City, Missouri 64106

www.andrewsmcmeel.com

12 13 14 15 16 WKT 10 9 8 7 6 5 4 3 2 1

ISBN: 978-1-4494-0239-6

Library of Congress Control Number: 2010937867

The information contained in this book is not intended to replace regular visits with your physician or to diagnose deficiencies in your diet. Before altering your diet you should always check with your physician about your specific needs. The information and recipes in this book are intended to benefit people with diabetes as part of a healthy diet in conjunction with a doctor's supervision. While every effort was made to assure that the information and recipes are nutritionally sound and balanced for diabetics, the author and publisher are not liable for any adverse effects you may experience.

www.divapro.com

Design: Diane Marsh
Photography: Penny De Los Santos
Food Stylist: Paige Fletcher
Prop Stylist: Laura McGuire
Assistant Food and Prop Stylist: Jo Ann Kugle
Art Director: Martha Hopkins

Contents

Acknowledgments
vi

Introduction
vii

CHAPTER 1: Flavor Infusions:
Dips, Dressings, Sauces, and Spice Mixes 1

CHAPTER 2: Jump-Start Your Day: Breakfast 15

CHAPTER 3: Midmorning Snacks and Afternoon Energizers 49

CHAPTER 4: Let's Do Lunch 71

CHAPTER 5: Delectable Dinners 113

CHAPTER 6: Sensational Side Dishes 189

CHAPTER 7: Sweet Finishes and Nighttime Nibbles 229

Photo Credits
264

Metric Conversions and Equivalents
265

Index
267

ACKNOWLEDGMENTS

Whenever I have the opportunity to write a cookbook, I always thank the Lord for giving me a passionate interest in all things culinary; for a gift for cooking; for Michael, my wonderful husband; and for my sweet family and friends. They fully and lovingly support my career and eat just about anything I dream up in the kitchen. Thank the Lord for all of you. I love you all dearly.

Thanks so much to Kirsty Melville and Jean Lucas at Andrews McMeel for their guidance and support of this project. I also want to thank Jackie Mills, MS, RD, for her insightful advice, her concise nutritional analysis, and for being such a joy to work with.

—Angela Shelf Medearis, 2011

Introduction

THE KITCHEN DIVA'S DIABETIC COOKBOOK was created because my husband, Michael, my mother, my father, my youngest sister, and many of my other family members and friends are diabetics. This is a user-friendly cookbook that addresses the health and dietary needs of prediabetics, juvenile diabetics, type 1 and type 2 diabetics, women with gestational diabetes related to pregnancy, those with diabetic-related complications, and anyone seeking to embrace a healthier diet and life-style. I'm not a diabetic, but my family medical history and challenges are a cautionary tale. I prepare meals that are suitable for my husband's needs as a type 2 diabetic and that also are satisfying for both of us. We also use these recipes when entertaining family and friends.

I've created a cookbook full of healthy, flavorful recipes, with a nutritional breakdown for each one. The information in this cookbook is designed to be inspirational for anyone with diabetes as well as for those who love and dine with them. I wanted to create a new collection of recipes based on comfort foods, but ones that incorporate healthy ingredients, spices, and cooking techniques designed to keep a diabetic's insulin levels in balance. A detailed nutritional and caloric analysis of each recipe was provided by Jackie Mills, MS, RD, to ensure that every recipe can be part of a healthful diet for anyone with diabetes.

The cookbook contains more than 150 easy-to-prepare, budget-friendly recipes that are great for diabetics and everyone else. These delicious recipes are specifically designed to meet the dietary needs of diabetics by providing flavorful low-sugar, low-sodium, lower-carb versions of traditional dishes and comfort foods. Each chapter includes fun, kid-friendly recipes, such as Peanut Butter Breakfast Bars, Barbecue Burgers, After-School Berry Smoothie, Crunchy Fish Sticks, and No-Bake Cookies, that will appeal to families while meeting the nutritional needs of children with diabetes.

The Kitchen Diva's Diabetic Cookbook was written to fill a void in the current collection of cookbooks for diabetics. This comprehensive guide not only addresses the lifestyle and dietary needs of those with various types of diabetes, it provides much-needed information as well as healthy, delicious recipes suitable for children, families, and entertaining.

The Kitchen Diva's Diabetic Cookbook provides diabetics with recipes that are specifically designed to:

- Help control the glucose levels in the blood

- Moderate portion size

- Assist with weight reduction or maintenance

- Assist parents to plan kid-friendly meals for children with diabetes

This cookbook is full of tips and information for selecting the best ingredients and stocking a healthy kitchen, along with time-saving techniques for getting healthy meals on the table faster. A variety of imaginative recipes for everything from flavor-enhancing herbal spice mixes to low-calorie sauces, and from hearty main courses to desserts that taste too decadent to be low in sugar and calories, fill the pages of this book, along with special recipes for holidays and celebrations.

I specialize in creating healthy, delicious versions of recipes for everything from ethnic and Southern dishes to traditional comfort foods. I love preparing inventive recipes that retain the intense flavors and luxurious textures of popular favorites while providing lower calorie counts, wholesome ingredients, and nutrients needed to maintain a healthy diet. The first step in this process is organizing your kitchen and pantry.

I've created a Healthy-Kitchen Guide to provide you with tips about how to create a healthy pantry, refrigerator, and freezer. There also are suggestions for budget-wise shopping strategies, ways to stretch your food dollars, and tips to turn your freezer into a "fast food" stop. I've also provided ways to teach your children healthy meal-planning skills.

The Healthy-Kitchen Guide

The following guide will help you create a healthy kitchen and pantry (as well as a healthy refrigerator and freezer). If you don't already have it, now is the time to invest in some basic kitchen equipment such as a good-quality 8- or 10-inch chef's knife, a large nonstick skillet, a large cast-iron pan, a large food processor, a blender, and a 3½- to 5-quart slow cooker.

The following lists will enable you to take advantage of sale foods and to stock foods in bulk for future use. Keeping the ingredients you need on hand enables you to easily create the recipes in this cookbook and maintain healthy eating habits.

This guide will help you stock your pantry or any other cool, dry place where you can store food items for a length of time, including kitchen cupboards, shelves, or a floor space in a closet. It also includes foods to keep on hand in your refrigerator and freezer.

Shopping for and selecting recipe ingredients wisely not only improves your health, it puts money in your pocket and saves preparation and cooking time in the kitchen. When shopping, keep the following tips in mind:

- Go through this cookbook and select the recipes you'd like to prepare for the week and create a meal plan. Check your pantry to see what ingredients you have on hand to avoid overspending or duplicating items.

- Make a list of the ingredients you'll need for each recipe and foods you're out of and need to purchase. Plan for a week's worth of menus—breakfast, lunch, and dinner, along with snacks.

- Plan for leftovers and use the variation suggestions in the cookbook. Add any additional foods to your list that you'll need to stretch one meal into two.

- If possible, let your children help with the meal planning, shopping, and cooking. Teaching them how to plan a meal, make a list, grocery shop, and cook healthy foods helps to ensure a lifetime of better food choices when they're adults. Assign them tasks while in the store (matching the coupon to the item on the shelf, selecting and weighing produce, etc.) to teach them about healthy choices and money.

- Check newspaper circulars, online coupons, and store coupons, and compare the discounted foods to the ingredients on your list. Note the foods that are on sale, and clip or print out coupons to save money. Attach the coupons to your grocery list so that you won't forget them.

- While shopping, check the unadvertised store specials and compare the unit pricing listed on the shelf under the items to make sure you're receiving the best price on your selected brand.

- Check store brands and compare them to name-brand products. Sometimes, store brands are comparable to name brands or even higher in quality, and the prices are lower.

- Use produce as soon after purchase as possible to benefit from the highest nutritional quality. Use frozen and canned vegetables and fruits at the end of the week.

- Prepare more than one meal at a time, especially if the meals have similar ingredients, such as chopped vegetables or meats that will be used in more than one recipe (for example, ground turkey or cooked chicken), or prepare and cook foods that bake at the same temperature at the same time.

- Put leftovers in single-serving containers for bag lunches or freeze them for quick microwave meals.

- Don't throw away leftovers; you're throwing away your money. Small amounts of leftover cooked meats and vegetables can be combined with low-sodium chicken, beef, or vegetable broth to make a soup or stew; to use as the base of a casserole; to wrap in a tortilla or pita bread to make a sandwich; or to serve with salad greens for lunch.

- Package and freeze leftovers in airtight microwave-safe containers to reheat and serve on busy nights.

Stocking the Healthy Kitchen

Keeping your kitchen stocked helps make budgeting and meal planning much easier. A well-stocked cool, dry space set aside for pantry foods enables you to have healthy ingredients on hand at all times. Arrange your pantry, refrigerator, and freezer purchases so that they can be used in order of purchase. The older purchased items should be close to the front or on the top, and the newer purchases in the back or on the bottom. The freezer also is part of a well-stocked kitchen, and the following lists include the foods to keep on hand there.

STOCKING THE PANTRY

Applesauce, unsweetened

Baking powder

Baking soda

Beans, canned low-sodium and dried: Black beans, black-eyed peas, cannellini beans, chickpeas (garbanzos), edamame, green beans, lentils, Mexican-style chili beans, navy or Great Northern beans, pinto beans, red kidney beans

Bread, sliced, whole-wheat

Bread crumbs: Whole-wheat panko (Japanese bread crumbs)

Croutons: Fat-free, whole-wheat (dry)

English muffins, whole-wheat

Pita breads, whole-wheat

Broth or bouillon: Low-sodium chicken, beef, and vegetable

Capers packed in brine

Cereal, dry: High-fiber, granola, wheat flakes

Chocolate, semisweet and dark: Chips, bars

Cocoa: Unsweetened powder, sugar-free mix

Coconut: Unsweetened, sweetened

Coffee: Instant, espresso coffee, coffee beans/ground coffee

Cookies: Reduced-fat vanilla wafers

Corn, canned: Whole-kernel and low-sodium

Cornmeal, yellow

Cornstarch

Crackers: Whole-grain, whole-grain goldfish, whole-grain melba toast

Cream of tartar

Flour: All-purpose white and whole-wheat, whole-wheat pastry flour

Fruit, canned in natural juices: Apples, cherries, peaches, pineapple

Fruit, dried: Apricots, blueberries, cherries, cranberries, figs, mixed fruit bits, prunes, raisins

Fruit juice: Apple, lemon, lime, orange, orange-pineapple

Graham crackers: Whole and crumbs

Grains: bulgur, whole-wheat couscous, quinoa

Green chiles, canned diced

Honey, raw

Lentils, dried

Liquid Smoke

Microwave low-fat popcorn

Milk: Dry, low-fat evaporated, skim, 1 percent low-fat

Nonstick spray coating, plain, olive, butter-flavored

Nuts, dry-roasted: Almonds, pecans, walnuts

Oats: Quick-cooking, old-fashioned

Oils: Canola, olive, vegetable, sesame, virgin coconut

Olives: Green, kalamata, black

Pasta, whole-wheat: Angel hair, buckwheat (soba), elbow, fettuccine, macaroni, spaghetti, tortellini, no-cook lasagna noodles

Peanut butter, no-sugar-added

Pickles: Dill, okra, Italian mixed vegetables

Pumpkin purée, canned

Rice: Brown, instant brown, wild

Salmon, canned, water-packed, or vacuum-packed

Salsa

Sardines, canned

Seeds, raw or roasted: Pumpkin (pepitas), sunflower

Soy nuts, dry-roasted

Spaghetti sauce, low-sodium organic

Split peas

Sugar: confectioners', stevia, Splenda no-calorie sweetener granulated, Splenda brown sugar blend

Sweet potato purée, canned

Syrup: Agave (plain, maple-flavored, honey-flavored)

Tea: Green, oolong peach

Tomatoes, canned low-sodium: Italian, diced with chiles and onions, diced fire-roasted

Tomato sauce, paste, marinara sauce

Tortilla: Corn, whole-wheat flour

Tortilla chips, baked

Tuna: Water-packed canned

Vinegar: Balsamic, no-sugar-added apple cider, distilled white, red wine, rice wine, white wine

Wheat germ, toasted

Worcestershire sauce

Yeast, active dry

Condiments

Barbecue sauce, low-sugar

Hot sauce

Ketchup, low-sugar

Mayonnaise, low-fat

Mustard (Dijon, stone-ground)

Pico de gallo

Salad dressing, light: Italian, peppercorn, ranch

Salsa

Soy sauce/tamari, low-sodium

Teriyaki sauce, low-sodium

Meat

Bacon or bacon bits

Beef: Lean ground, roast, lean stew, flank

Chicken: Whole, skinless breasts, parts, ground

Deli meats: Reduced-sodium sliced chicken, ham,
roast beef, turkey

Fish: Catfish, cod, haddock, salmon, tilapia, trout

Pork: Chops, loin roast, lean ground

Sausage: Chicken, turkey

Shellfish: Imitation crabmeat (surimi)

Turkey: Parts, ground breast meat, smoked parts

STOCKING THE REFRIGERATOR

Be sure to keep your refrigerator at 40°F or below, and check the temperature frequently with a refrigerator/ freezer thermometer.

Butter, whipped

Cheese, low-fat: American slices, blue, cream (Neufchâtel),
cottage, feta, shredded (Asiago, cheddar, Mexican
blend, Monterey, mozzarella, Parmesan), string

Eggs

Milk: Low-fat, buttermilk, plain soy milk, vanilla soy milk

Seeds: Poppy, sesame

Sour cream, low-fat

Tofu: Silken soft and firm

Yogurt, low-fat and nonfat: Plain, Greek

Fruits and Vegetables

Fresh fruits and vegetables are cheaper during their seasons, so be sure to take advantage of any lower prices. You can buy fresh fruit and produce in bulk and prepare and freeze them for later use. Apples should be kept unwashed until used in a plastic bag in the coldest part of the refrigerator away from broccoli, cabbage, cucumbers, greens, or cauliflower, as apples give off ethylene gas, and will cause the vegetables to ripen faster. Apples also can be stored in the pantry in a cool, dark place away from onions or garlic, as they absorb odors. Keep garlic, onions, and potatoes (white and sweet) on hand in a cool, dark place in the pantry. Onions and garlic are used in many main dishes, and a potato can be a meal in itself.

Herbs add freshness, flavor, and nutrients to your recipes. Using fresh, locally grown herbs that have been placed in a glass of water in the refrigerator, and produce are the best ways to create a healthy meal.

Apples: Gala, Fuji, Granny Smith, Jonagold, Mutsu, Rome, Winesap, York

Artichokes

Asparagus

Bananas

Bell peppers

Berries: Blueberries, blackberries, raspberries, strawberries

Broccoli

Brussels sprouts

Cabbage: napa, green

Carrots

Celery

Cherries

Chiles: Jalapeño, serrano, Scotch bonnet

Corn

Eggplants

Garlic

Ginger, fresh

Greens: Collards, mustard, kale

Fresh Herbs: Basil, cilantro, mint, parsley, rosemary, sage, thyme

Kohlrabi

Lemons

Limes

Mushrooms: Button, chanterelle, cremini, portobello, shiitake

Okra

Pantry: Onions: Green, red, Spanish, Vidalia, yellow

Pears: Anjou, Bartlett, Bosc, Comice

Peppers, bell

Pantry: Potatoes: Red, russet, Yukon Gold, sweet

Radicchio

Salad mix and lettuces

Spinach, baby

Sugar snap peas

Sunchokes (Jerusalem artichokes)

Tangerines

Tomatillos

Tomatoes

Turnips

Watermelon

Zucchini

SPICE IT UP!

The best way to reduce fat and salt without sacrificing flavor is to add herbs and spices to your recipes. Store dried herbs and spices in airtight containers in a cool, dry place for no longer than six months. Use the spice-mix recipes in this book (pages 13 and 14) for convenience.

When using spices and herbs, don't shake the container directly into the pot, as the heat and humidity may cause clumping in the container and affect the flavor. Use a measuring spoon or pour the desired amount into your hand or into a bowl, and then add it to the pot. Place whole spices in a tea ball or tie them in a piece of cheesecloth before placing them in the pot to make them easier to remove. Add whole spices to the pot at the beginning of cooking to allow more time for the flavor of the spice to release.

You can "refresh" ground spices by adding them to a dry pan and stirring them over medium-high heat. For slow-cooked recipes, add ground spices and/or fresh herbs to the pot close to the end of cooking to help them retain the most flavor.

If you're adding spices or herbs to a dish that doesn't require cooking, allow the dish to stand for a couple hours before serving so the flavors can mingle and intensify.

Allspice: Whole, ground

Basil, dried

Bay leaves

Cayenne pepper

Chile powder: Ancho, Mexican

Chili powder

Cinnamon: Ground, sticks

Cloves, ground

Coriander, ground

Cream of tartar

Cumin, ground

Curry powder

Garlic powder

Ginger, ground

Italian seasoning

Lemon pepper, no-salt-added

Liquid Smoke

Mustard, dry

Nutmeg: Ground, whole

Onion powder

Oregano

Paprika: Smoked, hot, sweet

Pepper: Black peppercorns, lemon pepper

Poultry seasoning

Red pepper flakes

Rosemary, dried

Sage, dried

Salt: Sea, kosher

Thyme, dried

Vanilla extract

STOCKING THE FREEZER

Prep and freeze sale foods, and cook double portions of your families' favorite dishes and freeze the extra; freeze leftovers, too. Freezing meals turns your freezer into a "fast food" stop for busy days.

Frozen foods should be thawed only in the refrigerator, in cold water, or in the microwave. Don't thaw foods on the counter or in hot water. Even if the center of the package is still frozen as it thaws on the counter, the outer layer of the food could be in the danger zone between 40° and 140°F, the range in which bacteria multiply rapidly.

Stocking your freezer with the foods listed below ensures that you'll have the nutritious ingredients used in these recipes on hand when you need to prepare food fast.

Asparagus

Broccoli, chopped

Carrots

Cauliflower

Edamame

Fruit: Berries, peaches, mixed fruit

Greens, chopped: Collards, kale, mustard

Ice cream, low-fat

Nuts, whole, raw: Almonds, pecans, walnuts

Okra, unbreaded

Peas

Seafood: Salmon, snapper, tilapia, trout (individually frozen fillets), shrimp (peeled and deveined)

Vegetables: Stir-fry, stewing

Waffles: Belgian, whole-wheat

Whipped topping, low-fat, sugar-free

Nutritional Information

In each chapter, I've provided a wealth of information to assist those who desire to take charge of their health by changing their attitudes, diets, and lifestyles.

Jackie Mills, MS, RD, calculated the nutritional content for these recipes using the most up-to-date analysis software available. To help you plan healthful meals that fit your specific dietary needs, each recipe lists the following information: calories, calories from fat, total fat, saturated fat, cholesterol, sodium, total carbohydrate, fiber, total sugars, and protein.

Carbohydrate choices and exchange list values also are provided to make it easy to plan diabetes-friendly meals. Because fiber is not completely digested, for dishes with more than 5 grams of fiber per serving, half of the fiber is subtracted from the total carbohydrate in the dish before calculating the carbohydrate choices.

If an ingredient is optional, it is not included in the analysis. If there are two options for an ingredient, the first option is the one used for the analysis. All measurements are rounded to the nearest whole number.

The values given for each recipe are as accurate as possible, but be aware that different brands of food products contain varying amounts of carbohydrate, sodium, fats, and calories. Read labels carefully and select only those foods that fit into your prescribed meal plan.

Happy and healthy eating!

Flavor Infusions:
Dips, Dressings, Sauces, and Spice Mixes

THERE'S NO REASON WHY YOU can't prepare and eat a dish that's both healthful and delicious, especially if you use the proper seasonings. One of the best ways to create wonderful dishes is to season them with herbs and spices. These flavor makers can elevate the most inexpensive ingredients to four-star dining quality.

This chapter was designed to provide you with spice and herb combinations that will transform even the most familiar dishes in this cookbook. It also includes recipes for well-loved dips, dressings, and sauces, as well as diabetic-friendly versions of popular convenience foods.

Restaurant dishes are often prepared with large amounts of fat and salt, two ingredients that add flavor, but which also add calories and high levels of sodium. I've used ethnic seasonings and cooking techniques to infuse the low-sodium and low-carb recipes in this book with unique and satisfying flavors.

I keep a shaker full of The Kitchen Diva's Seasoning Mix (page 13) handy in my kitchen to help boost the flavors of foods without having to take down numerous containers of spices. I also keep sauces such as Italian Garlic and Herb Salad Dressing (page 10) and Parsley–Walnut Pesto (page 3) on hand to flavor baked, broiled, or sautéed chicken, fish, turkey, pork, and lamb.

Having a ready-made dip such as Hot From-Texas Hummus (page 8) or Three-Cheese Dip (page 6) in your fridge and Spicy Pita Chips (page 5) in your pantry ensures that you'll have healthy snacks on hand at all times.

While a diabetes diagnosis may change the way you eat, it shouldn't impact the pure pleasure of a deliciously prepared meal. These spice-infused recipes allow you to add flavor to your food in a healthy, satisfying, and delicious way.

PARSLEY–WALNUT PESTO   3

SPICY PITA CHIPS   5

THREE-CHEESE DIP AND VARIATION:
    CHILI–CHEESE DIP   6, 7

HOT FROM-TEXAS HUMMUS   8

BLUE CHEESE DRESSING   9

ITALIAN GARLIC AND HERB SALAD DRESSING   10

SPICY VINAIGRETTE   11

KICKIN' BARBECUE SAUCE   12

THE KITCHEN DIVA'S SEASONING MIX   13

NO-SALT SPICE MIX   14

Parsley–Walnut Pesto

MAKES ¾ CUP

After filming a cooking show, I had an abundance of flat-leaf parsley left over, so I made a pesto using parsley in place of basil, and walnuts in place of pine nuts. When I researched the herb, I found that parsley was a good source of vitamins A, C, and K, as well as containing some iron and folate. This nutty, flavorful sauce can be used as a topping for fish, lamb, turkey, or chicken.

¾	cup chopped walnuts
2	slices whole-wheat bread, crusts trimmed
1	bunch, stemmed, fresh flat-leaf parsley
2	cloves garlic
½	cup grated Parmesan cheese
2	tablespoons nonfat plain yogurt
3	tablespoons extra-virgin olive oil
2	teaspoons grated lemon zest
2	tablespoons fresh lemon juice
½	teaspoon salt
1	teaspoon freshly ground black pepper

Toast the walnuts in a small, dry skillet over medium heat, stirring, until fragrant, 3 to 4 minutes. Transfer to a plate to cool.

Tear the bread into large pieces and pulse in a food processor to form fine crumbs. Add the parsley, garlic, cheese, and walnuts and pulse until finely chopped, scraping down the sides as needed. Combine the yogurt, oil, lemon zest, lemon juice, salt, and pepper in a small bowl. Add the oil mixture to the parsley mixture in a slow stream, pulsing to combine. Serve immediately or freeze.

To freeze the pesto, divide it into the preferred serving sizes and place it in small resealable plastic bags or plastic containers with airtight lids. Press excess air out of the plastic bags, if using, and freeze for up to 3 months.

NOTE: Wash fresh parsley right before using, since it is highly fragile. Put it in a bowl of cold water and swish it around with your hands, then place it on paper towels to dry.

SERVING SIZE: 1 tablespoon	**TOTAL FAT:** 9 g	**FIBER:** 1 g
EXCHANGE LIST VALUES: 2 fat	**SATURATED FAT:** 2 g	**TOTAL SUGARS:** 1 g
CARBOHYDRATE CHOICES: 0	**CHOLESTEROL:** 3 mg	**PROTEIN:** 3 g
CALORIES: 114	**SODIUM:** 176 mg	
CALORIES FROM FAT: 85	**TOTAL CARBOHYDRATE:** 5 g	

With Parsley–Walnut Pesto, page 3

Spicy Pita Chips

MAKES 24 CHIPS

I love the spice and texture of these whole-wheat pita chips alone or with one of the dips in this chapter. Making them at home is easy, and it saves money, and allows you to control the ingredients.

3   whole-wheat pita breads,
    each cut into 8 triangles

    Olive oil cooking spray

1   teaspoon chili powder

1   teaspoon ground cumin

1   teaspoon ground cinnamon

½   teaspoon ground coriander

½   teaspoon garlic powder

¼   teaspoon cayenne pepper

¼   teaspoon freshly ground black pepper

⅛   teaspoon salt

Preheat the oven to 350°F. Spread the pita triangles on a baking sheet and spray on both sides with cooking oil spray. Combine all the remaining ingredients in a large bowl and stir well to blend. Add the pita wedges and toss to coat. Spread the seasoned chips in a single layer on the baking sheet and sprinkle with any remaining spice mix.

Bake for about 15 minutes, tossing once, or until the chips are brown and crisp. Cool completely before serving. Store in an airtight container for up to 2 weeks.

SERVING SIZE: 4 pita chips
EXCHANGE LIST VALUES: 1 starch
CARBOHYDRATE CHOICES: 1
CALORIES: 94
CALORIES FROM FAT: 13

TOTAL FAT: 1 g
SATURATED FAT: 0 g
CHOLESTEROL: 0 mg
SODIUM: 220 mg
TOTAL CARBOHYDRATE: 18 g

FIBER: 3 g
TOTAL SUGARS: 0 g
PROTEIN: 3 g

Three-Cheese Dip

MAKES 4 CUPS

This dip is delicious with Spicy Pita Chips (page 5) or plain baked tortilla chips. Using full-flavored or extra-sharp cheeses reduces the amount you need to give this dish a rich flavor.

2   teaspoons olive oil

1   medium yellow onion, chopped

2   cloves garlic, minced

1½   cups 1 percent low-fat milk

3   tablespoons cornstarch

¼   cup salsa

1   cup shredded low-fat pepper Jack cheese

½   cup shredded low-fat Monterey Jack cheese

½   cup shredded low-fat extra-sharp cheddar cheese

1   (10-ounce) can diced tomatoes with green chilies, drained, or 1¼ cups canned fire-roasted tomatoes, drained and chopped

2   tablespoons fresh lime juice

1   tablespoon chili powder

1   tablespoon ground cumin

⅛   teaspoon cayenne pepper

¼   cup sliced green onions, including green parts

2   tablespoons chopped fresh cilantro

In a large microwaveable bowl, mix together the olive oil, onion, and garlic and cook on high, stirring, until soft, 2 to 3 minutes. Add 1 cup of the milk and cook on low (or defrost setting) until the milk begins to simmer, about 2 minutes.

Meanwhile, whisk together the remaining ½ cup of milk and the cornstarch in a small bowl. Add the cornstarch slurry to the onion mixture and cook on high for 2 minutes. Stir and cook for another 1 to 2 minutes, or until bubbling and thickened. Add the salsa and three cheeses and cook on low (or defrost setting) for 2 minutes. Stir and cook for another 1 to 2 minutes, or until melted. Stir in the tomatoes, lime juice, chili powder, cumin, and cayenne. Serve warm, garnished with the green onions and cilantro.

SERVING SIZE: ½ cup
EXCHANGE LIST VALUES:
    ½ carbohydrate, 1 medium-fat meat
CARBOHYDRATE CHOICES: ½
CALORIES: 135
CALORIES FROM FAT: 63

TOTAL FAT: 7 g
SATURATED FAT: 3 g
CHOLESTEROL: 20 mg
SODIUM: 301 mg
TOTAL CARBOHYDRATE: 10 g
FIBER: 1 g

TOTAL SUGARS: 4 g
PROTEIN: 9 g

Variation: Chili–Cheese Dip

Season 1 pound of lean ground beef or ground turkey with 1 teaspoon *each* of chili powder, ground cumin, and ¼ teaspoon cayenne pepper. Cook for 3 minutes in the microwave on low or defrost setting, then stir and mash to crumble. Cook for another 3 minutes, or until the meat is browned and cooked through. Drain off any juices and stir the meat into the dip.

SERVING SIZE: ½ cup	**CALORIES:** 206	**SODIUM:** 325 mg
EXCHANGE LIST VALUES:	**CALORIES FROM FAT:** 87	**TOTAL CARBOHYDRATE:** 10 g
½ carbohydrate, 2 medium-fat meat	**TOTAL FAT:** 10 g	**FIBER:** 1 g
CARBOHYDRATE CHOICES: ½	**SATURATED FAT:** 5 g	**TOTAL SUGARS:** 4 g
	CHOLESTEROL: 49 mg	**PROTEIN:** 20 g

Hot From-Texas Hummus

MAKES 3½ CUPS

The heat in chiles is due to a compound called capsaicin. Some studies have shown that capsaicin can lower cholesterol and help prevent arteriosclerosis. This hot and spicy hummus contains jalapeño chiles, a regular ingredient in the dishes we enjoy in my adopted state of Texas. I like serving this wonderful dip as a snack with Spicy Pita Chips (page 5) or as a spicy spread for sandwiches and wraps.

2   cloves garlic, smashed

1   large jalapeño chile, sliced

2   (15-ounce) cans low-sodium garbanzo beans, drained and rinsed

2   tablespoons no-sugar-added apple cider vinegar

½   teaspoon salt

½   cup olive oil

¾   cup packed fresh cilantro or parsley leaves

Process the garlic and jalapeño in a food processor or blender until minced. Add the beans, vinegar, and salt and purée until smooth. With the machine running, gradually add the olive oil in a steady stream. Process until the mixture is thick and smooth, 2 to 3 minutes. Add the cilantro or parsley and pulse until well combined, about 10 seconds.

Store in an airtight container in the refrigerator for up to 7 days. Bring to room temperature and stir to combine before serving.

SERVING SIZE: 2 tablespoons
EXCHANGE LIST VALUES: ½ fat
CARBOHYDRATE CHOICES: 0
CALORIES: 62
CALORIES FROM FAT: 39

TOTAL FAT: 4 g
SATURATED FAT: 1 g
CHOLESTEROL: 0 mg
SODIUM: 83 mg
TOTAL CARBOHYDRATE: 4 g

FIBER: 1 g
TOTAL SUGARS: 1 g
PROTEIN: 1 g

Blue Cheese Dressing

MAKES 1 CUP

Nonfat buttermilk adds richness to salad dressings and sauces. Buttermilk is a probiotic food, with health-promoting bacteria that may improve immune function. It's also a great source of calcium and protein. If you can't locate nonfat buttermilk in your local grocery store, you may want to buy it in powdered form or use ⅔ cup of nonfat plain yogurt in this recipe as a substitute. A small amount of blue cheese adds zest to this dressing while keeping it low in calories.

⅓   cup low-fat mayonnaise

⅓   cup nonfat buttermilk

⅓   cup nonfat plain yogurt

2   tablespoons no-sugar-added apple cider vinegar

1   tablespoon Dijon mustard

¼   teaspoon salt

½   teaspoon freshly ground black pepper

¼   cup crumbled blue cheese

Combine the mayonnaise, buttermilk, yogurt, vinegar, mustard, salt, and pepper in a medium bowl and whisk until smooth. Add the cheese and stir, mashing the cheese until incorporated. Cover and refrigerate for up to 1 week. Stir before using.

SERVING SIZE: 2 tablespoons
EXCHANGE LIST VALUES: ½ fat
CARBOHYDRATE CHOICES: 0
CALORIES: 59
CALORIES FROM FAT: 39

TOTAL FAT: 4 g
SATURATED FAT: 1 g
CHOLESTEROL: 7 mg
SODIUM: 267 mg
TOTAL CARBOHYDRATE: 3 g

FIBER: 0 g
TOTAL SUGARS: 2 g
PROTEIN: 2 g

Italian Garlic and Herb Salad Dressing

MAKES ¾ CUP

This flavorful dressing incorporates healthful low-calorie ingredients. You can use a blender, a food processor, or a glass jar with a tight-fitting lid to mix up the ingredients, but don't use an aluminum bowl, as the acid in the vinegar can react with the material, giving the dressing a metallic flavor.

2	unpeeled cloves garlic
½	cup no-sugar-added apple cider vinegar
2	tablespoons Italian seasoning
1½	teaspoons Dijon mustard
1	teaspoon agave syrup
½	teaspoon salt
1	teaspoon freshly ground black pepper
¼	cup extra-virgin olive oil

NOTE: All the ingredients should be at room temperature to make them easier to blend.

Heat a dry cast-iron or other heavy skillet over medium heat. Add the garlic and roast, turning occasionally with tongs, until blackened in spots and soft, about 10 minutes.

Squeeze the softened garlic clove out of the skin and combine it with the vinegar, Italian seasoning, mustard, syrup, salt, and pepper in a blender or food processor and process until smooth. With the machine running, gradually add the olive oil. Or, combine all the ingredients in a glass jar with a tight-fitting lid and shake until blended. Transfer to a glass jar with a tight-fitting lid if necessary and let the flavors meld at room temperature for 1 to 3 hours.

Store in the refrigerator for up to 3 weeks. Shake to blend before using.

SERVING SIZE: 1 tablespoon
EXCHANGE LIST VALUES: ½ fat
CARBOHYDRATE CHOICES: 0
CALORIES: 50
CALORIES FROM FAT: 42

TOTAL FAT: 5 g
SATURATED FAT: 1 g
CHOLESTEROL: 0 mg
SODIUM: 112 mg
TOTAL CARBOHYDRATE: 2 g

FIBER: 0 g
TOTAL SUGARS: 0 g
PROTEIN: 0 g

Spicy Vinaigrette

MAKES 2¼ CUPS

The chili powder and hot sauce add flavor and heat to this vinaigrette, and the capsaicin that makes these ingredients spicy is thought to lower cholesterol and help prevent arteriosclerosis. This also is a delicious low-fat marinade for turkey, chicken, or pork.

1¼   cups no-sugar-added apple cider vinegar

1½   tablespoons agave syrup or honey

2   cloves garlic

1   teaspoon chili powder

1   teaspoon hot sauce

1   teaspoon spicy brown mustard

1   teaspoon salt

1   teaspoon freshly ground black pepper

¾   cup extra-virgin olive oil

In a blender or food processor, blend the vinegar, syrup or honey, garlic, chili powder, hot sauce, mustard, salt, and pepper until smooth. With the machine running, gradually drizzle in the oil. Store in an airtight container in the refrigerator for up to 2 weeks. Shake to blend before using.

SERVING SIZE: 1 tablespoon
EXCHANGE LIST VALUES: ½ fat
CARBOHYDRATE CHOICES: 0
CALORIES: 49
CALORIES FROM FAT: 42

TOTAL FAT: 5 g
SATURATED FAT: 1 g
CHOLESTEROL: 0 mg
SODIUM: 69 mg
TOTAL CARBOHYDRATE: 2 g

FIBER: 0 g
TOTAL SUGARS: 1 g
PROTEIN: 0 g

Kickin' Barbecue Sauce

MAKES 3 CUPS

This recipe takes barbecue sauce to a new and healthier level by reducing the sugar and boosting the flavor. The salsa and the chiles provide spice without a lot of heat, and can be adjusted according to your preference.

3   cloves garlic, minced

1   large yellow onion, finely chopped

1   tablespoon olive oil

2   cups low-sugar ketchup

¼   cup agave syrup

¼   cup Splenda brown sugar blend

¼   cup medium-hot or hot salsa

2   tablespoons no-sugar-added
    apple cider vinegar

1   tablespoon Worcestershire sauce

2   teaspoons Dijon mustard

2   teaspoons chili powder

1   teaspoon ground cinnamon

1   teaspoon freshly ground black pepper

2   jalapeño or serrano chiles,
    pierced all over with a fork

Sauté the garlic and onion in the olive oil over medium-high heat in a heavy saucepan until the vegetables soften, about 3 minutes. Stir in all the remaining ingredients.

Bring the sauce to a boil, then reduce the heat to low and simmer, stirring frequently, until slightly thickened, 10 to 15 minutes. Let cool and discard the chiles. Store the sauce in an airtight container in the refrigerator for up to 2 weeks.

SERVING SIZE: 2 tablespoons
EXCHANGE LIST VALUE:
    1 carbohydrate
CARBOHYDRATE CHOICES: 1
CALORIES: 32

CALORIES FROM FAT: 5
TOTAL FAT: 1 g
SATURATED FAT: 0 g
CHOLESTEROL: 0 mg
SODIUM: 206 mg

TOTAL CARBOHYDRATE: 14 g
FIBER: 0 g
TOTAL SUGARS: 5 g
PROTEIN: 0 g

The Kitchen Diva's Seasoning Mix

MAKES ABOUT 2 CUPS

I created this seasoning mix so I could infuse my recipes with more flavor while monitoring the salt content. Combining the spices yourself provides you with control over the amount, freshness, and types used. And having a prepared spice blend saves time when cooking. This mix, which is easily multiplied, can be used in most of the savory recipes in this cookbook, especially if the recipe calls for just salt and pepper. It's delicious on chicken, fish, pork, and vegetables.

1   cup sea salt

1   (6-ounce) container garlic powder

1   (6-ounce) container onion powder

½   cup freshly ground black pepper

1   (.65 ounce) container poultry seasoning

1   tablespoon stevia granulated sweetener

1   teaspoon plain or Hungarian
     sweet paprika

¼   teaspoon ground cloves

¼   teaspoon cayenne pepper

Combine all the ingredients in a bowl and mix well. Taste a small amount to determine if the ingredients are balanced and flavorful, and adjust as necessary.

Store in an airtight container in a cool, dark place for up to 6 months.

SERVING SIZE: 1 teaspoon
EXCHANGE LIST VALUES: 0
CARBOHYDRATE CHOICES: 0
CALORIES: 4
CALORIES FROM FAT: 0

TOTAL FAT: 0 g
SATURATED FAT: 0 g
CHOLESTEROL: 0 mg
SODIUM: 112 mg
TOTAL CARBOHYDRATE: 1 g

FIBER: 0 g
TOTAL SUGARS: 0 g
PROTEIN: 0 g

No-Salt Spice Mix

MAKES ABOUT 1/3 CUP

If you've been advised to cut down on salt, this spice mix, which is easily multiplied, is perfect for you. Use it instead of the salt and pepper called for in the savory recipes in this book. (Sprinkling cooked foods such as fish, vegetables, and soups with 1 teaspoon of lemon juice or apple cider vinegar is another excellent way to replace salt without sacrificing flavor.)

2	teaspoons ground cumin
1	teaspoon ground coriander
1	teaspoon salt-free lemon pepper
½	teaspoon ancho chile powder
½	teaspoon sweet paprika
½	teaspoon ground cinnamon
¼	teaspoon ground allspice
¼	teaspoon ground ginger
⅛	teaspoon cayenne pepper
⅛	teaspoon ground cloves

Combine all the ingredients in a bowl and mix well. Store in an airtight glass jar in a cool, dark place for up to 6 months.

SERVING SIZE: ¼ teaspoon
EXCHANGE LIST VALUES: 0
CARBOHYDRATE CHOICES: 0
CALORIES: 1
CALORIES FROM FAT: 1

TOTAL FAT: 0 g
SATURATED FAT: 0 g
CHOLESTEROL: 0 mg
SODIUM: 0 mg
TOTAL CARBOHYDRATE: 0 g

FIBER: 0 g
TOTAL SUGARS: 0 g
PROTEIN: 0 g

Jump-Start Your Day:
Breakfast

WE ALL KNOW HOW IMPORTANT it is to start the day with a nutritious breakfast. The delicious recipes in this chapter provide quick and easy ways to jump-start your day, from protein-packed smoothies and microwave meals you can make in minutes to nutritious slow-cooker breakfast dishes you can prepare the night before. Now there is no excuse for missing breakfast.

A healthy breakfast can help with blood sugar control. When you don't eat breakfast, your blood sugar can drop too low, causing you to feel extreme pangs of hunger and to overeat at other meals. Even if your morning blood sugar level is normally high, it's still better to eat a small, high-protein meal than to skip breakfast.

A nutritious breakfast provides your body with much-needed vitamins and minerals to "break the fast" you undergo when sleeping. Eating within an hour of waking ensures that you have higher productivity throughout the morning, because you're better able to focus on the tasks at hand. A healthy breakfast also helps with appetite control, and one study found that eating breakfast lowers cholesterol, reducing your risk for heart disease.

According to the American Dietetic Association, breakfast is especially important for children and adolescents. Those who eat a healthy breakfast have better concentration and problem-solving skills, as well as improved hand-eye coordination; they also are more alert and creative, miss fewer days of school, and are more physically active.

Try these nutritious, vitamin-packed breakfast recipes to ensure that your entire family starts their day the healthy way.

FARMERS' MARKET VEGGIE JUICE   17

MEXICAN HOT CHOCOLATE   19

GREEN TEA CIDER REFRESHER   20

POWER SMOOTHIE   22

FRUITY TOFU SMOOTHIE   23

MOCHA MORNING SMOOTHIE   24

PEACH TEA SMOOTHIE   25

CANADIAN BACON   27

APPLE CIDER GLAZE FOR CANADIAN BACON   30

HOT PEPPER GLAZE FOR CANADIAN BACON   30

TURKEY CHORIZO   31

HEALTHY BREAKFAST SAUSAGE   32

PEANUT BUTTER BREAKFAST BARS   33

MICROWAVE BREAKFAST BOWL   34

MICROWAVE BREAKFAST SANDWICH   35

QUICK BLACK BEAN BREAKFAST TACOS   36

INSTANT OATMEAL   37

APPLE-STUFFED WAFFLE SANDWICHES   39

BUTTERMILK BRAN MUFFINS   40

SPINACH AND TOMATO CRUSTLESS QUICHE   41

MINI CHEESE QUICHES   42

DELUXE SLOW-COOKER OATMEAL   43

CINNAMON MULTIGRAIN BREAKFAST CEREAL   44

FRENCH TORTILLA TOAST   46

MINI OATMEAL PANCAKES WITH FRUIT BASKET BUTTER   47

Farmers' Market Veggie Juice

MAKES 4 SERVINGS

Start the day with a fresh, vitamin-packed drink based on produce at its seasonal peak. You can use tomatoes, zucchini, cucumbers, and/or yellow squash. Spinach, kale or Swiss chard, and carrots also blend beautifully in this drink. Fresh vegetables supply an abundance of nutrients and are low in calories. Salsa adds a little spice to this veggie juice.

1½	cups chopped tomatoes
2	tablespoons mild or hot salsa
1	red bell pepper, seeded, deribbed, and quartered
2	small zucchini, coarsely chopped
1	green onion, including green parts, coarsely chopped
1	stalk celery, chopped
½	small jalapeño chile, diced
	Juice of ½ lime
1	teaspoon stevia granulated sweetener
1	teaspoon freshly ground black pepper
⅛	teaspoon ground cloves

Working in batches, combine all the ingredients in a food processor and process on high until finely chopped. If necessary, gradually add a little water to reach the desired consistency.

SERVING SIZE: 8 ounces
EXCHANGE LIST VALUES: 2 vegetable
CARBOHYDRATE CHOICES: ½
CALORIES: 39
CALORIES FROM FAT: 4

TOTAL FAT: 1 g
SATURATED FAT: 0 g
CHOLESTEROL: 0 mg
SODIUM: 51 mg
TOTAL CARBOHYDRATE: 9 g

FIBER: 2 g
TOTAL SUGARS: 5 g
PROTEIN: 2 g

Mexican Hot Chocolate

SERVES 6

When consumed in moderation, a cup of flavonoid-rich hot chocolate made with dark, unprocessed cocoa is a nutritious breakfast drink. Chocolate and cocoa contain compounds called flavonols, which act as antioxidants and counteract some of the cellular damage that can lead to chronic diseases such as cancer and heart disease. The antioxidants in cocoa powder have been shown in some studies to lower blood pressure and improve blood flow, which is important for cardiovascular health.

Dutch cocoa has been treated with alkali, to produce a darker, richer taste. Unfortunately, this process drastically reduces flavonol content. Using unprocessed cocoa powder in this recipe reduces the calories without affecting the rich chocolate flavor of the drink. Mexican hot chocolate is traditionally flavored with cinnamon and enriched with heavy cream. Low-fat whipped topping sprinkled with a little cinnamon is a delicious substitute here.

¼ cup unsweetened powdered cocoa (not Dutch cocoa)

¼ cup stevia granulated sweetener or agave syrup

¾ teaspoon ground cinnamon, plus more for sprinkling

⅛ teaspoon salt

4 cups vanilla soy milk

Creamy Whipped Topping (page 257), optional

In a small bowl, combine the cocoa, stevia or syrup, the ¾ teaspoon ground cinnamon, and the salt. Heat 1 cup of the milk in a saucepan until bubbles form around the edges of the pan. Stir in the cocoa mixture and whisk until smooth. Bring to a simmer over low heat, stirring constantly. Stir in the remaining 3 cups of milk and return to a simmer. Immediately remove the pan from the heat and pour into serving cups. Top each with a dollop of whipped topping and sprinkle with cinnamon.

SERVING SIZE: 6 ounces
EXCHANGE LIST VALUES:
    1 carbohydrate, ½ fat
CARBOHYDRATE CHOICES: 1
CALORIES: 116

CALORIES FROM FAT: 27
TOTAL FAT: 3 g
SATURATED FAT: 0 g
CHOLESTEROL: 0 mg
SODIUM: 140 mg

TOTAL CARBOHYDRATE: 18 g
FIBER: 1 g
TOTAL SUGARS: 9 g
PROTEIN: 5 g

Green Tea Cider Refresher

MAKES 8 SERVINGS

Researchers have linked green tea to a multitude of health benefits, from preventing cancer and lowering cholesterol to relieving the symptoms of arthritis. Green tea contains more antioxidants than other types of tea, which may account for its healthful properties. But the best reason for drinking it is its refreshing flavor.

The apple cider vinegar may seem like a strange addition to this iced tea recipe, but it is an easy way to incorporate a kitchen staple that may help reduce blood glucose. It tastes similar to adding lemon juice to your tea.

8   green tea bags

4   cups boiling water

4   cups cold water

1   tablespoon no-sugar-added apple cider vinegar

1   cup stevia granulated sweetener

Place the tea bags in a 4-quart pitcher and add the boiling water. Cover and let steep for 5 minutes. Stir in the cold water, vinegar, and stevia, stirring to dissolve the stevia. Serve over ice.

SERVING SIZE: 8 ounces
EXCHANGE LIST VALUES: 0
CARBOHYDRATE CHOICES: 0
CALORIES: 17
CALORIES FROM FAT: 0

TOTAL FAT: 0 g
SATURATED FAT: 0 g
CHOLESTEROL: 0 mg
SODIUM: 7 mg
TOTAL CARBOHYDRATE: 4 g

FIBER: 0 g
TOTAL SUGARS: 4 g
PROTEIN: 0 g

Fruit Smoothies

If you've been skipping breakfast because you're pressed for time, a vitamin- and nutrient-rich antioxidant-packed smoothie is the answer. These healthy smoothie recipes get their good nutrient profile from ingredients such as fruits, vegetables, and soft tofu, along with wheat germ. This embryo of the wheat is a rich source of protein, fiber, unsaturated fat, phosphorus, zinc, thiamine, magnesium, and vitamins E, B1, B2, B5, and B6. Its natural antioxidants may help protect the muscles, blood, lungs, and eyes, and they also help strengthen your immune system and increase your ability to cope with stress. Soy milk and tofu contain high amounts of protein, omega-3 fats, calcium, selenium, other minerals, and antioxidants. Silken/soft tofu blends with other flavors while adding creaminess to your smoothie.

Smoothies easily can be adapted to add variety and interest to your morning. Frozen fruit and bananas or other fresh fruit add body, flavor, and nutrients, and black, green, white, or oolong teas add flavor and are packed with antioxidant polyphenols, which studies have suggested are powerful foes of cancer and heart disease. Adding coconut oil, steel-cut oats, ground flaxseed, or acai or goji berry juice are other good ways to increase the nutritional benefits of your drink. Just make sure the carbohydrate content of the ingredients you add fit into your recommended meal plan. Smoothies are easy to make, are filling, can be easily adapted to suit individual tastes, and, best of all, they're portable if you need a "breakfast to go."

You also can whip up an extra batch of smoothies or freeze leftovers for a snack or dessert. Pour the mixture into plastic molds, ice cube trays, or paper cups and freeze for when you crave something sweet or need a snack to go.

Power Smoothie

MAKES 6 SERVINGS

If you wake up feeling sluggish, this protein-packed power smoothie is the wake-up call you need. Protein powders are fairly expensive, but canned beans are not. High in protein and fiber, they provide a creamy texture to this smoothie, which can be prepared up to 2 days in advance. Pour into covered "to go" cups, cover, and refrigerate for busy mornings. The drink will thicken as it chills.

1	can (15 ounces) navy beans or Great Northern beans, drained and rinsed
1½	cups orange juice
2	cups quartered fresh or frozen strawberries or blueberries
2	tablespoons stevia granulated sweetener
1½	teaspoons ground cinnamon
⅛	teaspoon ground nutmeg
6 to 8 ice cubes, as needed (optional)	

Process all the ingredients, except the ice cubes, in a blender until smooth. If using fresh fruits, add ice and blend until smooth. If too thick, stir in additional orange juice or cold water as needed for the desired consistency.

SERVING SIZE: 6 ounces
EXCHANGE LIST VALUES: 1 starch, 1 fruit, 1 plant-based protein
CARBOHYDRATE CHOICES: 2
CALORIES: 136

CALORIES FROM FAT: 6
TOTAL FAT: 1 g
SATURATED FAT: 0 g
CHOLESTEROL: 0 mg
SODIUM: 204 mg

TOTAL CARBOHYDRATE: 27 g
FIBER: 5 g
TOTAL SUGARS: 9 g
PROTEIN: 7 g

Fruity Tofu Smoothie

MAKES 4 SERVINGS

Silken soft tofu is an inexpensive and nutritious form of protein. It naturally absorbs flavors, which allows it to blend seamlessly with everything from breakfast smoothies to main dishes.

1   cup silken soft tofu

1   banana, peeled and halved crosswise

½   cup soy milk or orange juice

½   cup low-fat vanilla yogurt

¼   cup fresh or frozen strawberries
    or blueberries

¼   cup wheat germ

1   tablespoon stevia granulated sweetener

In a blender, combine the tofu, 1 banana half, the soy milk or orange juice, and yogurt and blend until smooth. Add the berries and wheat germ and blend again. Add the remaining banana half, the stevia and blend until smooth. Serve immediately.

SERVING SIZE: 8 ounces
EXCHANGE LIST VALUES: ½ starch,
    ½ fruit, 1 plant-based protein
CARBOHYDRATE CHOICES: 1
CALORIES: 144

CALORIES FROM FAT: 37
TOTAL FAT: 4 g
SATURATED FAT: 0 g
CHOLESTEROL: 2 mg
SODIUM: 34 mg

TOTAL CARBOHYDRATE: 18 g
FIBER: 2 g
TOTAL SUGARS: 9 g
PROTEIN: 10 g

Mocha Morning Smoothie

MAKES 2 SERVINGS

Adding ground flaxseed is a great way to incorporate nutrition into this coffee-based smoothie. Flaxseeds are high in omega-3 fatty acids, which are thought to reduce the risk of heart attacks, stroke, and blood clots, as well as lowering blood pressure and cholesterol.

1	cup low-fat vanilla yogurt
½	cup low-fat or vanilla soy milk
½	cup brewed strong coffee, chilled
1	teaspoon stevia granulated sweetener
1	cup ice cubes
2	tablespoons ground flaxseed

Blend all the ingredients on high speed in a blender or food processor until smooth, 15 to 20 seconds. Serve immediately.

SERVING SIZE: 8 ounces
EXCHANGE LIST VALUES:
   ½ carbohydrate, 1 reduced-fat milk,
   ½ fat
CARBOHYDRATE CHOICES: 1½

CALORIES: 168
CALORIES FROM FAT: 48
TOTAL FAT: 5 g
SATURATED FAT: 1 g
CHOLESTEROL: 6 mg

SODIUM: 110 mg
TOTAL CARBOHYDRATE: 24 g
FIBER: 3 g
TOTAL SUGARS: 19 g
PROTEIN: 9 g

Peach Tea Smoothie

MAKES 3 SERVINGS

You can make the tea for this smoothie the night before and store it in the refrigerator to save time. For a change of pace, add 1 cup of chopped mango, apple, or melon instead of the banana.

2   black, green, white, or oolong peach tea bags

2   cups water

1   cup low-fat plain Greek yogurt

1   banana, peeled and sliced

2   teaspoons stevia granulated sweetener

6 to 8 ice cubes

Place the tea bags and water in a large microwaveable cup and bring it to a boil in a microwave on high for 3 to 4 minutes. Cover the cup with a saucer and let steep for at least 5 minutes. Add the brewed tea, yogurt, banana, and stevia to a blender and blend for 10 seconds. Add the ice cubes and blend for 15 seconds.

SERVING SIZE: 8 ounces
EXCHANGE LIST VALUES: ½ fruit, ½ reduced-fat milk
CARBOHYDRATE CHOICES: 1
CALORIES: 89

CALORIES FROM FAT: 15
TOTAL FAT: 2 g
SATURATED FAT: 1 g
CHOLESTEROL: 5 mg
SODIUM: 32 mg

TOTAL CARBOHYDRATE: 13 g
FIBER: 1 g
TOTAL SUGARS: 9 g
PROTEIN: 7 g

Canadian Bacon

MAKES 20 SERVINGS

If you're trying to find breakfast meats that are lower in fat and sodium than regular bacon or pork sausage, Canadian bacon is a good choice.

Making your own Canadian bacon takes a little time, but it saves lots of money! The meat, although quite lean, is particularly juicy because of the brining process. You can slice and portion the meat into servings, then freeze it for later use as a breakfast meat, as part of a lunchtime salad or soup, to add to casseroles, or to serve as the main-course meat for dinner. Poultry seasoning typically contains ground rosemary, thyme, sage, black pepper, and nutmeg, the perfect spices for pork, chicken, and fish. Adding the Apple Cider Glaze (page 30) or the Hot Pepper Glaze (page 30) adds another dimension of flavor to the dish.

1	cup kosher salt
1	cup agave syrup or maple-flavored agave syrup
1	gallon warm water
¼	cup whole cloves
3	cinnamon sticks, or 3 tablespoons ground cinnamon
3	tablespoons plus 2 teaspoons poultry seasoning

1	large pork loin (5 pounds), trimmed of all fat
2	tablespoons olive oil
2	cups cornmeal
¼	cup water
	Apple Cider Glaze (page 30) or Hot Pepper Glaze (page 30), optional

Continued on page 28

SERVING SIZE: 3 ounces
EXCHANGE LIST VALUES: 1 starch, 1 lean meat
CARBOHYDRATE CHOICES: 1
CALORIES: 209

CALORIES FROM FAT: 67
TOTAL FAT: 7 g
SATURATED FAT: 2 g
CHOLESTEROL: 66 mg
SODIUM: 367 mg

TOTAL CARBOHYDRATE: 13 g
FIBER: 1 g
TOTAL SUGARS: 2 g
PROTEIN: 22 g

Mix the salt and syrup in the warm water in a large bowl until the syrup dissolves. Add the cloves, cinnamon, and 3 tablespoons of the poultry seasoning and stir to combine. Pour the mixture into a large resealable bag. Place the bag in a baking pan and add the pork loin to the bag. Press out any air from the bag to make sure the meat is submerged. Place in the refrigerator for 24 to 72 hours, turning the bag once or twice each day.

Preheat the oven to 325°F. Remove the meat from the bag and discard the brining liquid. Rinse the meat with cold water to remove any excess salt. Pat the meat dry with paper towels, then rub it with the olive oil. Mix together the remaining 2 teaspoons of poultry seasoning and the cornmeal. Roll the meat in the cornmeal mixture to give it a crust. Place the meat on a rack in a baking pan. Pour the water into the pan to prevent the meat from drying out.

Bake for about 30 minutes, or until an instant-read thermometer inserted in the center of the pork registers 145°F. Remove the meat from the oven. Cool for 30 minutes. Cut into 1/4-inch-thick slices. Before serving, brush both sides of each slice with one of the glazes.

Or, divide the meat into serving portions, wrap it in plastic wrap and a layer of aluminum foil, place it in a resealable plastic bag, and store it in the refrigerator. The slices also can be brushed with the glaze, divided into serving portions, wrapped in plastic, placed in a plastic freezer bag, and frozen for up to 6 months. Thaw in the refrigerator. Reheat the bacon on high in the microwave for 1 to 2 minutes, or over medium-high heat for 1 to 2 minutes on each side in a nonstick skillet.

Apple Cider Glaze

MAKES 1 CUP

1   cup unsweetened apple juice

3   tablespoons Splenda brown sugar blend

2   tablespoons no-sugar-added
    apple cider vinegar

1   teaspoon ground ginger

½   teaspoon ground cinnamon

Combine all the ingredients in a microwaveable bowl. Microwave on high for 3 to 4 minutes.

SERVING SIZE: 2 teaspoons
EXCHANGE LIST VALUES: 0
CARBOHYDRATE CHOICES: 0
CALORIES: 13
CALORIES FROM FAT: 0

TOTAL FAT: 0 g
SATURATED FAT: 0 g
CHOLESTEROL: 0 mg
SODIUM: 0 mg
TOTAL CARBOHYDRATE: 3 g

FIBER: 0 g
TOTAL SUGARS: 3 g
PROTEIN: 0 g

Hot Pepper Glaze

MAKES 1¼ CUPS

1   cup unsweetened orange-pineapple juice

3   tablespoons Splenda brown sugar blend

3   tablespoons hot sauce

1   tablespoon stone-ground or spicy mustard

½   tablespoon freshly ground black pepper

Mix together all the ingredients in a microwaveable bowl. Microwave on high for 3 to 4 minutes.

SERVING SIZE: 2 teaspoons
EXCHANGE LIST VALUES: 0
CARBOHYDRATE CHOICES: 0
CALORIES: 11
CALORIES FROM FAT: 0

TOTAL FAT: 0 g
SATURATED FAT: 0 g
CHOLESTEROL: 0 mg
SODIUM: 45 mg
TOTAL CARBOHYDRATE: 2 g

FIBER: 0 g
TOTAL SUGARS: 2 g
PROTEIN: 0 g

Turkey Chorizo

MAKES 4 SERVINGS

Chorizo is made from ground pork, fat, and spices. This turkey version retains all the flavor of the original without the unhealthy fat. Add to scrambled eggs, tacos, quiches, and pasta sauces.

1	pound ground turkey breast meat
2	tablespoons olive oil
2	tablespoons no-sugar-added apple cider vinegar
2	cloves garlic, minced
1	tablespoon sweet paprika
1	teaspoon ground cumin
1	teaspoon salt
1	teaspoon freshly ground black pepper
¼	teaspoon cayenne pepper
¼	teaspoon dried oregano
⅛	teaspoon ground cloves

Place the turkey in a medium bowl. Add 1 tablespoon of the olive oil, the vinegar, garlic, and all of the spices to the meat. Blend well to combine. Cover and refrigerate for 30 minutes.

Add the remaining 1 tablespoon of oil to a large skillet. Over high heat, brown the meat, breaking it up with a potato masher or a slotted spoon. Remove from the heat and let cool. Store in a covered container in the refrigerator for up to 7 days.

SERVING SIZE: 3 ounces
EXCHANGE LIST VALUES: 4 lean meat, 1 fat
CARBOHYDRATE CHOICES: 0
CALORIES: 220

CALORIES FROM FAT: 87
TOTAL FAT: 10 g
SATURATED FAT: 1 g
CHOLESTEROL: 45 mg
SODIUM: 358 mg

TOTAL CARBOHYDRATE: 5 g
FIBER: 1 g
TOTAL SUGARS: 0 g
PROTEIN: 29 g

Healthy Breakfast Sausage

MAKES 12 PATTIES

Making your own breakfast sausage allows you to control the ingredients. Here, turkey and oatmeal are added to pork to reduce the fat content and provide a healthy boost of fiber. Brown and serve the patties immediately, or separate them into serving portions and freeze for up to 6 months.

1	pound ground turkey breast
8	ounces lean ground pork
¼	cup quick-cooking oatmeal
1	tablespoon poultry seasoning
1	tablespoon Worcestershire sauce
1	teaspoon stone-ground mustard
1	teaspoon garlic powder
1	teaspoon onion powder
1	teaspoon freshly ground black pepper
1	teaspoon dried oregano
¼	teaspoon red pepper flakes
1	tablespoon cold water

Combine the turkey, pork, oatmeal, poultry seasoning, Worcestershire sauce, mustard, garlic powder, onion powder, black pepper, oregano, and red pepper flakes in a large bowl. Mix well. Sprinkle the cold water over the mixture and let it marinate for 30 minutes.

Form the mixture into 12 patties. Lightly coat a large nonstick skillet with cooking oil spray and heat over medium heat. Brown the patties for about 4 minutes on each side, or until cooked through. Serve hot.

SERVING SIZE: 1 patty
EXCHANGE LIST VALUES: 2 lean meat
CARBOHYDRATE CHOICES: 0
CALORIES: 75
CALORIES FROM FAT: 13

TOTAL FAT: 1 g
SATURATED FAT: 0 g
CHOLESTEROL: 26 mg
SODIUM: 160 mg
TOTAL CARBOHYDRATE: 2 g

FIBER: 0 g
TOTAL SUGARS: 0 g
PROTEIN: 14 g

Peanut Butter Breakfast Bars

MAKES 8 SERVINGS

My husband, Michael, is often in a rush in the mornings and needs something quick to eat, such as a breakfast bar, so he can take his diabetes medicine. These bars also are perfect for midmorning snacks.

¾ cup unsweetened applesauce

3   tablespoons firmly packed Splenda brown sugar blend

⅓ cup no-sugar peanut butter

½ teaspoon ground cinnamon

½ cup old-fashioned oats

½ cup chopped walnuts

⅓ cup toasted wheat germ

¼ cup dry-roasted sunflower seeds

2   cups wheat flakes

In a large microwaveable bowl, combine the applesauce and brown sugar blend. Heat in the microwave on high for 4 to 5 minutes. Stir and cook for another 2 minutes. Stir in the peanut butter and cook on high for 1 to 2 minutes, or until melted. Stir in the cinnamon, rolled oats, walnuts, wheat germ, and sunflower seeds until well combined. Add the wheat flakes, stirring to coat.

Press the mixture very firmly and evenly into an ungreased 8-inch square pan (or the bars will crumble). Refrigerate for at least 1 hour to set. Cut into 8 bars. Store in an airtight container in the refrigerator for up to 2 days.

SERVING SIZE: 1 bar

EXCHANGE LIST VALUES:
    ½ carbohydrate, 1½ starch, 1½ fat

CARBOHYDRATE CHOICES: 1½

CALORIES: 237

CALORIES FROM FAT: 119

TOTAL FAT: 13 g

SATURATED FAT: 2 g

CHOLESTEROL: 0 mg

SODIUM: 121 mg

TOTAL CARBOHYDRATE: 25 g

FIBER: 5 g

TOTAL SUGARS: 10 g

PROTEIN: 8 g

Microwave Breakfast Bowl

MAKES 1 SERVING

The beauty of this breakfast bowl is that you can prepare it in less than 10 minutes at home, or mix up all of the ingredients and microwave it at work. You also can turn it into a casserole by multiplying the ingredients and cooking it in a larger dish.

1	large egg, lightly beaten
¼	cup diced Canadian bacon (page 27), Turkey Chorizo (page 31), or diced low-sodium deli ham
3	tablespoons 1 percent low-fat milk
3	tablespoons shredded reduced-fat cheddar cheese
¼	teaspoon ground nutmeg
⅛	teaspoon salt
⅛	teaspoon freshly ground black pepper
⅛	teaspoon Worcestershire sauce
1	slice day-old whole-wheat bread, crust removed, cubed

Mix together all the ingredients, except the bread cubes, in a microwaveable bowl until well blended. Gently stir in the bread cubes, but don't overmix or the bread will disintegrate. Cover the bowl tightly with plastic wrap. Poke a couple of holes in the plastic for venting.

Microwave on medium-high for about 5 minutes, or until the egg is set. Rotate the bowl midway through cooking if your microwave doesn't automatically rotate. Let stand in the microwave a minute or two once cooking is complete. Serve warm.

SERVING SIZE: 8 ounces

EXCHANGE LIST VALUES: 1 starch, 1 lean meat, 1 medium-fat meat

CARBOHYDRATE CHOICES: 1

CALORIES: 271

CALORIES FROM FAT: 104

TOTAL FAT: 12 g

SATURATED FAT: 5 g

CHOLESTEROL: 218 mg

SODIUM: 426 mg

TOTAL CARBOHYDRATE: 19 g

FIBER: 3 g

TOTAL SUGARS: 4 g

PROTEIN: 21 g

Microwave Breakfast Sandwich

MAKES 1 SERVING

This breakfast sandwich is healthier, faster, and much less expensive than similar ones sold at fast-food restaurants. You can multiply this recipe, wrap the sandwiches individually, freeze them, then reheat them in the microwave.

1   large egg

1   teaspoon mild to hot salsa

½   teaspoon freshly ground black pepper

1   slice reduced-fat American cheese

1   whole-wheat English muffin,
    lightly toasted

Lightly grease a small microwaveable bowl with cooking oil spray. Break the egg into the bowl. Add the salsa and pepper and beat lightly. Tear the cheese into small pieces and stir it into the egg. Microwave the mixture for 50 to 60 seconds, until set. Make a sandwich with the English muffin and the cooked egg mixture.

SERVING SIZE: 1 sandwich

EXCHANGE LIST VALUES: 2 starch,
   1 medium-fat meat

CARBOHYDRATE CHOICES: 2

CALORIES: 256

CALORIES FROM FAT: 89

TOTAL FAT: 10 g

SATURATED FAT: 3 g

CHOLESTEROL: 196 mg

SODIUM: 593 mg

TOTAL CARBOHYDRATE: 29 g

FIBER: 4 g

TOTAL SUGARS: 7 g

PROTEIN: 16 g

Quick Black Bean Breakfast Tacos

MAKES 8 TACOS

These black bean tacos are a good source of protein and fiber. Wrap the tacos individually to freeze, then reheat them in the microwave.

1   (15-ounce) can fat-free refried beans

2   tablespoons mild to medium-hot salsa

1   teaspoon chili powder

1   teaspoon freshly ground black pepper

8   (6-inch) corn or whole-wheat flour tortillas

½   cup shredded reduced-fat cheddar cheese

Mix together the beans, salsa, chili powder, and pepper in a bowl. Place the tortillas on a microwave-safe plate. Top each tortilla with 2 tablespoons of the bean mixture, sprinkle it with the cheese, and fold it in half. Cover with a damp paper towel. Heat on high in the microwave until the filling is warm and the cheese is melted, 20 to 30 seconds.

SERVING SIZE: 1 taco
EXCHANGE LIST VALUES: 1½ starch, ½ medium-fat meat
CARBOHYDRATE CHOICES: 1½
CALORIES: 213

CALORIES FROM FAT: 54
TOTAL FAT: 6 g
SATURATED FAT: 3 g
CHOLESTEROL: 10 mg
SODIUM: 686 mg

TOTAL CARBOHYDRATE: 28 g
FIBER: 7 g
TOTAL SUGARS: 1 g
PROTEIN: 10 g

Instant Oatmeal

MAKES 4 SERVINGS

Making your own "instant" oatmeal instead of buying the packaged variety is a much healthier way to enjoy the nutritional benefits of this cereal. Mixing an ounce of dried fruit into the oatmeal and eating 4 ounces of low-fat Greek yogurt or cottage cheese makes this a nutritious, quick, and easy breakfast.

1⅓ cups quick-cooking oats

2⅔ cups water

1 teaspoon ground cinnamon

1 teaspoon agave syrup or stevia granulated sweetener

¼ teaspoon salt

Combine all the ingredients in a large microwaveable bowl. Microwave on high for 1 minute and 15 seconds. Stir and microwave for an additional minute. Let stand in the microwave for 2 minutes to thicken before serving.

VARIATIONS: Stir in some or all of these ingredients to make your oatmeal extra special: 1 peeled and chopped apple, 2 tablespoons of coarsely chopped walnuts or pecans, and 2 tablespoons of raisins.

SERVING SIZE: ⅓ cup

EXCHANGE LIST VALUES: 1 starch

CARBOHYDRATE CHOICES: 1

CALORIES: 105

CALORIES FROM FAT: 17

TOTAL FAT: 2 g

SATURATED FAT: 0 g

CHOLESTEROL: 0 mg

SODIUM: 151 mg

TOTAL CARBOHYDRATE: 20 g

FIBER: 3 g

TOTAL SUGARS: 2 g

PROTEIN: 4 g

Apple-Stuffed Waffle Sandwiches

MAKES 4 SERVINGS

This dual-purpose recipe makes a wonderful, kid-pleasing breakfast or a tasty after-school snack. To save time, make the apple topping and the syrup ahead of time, and store them in airtight containers for a week. For a delicious variation, use a pear in place of the apple. The syrup also is delicious with other breakfast dishes.

APPLE–CINNAMON SYRUP (OPTIONAL)

2   tablespoons stevia granulated sweetener

¼   cup unsweetened apple juice

1   teaspoon fresh lemon juice

1   teaspoon ground cinnamon

1   crisp red apple (York, Rome Beauty, or Winesap), cored and diced

2   tablespoons stevia granulated sweetener

¼   cup unsweetened apple juice

4   frozen whole-grain waffles or Belgian waffles, toasted

4   tablespoons no-sugar peanut butter

To make the optional apple-cinnamon syrup, place all the ingredients in a small microwaveable bowl and heat on medium (or defrost setting) for 3 to 4 minutes. Cover the bowl with plastic wrap and set aside.

In a medium microwaveable bowl, combine the apple, stevia, and apple juice and cook on high for 4 to 5 minutes, stirring once, until the apple is lightly caramelized and crisp-tender.

For each serving, place a waffle on a plate. Spread with 1 tablespoon of peanut butter and 2 tablespoons of the apple mixture. Top with another waffle. Cut the sandwich in half and drizzle with 1 to 2 teaspoons of the apple-cinnamon syrup, if desired.

SERVING SIZE: ½ sandwich
EXCHANGE LIST VALUES: 1 starch, 1 fruit, 1½ fat
CARBOHYDRATE CHOICES: 2
CALORIES: 232

CALORIES FROM FAT: 100
TOTAL FAT: 11 g
SATURATED FAT: 2 g
CHOLESTEROL: 0 mg
SODIUM: 272 mg

TOTAL CARBOHYDRATE: 28 g
FIBER: 4 g
TOTAL SUGARS: 11 g
PROTEIN: 6 g

Buttermilk Bran Muffins

MAKES 12 MUFFINS

I like using whole-grain cereals in my recipes, particularly in these muffins. Fiber, especially the insoluble kind such as the whole bran in these muffins, fills you up and keeps your digestive system on track. The buttermilk in the batter makes the muffins moist and tender.

2   cups whole-bran cereal

1⅔ cups low-fat buttermilk

2   large eggs, lightly beaten

⅓   cup packed Splenda brown sugar blend

2   tablespoons agave syrup or maple-flavored agave syrup

3   tablespoons canola oil

1   cup whole-wheat flour

1¾ teaspoons baking powder

1   teaspoon ground cinnamon

¼   teaspoon baking soda

¼   cup mixed dried fruit or raisins, chopped

½   cup chopped walnuts

Preheat the oven to 350°F. Using cooking oil spray, lightly coat the cups in a 12-cup muffin pan; set aside.

In a large bowl, mix together the bran cereal and buttermilk. Let stand for 5 to 10 minutes, or until the cereal is softened. Stir the eggs, brown sugar blend, syrup, and oil into the bran mixture.

In a small bowl, stir together the flour, baking powder, cinnamon, and baking soda. Add the flour mixture to the bran mixture and stir just until combined. Stir in the dried fruit and nuts. Spoon the batter evenly into the prepared muffin cups, filling each three-quarters full.

Bake for 25 to 30 minutes, or until the tops spring back when touched and a toothpick inserted in the center comes out clean. Cool in the pan on a wire rack for 5 minutes. Unmold onto the rack and let cool completely. Store in an airtight container for up to 7 days.

SERVING SIZE: 1 muffin

EXCHANGE LIST VALUES:
    ½ carbohydrate, 1½ starch, 1 fat

CARBOHYDRATE CHOICES: 2

CALORIES: 198

CALORIES FROM FAT: 77

TOTAL FAT: 9 g

SATURATED FAT: 1 g

CHOLESTEROL: 33 mg

SODIUM: 166 mg

TOTAL CARBOHYDRATE: 28 g

FIBER: 5 g

TOTAL SUGARS: 13 g

PROTEIN: 6 g

Spinach and Tomato Crustless Quiche

MAKES 8 SERVINGS

This salad-topped quiche is delicious for brunch, lunch, or dinner. Best of all, it looks beautiful and it's easy to make. Eggs are an inexpensive, high-quality source of protein, vitamins D and B12, and lutein, which is thought to be important for healthy vision.

½   cup 1 percent low-fat milk

2   tablespoons all-purpose flour

3   large eggs

1   cup low-fat cottage cheese

2   ounces reduced-fat cream cheese (preferably Neufchâtel), cubed

1   cup shredded reduced-fat sharp cheddar cheese or Monterey Jack cheese

1   teaspoon stevia granulated sweetener

1   tablespoon poultry seasoning

½   teaspoon salt

1   teaspoon freshly ground black pepper

3   tablespoons olive oil

1   tablespoon no-sugar-added apple cider vinegar

8   cherry tomatoes, halved

1   cup baby spinach leaves

Preheat the oven to 350°F. In a medium bowl, gradually whisk the milk into the flour until smooth. Whisk in the egg, cottage cheese, and cream cheese (the mixture will not be smooth). Stir in the cheese, stevia, ½ tablespoon of the poultry seasoning, the salt, and ½ teaspoon of the pepper.

Pour the mixture into a lightly greased 9-inch pie plate. Bake for 45 to 50 minutes, or until puffed and golden and a knife inserted near the center comes out clean.

In a medium bowl, mix together the remaining ½ tablespoon of poultry seasoning, the remaining ½ teaspoon of pepper, the olive oil, and apple cider vinegar. Toss the tomatoes and spinach in the dressing. Cut the quiche into 8 slices. Top each slice of the quiche with the spinach salad and serve immediately.

SERVING SIZE: ⅛ of quiche

EXCHANGE LIST VALUES: 1 medium-fat meat, ½ high-fat meat, 1 fat

CARBOHYDRATE CHOICES: 0

CALORIES: 182

CALORIES FROM FAT: 121

TOTAL FAT: 13 g

SATURATED FAT: 5 g

CHOLESTEROL: 89 mg

SODIUM: 420 mg

TOTAL CARBOHYDRATE: 4 g

FIBER: 0 g

TOTAL SUGARS: 2 g

PROTEIN: 10 g

Mini Cheese Quiches

MAKES 6 SERVINGS

These mini cheese quiches can be individually wrapped in plastic and refrigerated for up to 3 days or frozen for up to 1 month. To reheat, remove the plastic, wrap the quiches in a microwave-safe paper towel, and microwave on high for 30 to 60 seconds.

A nonstick muffin pan works best for this recipe. If you don't have one, line a regular muffin tin with paper cupcake liners, or prepare this dish in a 13 by 9-inch prepared baking pan and add an additional 5 to 7 minutes to the cooking time. Substitute 8 slices of Canadian bacon, finely diced, for the sausage for a delicious twist on this dish.

1	package (8 ounces) ground turkey sausage
1	teaspoon olive oil
¼	cup sliced green onions, including green parts
¼	cup finely diced red bell pepper
1	tablespoon poultry seasoning
5	large eggs
3	large egg whites
½	cup soy milk
1	teaspoon freshly ground black pepper
½	teaspoon salt
¼	cup shredded reduced-fat Swiss or Monterey Jack cheese

Position a rack in the center of the oven and preheat the oven to 325°F. Coat the cups of a 6-cup nonstick muffin pan generously with cooking spray.

In a large microwaveable bowl, combine the sausage, oil, onions, bell pepper, and poultry seasoning and microwave on high until the sausage is golden brown, 6 to 8 minutes. Set aside to cool.

Whisk together the eggs, egg whites, milk, pepper, and salt in a medium bowl. Fill the muffin cups two-thirds full with the egg mixture. Place 1 heaping tablespoon of the sausage mixture in each cup. Sprinkle each cup with some of the cheese.

Bake until the tops are just beginning to brown and the centers are set, about 25 minutes. Let cool on a wire rack for 5 minutes. Place a wire rack on top of the muffin pan, flip it over, and turn the quiches out onto the rack. Turn upright and let cool completely.

SERVING SIZE: 1 mini quiche
EXCHANGE LIST VALUES: 2 lean meat
CARBOHYDRATE CHOICES: 0
CALORIES: 168
CALORIES FROM FAT: 79

TOTAL FAT: 9 g
SATURATED FAT: 3 g
CHOLESTEROL: 187 mg
SODIUM: 443 mg
TOTAL CARBOHYDRATE: 3 g

FIBER: 1 g
TOTAL SUGARS: 1 g
PROTEIN: 18 g

Deluxe Slow-Cooker Oatmeal

MAKES 8 SERVINGS

You won't need an alarm clock to wake you with the fragrance of apples and cinnamon wafting through your house in the morning. This is a great way to start the day!

⅓	cup Splenda brown sugar blend
2	teaspoons ground cinnamon
1	apple (York, Rome Beauty, or Winesap), peeled, cored, and diced
2	cups old-fashioned or steel-cut oats
2	cups vanilla soy milk
2	cups water
½	teaspoon salt
¼	cup raisins or dried mixed berries, chopped
¼	cup chopped walnuts or almonds

Lightly spray a slow cooker with cooking oil spray. Add the brown sugar blend, 1 teaspoon of the cinnamon, and the apple to the cooker, stirring to coat the apple well. In a medium bowl, mix together the oats, soy milk, water, the remaining 1 teaspoon of cinnamon, and the salt.

Pour the oatmeal mixture on top of the apple mixture in the slow cooker and stir. Cover and cook overnight for 8 to 9 hours on low. In the morning, stir in the raisins or berries and the nuts, stirring thoroughly. Serve immediately.

SERVING SIZE: ½ cup
EXCHANGE LIST VALUES: ½ carbohydrate, 1 starch, ½ fruit, ½ fat
CARBOHYDRATE CHOICES: 2
CALORIES: 202

CALORIES FROM FAT: 45
TOTAL FAT: 5 g
SATURATED FAT: 1 g
CHOLESTEROL: 0 mg
SODIUM: 183 mg

TOTAL CARBOHYDRATE: 34 g
FIBER: 3 g
TOTAL SUGARS: 17 g
PROTEIN: 5 g

Cinnamon Multigrain Breakfast Cereal

MAKES 6 SERVINGS

Start the slow cooker the night before and wake up to a delicious breakfast. This cinnamon-flavored, fruit-filled cereal also contains barley, millet, amaranth, oats, bulgur, and brown rice—whole grains that contain fiber, which has been found to help control blood glucose levels. These types of grains also are a rich source of magnesium, a mineral that acts as a cofactor (a compound needed by an enzyme to carry out the reaction it catalyzes) for more than three hundred enzymes, including those involved in the body's use of glucose and insulin secretion. Most of these grains require long cooking times, so a slow cooker is the perfect way to prepare this power-packed cereal. Enjoy a hearty breakfast and get the benefits of both whole grains and dairy by serving a hot bowl of this multigrain cereal with low-fat milk.

2	tablespoons barley
2	tablespoons millet
2	tablespoons amaranth
1	cup quick-cooking oats
2½	tablespoons bulgur wheat
2½	tablespoons brown rice
½	cup mixed dried fruit, chopped
1½	teaspoons ground cinnamon
½	teaspoon salt
3½	cups water
1	tablespoon vanilla extract

Combine all the grains, the dried fruit, cinnamon, and salt in a slow cooker. Stir in the water and vanilla. Cover and cook for 6 to 8 hours on low. Stir before serving and add more water if needed. Serve hot.

SERVING SIZE: ½ cup
EXCHANGE LIST VALUES: 1 starch, 1½ fruit
CARBOHYDRATE CHOICES: 2½
CALORIES: 179

CALORIES FROM FAT: 15
TOTAL FAT: 2 g
SATURATED FAT: 0 g
CHOLESTEROL: 0 mg
SODIUM: 219 mg

TOTAL CARBOHYDRATE: 35 g
FIBER: 5 g
TOTAL SUGARS: 11 g
PROTEIN: 5 g

Amaranth

The grain amaranth has been used for food by humans for centuries. The most common usage is to grind it into a flour for use in breads, noodles, pancakes, cereals, granola, cookies, and other flour-based products. It can be popped like popcorn or flaked like oatmeal. More than forty products containing amaranth are currently on the market in the United States.

One of the reasons for the recent interest in amaranth is its nutritional qualities. The grain has 12 to 17 percent protein and is high in fiber and in lysine, an essential amino acid in which cereal crops are low. Amaranth comes in several varieties, with mild, sweet, nutty, and maltlike flavors. Eating this grain can benefit people with hypertension and cardiovascular disease, as regular consumption has been found to reduce blood pressure and cholesterol levels.

French Tortilla Toast

MAKES 4 SERVINGS

Whole-wheat tortillas are a pantry staple at our house. We use tortillas for everything, including traditional Mexican dishes, sandwich wraps, pizzas, and this delicious nontraditional French toast.

2	large eggs
¼	cup water plus 2 tablespoons
¼	teaspoon salt
1½	teaspoons ground cinnamon
1	teaspoon agave syrup
4	(10-inch) whole-wheat flour tortillas, cut into quarters
3	tablespoons sugar-free jam in your flavor of choice
¼	cup blueberries or sliced strawberries

Beat the eggs with ¼ cup of the water and the salt until frothy. Stir in the cinnamon and syrup. Dip the tortilla pieces in the egg mixture for 10 to 15 seconds on each side, coating them evenly.

Spray a large, heavy skillet with cooking oil spray. Turn the heat to medium-high. Fry 3 or 4 tortilla wedges at a time until browned lightly on each side. Spray the skillet with more cooking oil as needed. Place 4 tortilla quarters on each plate, overlapping them slightly.

Mix the jam with the remaining 2 tablespoons of water in a microwaveable bowl and microwave for 45 seconds on low or defrost setting, stirring to combine. Sprinkle the tortillas with the blueberries or strawberry slices. Drizzle with the jam topping and serve immediately.

SERVING SIZE: 4 tortilla quarters	**TOTAL FAT:** 8 g	**FIBER:** 6 g	
EXCHANGE LIST VALUES: 2 starch	**SATURATED FAT:** 2 g	**TOTAL SUGARS:** 4 g	
CARBOHYDRATE CHOICES: 2	**CHOLESTEROL:** 93 mg	**PROTEIN:** 8 g	
CALORIES: 213	**SODIUM:** 506 mg		
CALORIES FROM FAT: 69	**TOTAL CARBOHYDRATE:** 30 g		

Mini Oatmeal Pancakes with Fruit Basket Butter

MAKES 8 SERVINGS

My family loves pancakes for breakfast, and these mini pancakes are perfect for everyone. The pancakes use steel-cut oats, which makes them more nutritious and satisfying than traditional pancakes. You can make these mini-pancakes in advance, let them cool, wrap them in portion sizes, freeze, and reheat them in the microwave for a quick breakfast. The fruit butter is the perfect sweet topping, or you can use regular or maple-flavored agave syrup.

2	cups steel-cut or quick-cooking oatmeal
¼	cup whole-wheat flour
2	teaspoons baking powder
⅛	teaspoon salt
1	cup vanilla soy milk
2	teaspoons agave syrup
1	teaspoon fresh lemon juice
1	egg white
1	teaspoon ground cinnamon
⅛	teaspoon ground nutmeg
	Cooking oil spray
	Fruit Basket Butter (recipe follows)

Grind the oatmeal in a food processor until it forms a powdery, flourlike consistency. Combine the ground oatmeal, flour, baking powder, and salt in a medium bowl and stir with a whisk to blend.

Form a well in the center of the oatmeal mixture and add the soy milk, syrup, lemon juice, egg white, cinnamon, and nutmeg. Gently stir until well blended and most (but not all) of the lumps are gone. Let rest for about 10 minutes. If you prefer a thinner, lighter pancake, add 2 tablespoons of water to the batter.

Heat the oven to 200°F. Spray a large, nonstick skillet with cooking oil spray and place it over medium-high heat. Scoop one-third cupfuls of batter and pour into the skillet in batches. Cook until the edges are lightly browned, then turn and cook until golden brown on the second side. Place the pancakes on a sheet pan and place them in the oven to keep warm until serving time. Spread each pancake with ½ teaspoon of fruit butter.

SERVING SIZE: 4 pancakes
EXCHANGE LIST VALUES: 1½ starch, ½ fruit
CARBOHYDRATE CHOICES: 2
CALORIES: 150

CALORIES FROM FAT: 17
TOTAL FAT: 2 g
SATURATED FAT: 0 g
CHOLESTEROL: 0 mg
SODIUM: 197 mg

TOTAL CARBOHYDRATE: 29 g
FIBER: 3 g
TOTAL SUGARS: 11 g
PROTEIN: 4 g

Fruit Basket Butter

MAKES ¾ CUP

I created this "butter" out of the fruits left in the basket that sits on my counter. Sometimes, the fruits we've purchased start to look a little aged before we get a chance to eat them. We use this fruit butter on pancakes, waffles, bagels, or as a spread on cheese and crackers.

2	pieces fruit (apples, pears, peaches or plums, in any combination)
½	cup water or apple juice
2	tablespoons Splenda brown sugar blend
1	teaspoon fresh lime or lemon juice
½	teaspoon vanilla extract
⅛	teaspoon salt

Peel, core or pit, and slice the fruit as necessary.

In a microwaveable bowl, combine the sliced fruit and all the remaining ingredients. Microwave on high for 3 to 4 minutes. Mash the fruit with a fork. Microwave for another 2 minutes, then mash with a fork again. Let the fruit stand in the microwave for 2 minutes to allow the mixture to thicken. Serve immediately.

SERVING SIZE: 1 tablespoon
EXCHANGE LIST VALUES: ½ fruit
CARBOHYDRATE CHOICES: ½
CALORIES: 35
CALORIES FROM FAT: 0

TOTAL FAT: 0 g
SATURATED FAT: 0 g
CHOLESTEROL: 0 mg
SODIUM: 37 mg
TOTAL CARBOHYDRATE: 8 g

FIBER: 1 g
TOTAL SUGARS: 7 g
PROTEIN: 0 g

Midmorning Snacks

and

Afternoon Energizers

SNACKS, AS PART OF A well-balanced meal plan, can help some diabetics keep their blood sugar, or glucose, levels from dropping or spiking. Opt for snacks of 125 calories or less to stay within your daily calorie goal. Eating snacks helps to keep your blood glucose levels in balance, provides you with a power boost between breakfast and lunch, and gives you a surge of energy in the afternoons. It's important to select snack foods that satisfy your hunger in a healthy way, supply your body with energy, and provide important nutrients. Recipes containing beans; berries; breads, cereals, and grains; dairy; eggs; fruits; lean meats; nuts and seeds; seafood; and vegetables are all included in this chapter. These building blocks are a good foundation for creating nutritious snacks for both children and adults.

Eating three small, well-balanced meals and two or three healthy snacks is a good way to protect your health and your heart. Research shows that people who eat a healthy breakfast, lunch, and dinner along with two or three healthy snacks each day are less likely to overeat and gain weight. One of the biggest challenges in maintaining a healthy weight is watching portion size. Healthy snacks keep you from feeling hungry while allowing you to eat smaller meals at breakfast, lunch, and dinner, thereby lowering your calorie intake.

If you love chocolate, as I do, 2 ounces of dark chocolate or an 8-ounce mug of sugar-free hot chocolate is a healthier snack than a milk-chocolate candy bar. The best way to avoid eating junk food and to save money is to make your own snacks at home. Keep plenty of fresh fruit and vegetables refrigerated in small plastic bags, ready to grab and go. Whole-wheat pretzels, baked tortilla chips, and rice cakes are delicious with low-fat toppings such as spicy mustard or salsa. Spice up air-popped popcorn with a little cayenne pepper or garlic powder. Dried fruit such as raisins or cranberries mixed with walnuts and whole-grain cereal is easy to pack in small plastic bags for a quick and healthy homemade trail mix.

Choose low-fat or nonfat versions of dairy products so you can reap the benefits of adding calcium to your diet with only a small amount of added fat. Read labels and look for added sugars, as "light" doesn't always mean that a food is low in sugar.

Substitute nonfat frozen yogurt or sorbet for ice cream to save about one-third of the calories. You also can whip up an extra batch of smoothies and freeze leftovers for a snack (see recipe, page 55). Pour the smoothie into plastic molds, ice cube trays, or paper cups and freeze the mixture for whenever you crave something sweet, or need a snack to go.

Healthy snacks contain complex carbohydrates such as whole-grain breads and cereals. Combining complex carbohydrates such as whole grains with protein-rich foods such as unsweetened or artificially sweetened low-fat or nonfat yogurt, peanut butter, or low-fat cheese creates a satisfying snack.

A snack should provide some health benefits, such as fiber or antioxidants. Avoid foods with lots of simple carbohydrates (sugars), such as candy bars or soda. Giant portions can turn a healthy snack into a calorie-packed feast. Some ways to keep the portions appropriate include using a small plate, drinking water between bites, and portioning out an amount that's 125 calories or less, rather than just eating out of the box or bag. If you enjoy snacks, then your meals can be made smaller to keep your caloric intake in balance. The total calorie count for a snack should consistently be about 125 calories or less. Calorie counts can be calculated from online sites such as www.thecaloriecounter.com.

If you occasionally need to buy prepackaged snacks, read food labels and check the nutrition information. Just because something is labeled as "low fat," "all natural," or "pure" doesn't necessarily mean that it's nutritious. Many low-fat snacks contain unhealthy amounts of sugar and as many calories as full-fat snacks.

Do the math when reading the serving size information on the label, as most snack foods are meant to be two or more servings. You may need to double or triple the amount of fat, calories, or sugar shown on the label to get an accurate caloric count. While prepackaged 100-calorie snacks are convenient, you can make your own versions of low-calorie, grab-and-go snacks at home using the recipes in this chapter.

Avoid overeating or going hungry between meals by including nutritious snacks in your diet. These healthful choices will help you avoid fattening junk food while enjoying a satisfying between-meal treat.

SOUL FOOD SPREAD   52

CRUNCHY CHILI BEANS   53

AFTER-SCHOOL BERRY SMOOTHIE   55

CINNAMON–APPLE CHIPS   56

CRUNCHY KOHLRABI STICKS   57

SUSHI-STYLE CRAB ROLL   58

FROZEN YOGURT–DIPPED BANANA POPS   60

BUFFALO-STYLE STUFFED EGGS   63

CRACKER SNACK MIX   64

CHOCOLATE POPCORN   65

CAJUN POPCORN   67

TACO-SPICED PUMPKIN SEEDS   68

SWEET BALSAMIC-GLAZED ALMONDS   69

CINNAMON-SPICED WALNUTS   70

Soul Food Spread

ABOUT 1¼ CUPS

Using beans as the creamy base for spreads and dips adds protein and fiber while reducing the fat typically added from dairy products such as sour cream or cream cheese. This dip is delicious with raw vegetables or Spicy Pita Chips (page 5).

1 (15-ounce) can no-salt-added black-eyed peas, drained and rinsed, or 1½ cups cooked black-eyed peas, drained

¼ cup tightly packed fresh flat-leaf parsley

2 tablespoons fresh lemon juice

2 tablespoons extra-virgin olive oil

1 tablespoon Italian seasoning

1 large clove garlic, minced

¼ teaspoon salt

¼ teaspoon freshly ground black pepper

Reserve a few black-eyed peas for garnish, and combine the remaining peas in a food processor with all the remaining ingredients. Process until smooth. Transfer to a serving bowl and garnish with the reserved peas. Serve now, or cover and refrigerate for up to 2 days.

Quick Snack Fix SOY NUTS AND EDAMAME ARE A GREAT SOURCE OF PROTEIN AND FIBER, AND A QUICK AND EASY SNACK. ONE-QUARTER CUP OF ROASTED SOY NUTS IS ABOUT 120 CALORIES, WHILE ½ CUP SHELLED EDAMAME IS ABOUT 100 CALORIES.

SERVING SIZE: ¼ cup
EXCHANGE LIST VALUES: 1 starch, 1 plant-based protein, 1 fat
CARBOHYDRATE CHOICES: 1
CALORIES: 117

CALORIES FROM FAT: 57
TOTAL FAT: 6 g
SATURATED FAT: 1 g
CHOLESTEROL: 0 mg
SODIUM: 136 mg

TOTAL CARBOHYDRATE: 12 g
FIBER: 3 g
TOTAL SUGARS: 1 g
PROTEIN: 4 g

Crunchy Chili Beans

MAKES ABOUT 3 CUPS

Seasoning garbanzo beans with spices and then roasting them makes the beans crisp and flavorful on the outside and creamy on the inside. Garbanzo beans are a good source of cholesterol-lowering fiber, which can help to prevent blood sugar levels from rising too rapidly after a meal. The significant quantities of folate in them helps form red blood cells and metabolize protein, and the magnesium content helps maintain a steady heartbeat.

Garbanzo beans are high in protein and iron, and because of their high starch and fiber content, they are digested slowly and can make you feel fuller longer. They are a great choice for pregnant women (especially those with gestational diabetes) and lactating women who need a higher intake of iron and protein.

2	(15-ounce) cans garbanzo beans (chickpeas)
1	tablespoon Worcestershire sauce
1	tablespoon chili powder
2	teaspoons Liquid Smoke
1	teaspoon ground cinnamon
½	teaspoon garlic powder
½	teaspoon hot sauce

Drain the garbanzo beans and rinse them several times in cold water. Spread the beans on a paper towel to dry. Mix together all the remaining ingredients in a medium bowl. Add the beans to the mixture and marinate for 30 minutes. Stir to coat.

Preheat the oven to 350°F. Spray a baking sheet with cooking oil spray and spread out the beans in a single layer. Bake for about 30 minutes, stirring occasionally, or until lightly golden brown. Let cool before eating. Store in an airtight container for up to 7 days.

Quick Snack Fix FROZEN BLUEBERRIES OR GRAPES ARE AN ICY SWEET SNACK DURING WARMER MONTHS. FREEZING DOESN'T ALTER THE NUTRITIONAL BENEFIT OF THE FRUIT.

SERVING SIZE: ⅓ cup
EXCHANGE LIST VALUES: 1 starch, 1 plant-based protein
CARBOHYDRATE CHOICES: 1
CALORIES: 83

CALORIES FROM FAT: 12
TOTAL FAT: 1 g
SATURATED FAT: 0 g
CHOLESTEROL: 0 mg
SODIUM: 169 mg

TOTAL CARBOHYDRATE: 14 g
FIBER: 3 g
TOTAL SUGARS: 2 g
PROTEIN: 4 g

After-School Berry Smoothie

MAKES 3 SERVINGS

This is the perfect after-school snack to make ahead of time and keep in a covered container in the refrigerator. Give it a shake to remix. Or, you can freeze it in ice pop molds or an ice cube tray to make a cool dessert.

1	banana
½	cup orange juice
½	cup vanilla soy yogurt
½	cup mixed fresh or frozen berries (blueberries, strawberries, or raspberries; you can also use cherries)
1	tablespoon agave nectar

In a blender, combine all the ingredients and purée until smooth.

Quick Snack Fix

- TWO TANGERINES CONTAIN A GOOD AMOUNT OF FIBER AND 20 FEWER CALORIES THAN AN 8-OUNCE GLASS OF ORANGE JUICE.

- ONE SMALL SNACK BOX (1.5 OUNCES) OF RAISINS OR 4 PRUNES; BOTH ARE HIGH IN ANTIOXIDANTS.

- A 4-OUNCE CUP OF DICED PEACHES IN JUICE ONLY HAS 80 CALORIES.

SERVING SIZE: 8 ounces
EXCHANGE LIST VALUES:
  1 carbohydrate, 1 fruit
CARBOHYDRATE CHOICES: 2
CALORIES: 121

CALORIES FROM FAT: 9
TOTAL FAT: 1 g
SATURATED FAT: 0 g
CHOLESTEROL: 0 mg
SODIUM: 6 mg

TOTAL CARBOHYDRATE: 28 g
FIBER: 2 g
TOTAL SUGARS: 20 g
PROTEIN: 2 g

Cinnamon–Apple Chips

MAKES 4 SERVINGS

My daughter, Deanna, loves these apple chips. They're easy to prepare and more nutritious than commercially packaged snacks.

4   small Granny Smith or other tart apples

2   tablespoons stevia granulated sweetener

1   tablespoon ground cinnamon

    Butter-flavored cooking spray

Preheat the oven to 250°F. Line 2 baking sheets with parchment paper or aluminum foil. Cut the apples into quarters. Cut out the core and remove the seeds. Slice the apples as thinly as possible; the slices don't have to be uniform.

Combine the stevia and cinnamon in a large bowl and mix well. Add the apple slices and toss until well coated. Place the apples in a single layer on the prepared baking sheets. Lightly spray the apples with butter-flavored cooking spray. Bake for 1 hour, then stir and spray the apples with a little more of the cooking spray. Continue baking until the apples are lightly browned and crisp, about 1 additional hour. Set aside to cool. Store in an airtight jar or a resealable plastic bag for up to 3 days.

SERVING SIZE: About 14
EXCHANGE LIST VALUES: 1½ fruit
CARBOHYDRATE CHOICES: 1½
CALORIES: 99
CALORIES FROM FAT: 17

TOTAL FAT: 2 g
SATURATED FAT: 0 g
CHOLESTEROL: 0 mg
SODIUM: 2 mg
TOTAL CARBOHYDRATE: 23 g

FIBER: 5 g
TOTAL SUGARS: 16 g
PROTEIN: 0 g

Crunchy Kohlrabi Sticks

MAKES 1 SERVING

Raw kohlrabi tastes like a cross between an apple, a potato, and a water chestnut. A medium-sized kohlrabi has about 40 calories and 8 grams of carbs. They are high in vitamin C, potassium, and fiber. This recipe provides a spicy crunch when you're in need of a snack.

½   cup cold water

1   tablespoon no-sugar-added apple cider vinegar

1   tablespoon hot sauce

1   teaspoon whole-grain mustard

½   teaspoon agave syrup

1   medium kohlrabi, washed and peeled

2   green onions, including green parts, finely chopped

Whisk together the water, vinegar, hot sauce, mustard, and syrup in a medium bowl. Slice the kohlrabi into thick rounds, about ½-inch thick. Then stack the pieces, and cut into ¼-inch-wide sticks. Stir the kohlrabi and onions into the marinade, coating the pieces evenly. Cover and refrigerate for 2 to 3 days, stirring occasionally. Drain off the marinade and serve the sticks cold or at room temperature.

Quick Snack Fix THINLY SLICED LEAN DELI MEATS ARE A GREAT SOURCE OF QUICK PROTEIN.

- WRAP REDUCED-SODIUM HAM, TURKEY, OR ROAST BEEF SLICES AROUND STICKS OF RAW KOHLRABI, CELERY, ASPARAGUS, SNOW PEAS, OR LOW-FAT STRING CHEESE FOR A PROTEIN-PACKED SNACK.

SERVING SIZE: 2 cups
EXCHANGE LIST VALUES: 1 vegetable
CARBOHYDRATE CHOICES: ½
CALORIES: 39
CALORIES FROM FAT: 2

TOTAL FAT: 0 g
SATURATED FAT: 0 g
CHOLESTEROL: 0 mg
SODIUM: 143 mg
TOTAL CARBOHYDRATE: 9 g

FIBER: 4 g
TOTAL SUGARS: 4 g
PROTEIN: 2 g

Sushi-Style Crab Roll

MAKES 2 SERVINGS

I love using imitation crabmeat, also called surimi, because it's a delicious, nutritious, and budget-friendly food that has been made for centuries in Japan. Pollack, hake, or other types of white fish are minced, cooked, and flavored to mimic the texture and color of the meat of lobster, crab, shrimp, and other shellfish. Nori is a healthy wrap made from seaweed that has been pressed and dried into thin sheets. If you have trouble finding it, substitute a butter lettuce leaf. Imitation crabmeat sticks make a wonderful snack in this sushi-style roll. It also can be flaked and placed on rice cakes or crackers with a few drops of sriracha chili sauce or wasabi paste to make a quick snack.

1½	tablespoons low-fat mayonnaise
¼	ripe avocado, pitted and sliced
1	teaspoon sriracha chili sauce
1	tablespoon reduced-sodium soy sauce
1	nori seaweed wrap
2	sticks reduced-sodium imitation crabmeat
½	cucumber, peeled, seeded, and sliced lengthwise into strips
1	stalk celery, sliced lengthwise into sticks
1	green onion, including green parts, sliced into strips

Combine 1 tablespoon of the mayonnaise, the avocado, ¾ teaspoon of the sriracha chili sauce, and the soy sauce in a small bowl and stir until smooth. Wrap the nori sheet in a damp paper towel and microwave on high for 10 to 15 seconds or until pliable.

Place the nori sheet shiny side down on a plastic wrap–covered bamboo sushi mat or a layer of plastic wrap on top of a dish towel. Spread the avocado mixture over the nori sheet to cover the entire surface except for a 1-inch border on two opposite ends of the nori sheet. Place the crab sticks, cucumber, celery, and green onion across the center of the nori sheet, parallel to the two ends without the avocado spread.

Grasp one end of the mat or dish towel, parallel to one of the ends of the nori with the bare border, and bring the mat or plastic wrap and towel over the line of filling ingredients in the center of the roll.

SERVING SIZE: 3 pieces
EXCHANGE LIST VALUES: 1 vegetable, 1½ fat
CARBOHYDRATE CHOICES: ½
CALORIES: 123

CALORIES FROM FAT: 69
TOTAL FAT: 8 g
SATURATED FAT: 1 g
CHOLESTEROL: 10 mg
SODIUM: 664 mg

TOTAL CARBOHYDRATE: 10 g
FIBER: 3 g
TOTAL SUGARS: 4 g
PROTEIN: 4 g

Tuck the end of the nori under the filling ingredients and, applying firm and even pressure along the length, roll the rest of the sushi. Pull the mat or towel and plastic wrap back as you roll to keep those out of the finished sushi.

Roll until only the last 1 inch of nori remains. Dab water along the nori strip to moisten and pull it up and over the sushi roll, pressing it in place to make it stick to the rest of the roll and seal the roll.

Pull the plastic wrap off the outside of the roll and use a sharp knife to cut the roll into 6 pieces. Turn 3 pieces on their sides on each of two small plates. Mix together the remaining ½ tablespoon of mayonnaise and ¼ teaspoon of sriracha chili sauce and dab a little on the top of each sushi roll. Serve immediately.

Quick Snack Fix IMITATION CRABMEAT AND WATER-PACKED CANNED SARDINES, SALMON, OR TUNA ARE CONVENIENCE FOODS THAT ARE GOOD SOURCES OF PROTEIN.

- PLACE 2 TO 3 SARDINES ON A WHOLE-GRAIN SCANDINAVIAN-STYLE CRACKER, SUCH AS WASA, RY KRISP, RYVITA, OR KAVLI, OR ON WHOLE-GRAIN MELBA TOAST. FINISH WITH A SQUEEZE OF LEMON.

Quick Snack Fix VEGETABLES MAKE A GREAT SNACK BECAUSE THEY'RE LOW IN FAT AND CALORIES AND HIGH IN VITAMINS, FIBER, MINERALS, AND OTHER NUTRIENTS.

- 2 CUPS OF BABY CARROTS ARE 100 CALORIES.

- STUFF A FEW STICKS OF CELERY WITH A MIX OF CRUSHED PINEAPPLE AND PART-SKIM RICOTTA CHEESE.

- STUFF PICKLED ITALIAN-STYLE GIARDINIERA VEGETABLES IN A SMALL WHOLE-WHEAT PITA POCKET.

Frozen Yogurt–Dipped Banana Pops

MAKES 8 POPS

These easy-to-make fruit pops are real kid pleasers, and making them is a wonderful way to get kids into the kitchen to learn how to prepare healthy dishes. The secret to these frozen bananas is to use ripe bananas with black spots on them, as they are full of natural sugar. You will need 8 wooden craft sticks for these pops, which can be served for a healthy snack or dessert.

4	ripe bananas
1	small (4-ounce) container plain low-fat Greek yogurt
½	tablespoon stevia granulated sweetener
1	teaspoon vanilla extract
1¾	cups low-fat granola

Peel the bananas and cut them in half crosswise. Insert a wooden craft stick into the large end of each banana. Mix together the yogurt, stevia, and vanilla in a small bowl. Dip the banana into the yogurt, or use a pastry brush to cover it completely with yogurt. Place the granola on a plate and roll the bananas in the granola mixture until well coated. Freeze the pops, uncovered, on a waxed paper–covered plate until solid—about 4 hours or overnight.

SERVING SIZE: 1 pop
EXCHANGE LIST VALUES: ½ starch, 1 fruit
CARBOHYDRATE CHOICES: 1½
CALORIES: 121

CALORIES FROM FAT: 12
TOTAL FAT: 1 g
SATURATED FAT: 0 g
CHOLESTEROL: 1 mg
SODIUM: 42 mg

TOTAL CARBOHYDRATE: 25 g
FIBER: 3 g
TOTAL SUGARS: 11 g
PROTEIN: 4 g

How to Make

Hard-Cooked Eggs

Bring the eggs to room temperature. Place the eggs in room-temperature water in a large pot. Bring to a boil, then turn down to a low boil and cook for 12 minutes. Quickly chill the eggs in ice-cold water. Peel and use as directed, or store in the refrigerator for up to 1 week.

The greenish color around the yolk of hard-cooked eggs is a natural result of sulfur and iron reacting at the surface of the yolk. It may occur when eggs are cooked too long or at too high temperature. Although the color may be unappealing, the eggs are still wholesome and nutritious and their flavor is unaffected. Greenish yolks can best be avoided by using the proper cooking time and temperature (avoid intense boiling), and by rapidly cooling the cooked eggs.

Buffalo-Style Stuffed Eggs

MAKES 12 STUFFED EGGS

These eggs have all of the flavors of buffalo chicken wings without the calories. You can make them ahead and store them in an airtight container in the refrigerator for up to a week for quick snacks.

6   large eggs, hard cooked (see page 62)

¼   cup crumbled blue cheese

2   tablespoons low-fat mayonnaise

1½   teaspoons minced fresh flat-leaf parsley

1½   tablespoons hot sauce

½   teaspoon salt

⅛   teaspoon freshly ground black pepper

1   stalk celery, diced

Shell and cut the eggs in half lengthwise. Remove the egg yolks and place them in a bowl. Mash the yolks and mix well with the cheese, mayonnaise, parsley, hot sauce, salt, and pepper. Spoon the yolk mixture back into the shells. Garnish with the celery.

Quick Snack Fix HARD-COOKED EGGS CAN BE PREPARED DAYS IN ADVANCE AND TRANSFORMED INTO A VARIETY OF HEALTHY SNACKS. ONE HARD-COOKED EGG IS A QUICK, LOW-CALORIE SNACK (ONLY 72 CALORIES) AND A GREAT SOURCE OF PROTEIN.

SERVING SIZE: 1 stuffed egg half
EXCHANGE LIST VALUES:
    ½ medium-fat meat
CARBOHYDRATE CHOICES: 0
CALORIES: 55

CALORIES FROM FAT: 36
TOTAL FAT: 4 g
SATURATED FAT: 1 g
CHOLESTEROL: 96 mg
SODIUM: 241 mg

TOTAL CARBOHYDRATE: 1 g
FIBER: 0 g
TOTAL SUGARS: 0 g
PROTEIN: 4 g

Cracker Snack Mix

MAKES ABOUT 3 CUPS

Crunchy snacks have been found to relieve stress because they allow you to relieve some of your anxiety through chewing and the comfort of food. Healthy, crunchy snacks such as nuts, whole-grain chips, and crunchy fruits and vegetables are a great alternative to high-carb snack foods. This crunchy mix is the perfect snack food for a stressful day.

1	cup low-fat whole-grain pretzels
1	cup whole-grain cereal squares
1	cup whole-grain goldfish crackers
1½	teaspoons Worcestershire sauce
2	teaspoons toasted wheat germ
2	teaspoons chili powder
1	teaspoon onion powder
1	teaspoon garlic powder

Preheat the oven to 350°F. Spray a baking sheet with cooking oil spray. Mix together all of the ingredients in a large bowl. Spread the mixture in a single layer on the prepared baking sheet and bake for 15 minutes, stirring every 5 minutes for even browning. Remove from the oven and let cool before eating. Store in an airtight container for up to 7 days.

SERVING SIZE: ½ cup
EXCHANGE LIST VALUES: 1 starch
CARBOHYDRATE CHOICES: 1
CALORIES: 86
CALORIES FROM FAT: 16

TOTAL FAT: 2 g
SATURATED FAT: 0 g
CHOLESTEROL: 1 mg
SODIUM: 203 mg
TOTAL CARBOHYDRATE: 16 g

FIBER: 2 g
TOTAL SUGARS: 2 g
PROTEIN: 2 g

Chocolate Popcorn

MAKES 4 CUPS

If you're a chocoholic like me, sugar-free cocoa mix is the answer to your cravings. It provides a healthy and delicious chocolate coating for this popcorn treat.

4 cups air-popped popcorn, or 1 bag (3½-ounce) low-fat popcorn

1 package sugar-free cocoa mix

1 teaspoon ground cinnamon

Prepare the popcorn according to the package directions. Mix together the cocoa mix and cinnamon in a large resealable plastic bag. Transfer the popcorn to the plastic bag with the cocoa mixture. Seal the bag and shake well until the cocoa mixture coats the popcorn. Store in an airtight container for up to 7 days.

Quick Snack Fix

- LOW-FAT MILK, CHEESE, YOGURT, AND OTHER DAIRY PRODUCTS ARE GOOD SOURCES OF CALCIUM AND PROTEIN, AND MAKE A FILLING SNACK.

- SPREAD 1 TABLESPOON PART-SKIM RICOTTA CHEESE OVER ONE HALF OF A SMALL CINNAMON-RAISIN BAGEL. SPRINKLE WITH CINNAMON, IF DESIRED, AND TOP WITH A FEW THIN SLICES OF PEAR OR APPLE.

SERVING SIZE: 1 cup
EXCHANGE LIST VALUES: ½ starch
CARBOHYDRATE CHOICES: ½
CALORIES: 47
CALORIES FROM FAT: 4

TOTAL FAT: 0 g
SATURATED FAT: 0 g
CHOLESTEROL: 0 mg
SODIUM: 34 mg
TOTAL CARBOHYDRATE: 9 g

FIBER: 2 g
TOTAL SUGARS: 2 g
PROTEIN: 2 g

Clockwise from top left: Cajun
Popcorn, Cinnamon-Spiced Walnuts,
Sweet Balsamic-Glazed Almonds,
and Taco-Spiced Pumpkin Seeds

Cajun Popcorn

MAKES 4 CUPS

Tossing spices into air-popped or low-fat popcorn adds a punch of flavor to a quick and easy snack.

4   cups air-popped popcorn, or 1 bag
    (3½ ounces) low-fat microwave popcorn

2   teaspoons chili powder

1   teaspoon ground cinnamon

½   teaspoon garlic powder

⅛   teaspoon cayenne pepper

Prepare the popcorn according to the package directions. Mix together all the remaining ingredients in a large resealable plastic bag. Transfer the cooked popcorn to the plastic bag with the spices. Seal the bag and shake well until the spices coat the popcorn. Store in an airtight container for up to 7 days.

Quick Snack Fix

• SPREAD 1 TABLESPOON OF NUT BUTTER ON A RICE CAKE FOR A QUICK AND SATISFYING SNACK.

NUTS AND SEEDS CONTAIN HEALTHY MONOUNSATURATED FATS OUR BODIES NEED. THESE OMEGA-3 AND OMEGA-6 FATTY ACIDS ARE VITAL TO THE HEALTH OF OUR BRAINS AND IMMUNE AND CARDIOVASCULAR SYSTEMS. NUTS ALSO ARE RICH IN PROTEIN AND FIBER, SO THEY CAN HELP YOU FEEL FULLER LONGER.

NUTS, SEEDS, AND PEANUT, ALMOND, AND CASHEW BUTTERS ARE HEALTHY SNACKS, BUT ARE HIGH IN CALORIES AND SHOULD BE EATEN UNSALTED. FOR EXAMPLE, 2 TABLESPOONS OF PEANUTS HAVE 100 CALORIES. USE PORTION CONTROL TO KEEP THE CALORIES IN NUTS AND SEEDS IN THE 100- TO 125-CALORIE RANGE.

SERVING SIZE: 1 cup
EXCHANGE LIST VALUES: ½ starch
CARBOHYDRATE CHOICES: ½
CALORIES: 34
CALORIES FROM FAT: 3

TOTAL FAT: 0 g
SATURATED FAT: 0 g
CHOLESTEROL: 0 mg
SODIUM: 1 mg
TOTAL CARBOHYDRATE: 7 g

FIBER: 2 g
TOTAL SUGARS: 0 g
PROTEIN: 1 g

Taco-Spiced Pumpkin Seeds

MAKES 2 CUPS

Pumpkin seeds (also called pepitas) are a nutritious snack, but adding the chili powder and cinnamon takes these protein-packed seeds to a whole new level.

2   tablespoons firmly packed Splenda brown sugar blend

1   teaspoon chili powder

1   teaspoon ground cinnamon

1   teaspoon ground cumin

½   teaspoon salt

¼   teaspoon garlic powder

2   cups shelled pumpkin seeds

     Butter-flavored cooking oil spray

Preheat the oven to 300°F. Stir together the brown sugar blend, chili powder, cinnamon, cumin, salt, and garlic powder in a small bowl. Spread the pumpkin seeds in an even layer on a rimmed baking sheet. Spray the pumpkin seeds with the cooking oil spray, tossing and spraying until well coated. Sprinkle the pumpkin seeds with the spice mix. Toss until well combined. Bake for 8 to 10 minutes, stirring occasionally. Remove from the oven and let cool. Store in an airtight container for up to 7 days.

SERVING SIZE: 1½ tablespoons
EXCHANGE LIST VALUES: 1½ fat
CARBOHYDRATE CHOICES: 0
CALORIES: 104
CALORIES FROM FAT: 74

TOTAL FAT: 8 g
SATURATED FAT: 1 g
CHOLESTEROL: 0 mg
SODIUM: 58 mg
TOTAL CARBOHYDRATE: 3 g

FIBER: 1 g
TOTAL SUGARS: 1 g
PROTEIN: 4 g

Sweet Balsamic-Glazed Almonds

MAKES 2 CUPS

Almonds are a heart-healthy snack packed with monounsaturated fat, protein, potassium, calcium, phosphorous, iron, vitamin E, magnesium, selenium, and fiber. Here, the brown sugar blend and vinegar provide the almonds with a fabulous flavor. The sugar forms a caramel-like coating on the almonds, and the spices provide a little heat with each bite.

2   cups raw almonds

½   cup firmly packed Splenda brown sugar blend

⅔   cup balsamic vinegar

½   teaspoon salt

½   teaspoon ground cinnamon

¼   teaspoon chili powder or cayenne pepper (optional)

Line a baking pan with parchment or waxed paper and set aside. Place the almonds in a large, heavy skillet. Cook over medium heat for 3 to 5 minutes, until lightly toasted. Turn the heat to low and add the brown sugar blend, vinegar, salt, and cinnamon. Stir until the sugar melts, the almonds are well coated, and no liquid is left in the bottom of the pan. If using chili powder or cayenne pepper, sprinkle it over the nuts evenly and toss. Transfer the almonds to the prepared baking pan and separate the individual nuts. Set aside and let cool before serving. Store in an airtight container for up to 7 days.

SERVING SIZE: 1½ tablespoons
EXCHANGE LIST VALUES:
       ½ carbohydrate, 1½ fat
CARBOHYDRATE CHOICES: ½
CALORIES: 108

CALORIES FROM FAT: 61
TOTAL FAT: 7 g
SATURATED FAT: 1 g
CHOLESTEROL: 0 mg
SODIUM: 57 mg

TOTAL CARBOHYDRATE: 9 g
FIBER: 2 g
TOTAL SUGARS: 6 g
PROTEIN: 3 g

Cinnamon-Spiced Walnuts

MAKES 2 CUPS

Spiced nuts, eaten in moderation, are a healthy snack. Some researchers have found that eating cinnamon every day can help lower blood glucose—and it gives a savory bite to these crunchy walnuts.

2   cups walnut halves

      Butter-flavored cooking oil spray

2   tablespoons firmly packed
      Splenda brown sugar blend

1   teaspoon ground cinnamon

¼   teaspoon salt

Preheat the oven to 300°F. Spread the walnuts in an even layer in a baking pan. Spray the walnuts with the cooking oil spray until well coated. Stir together the brown sugar blend, cinnamon, and salt in a medium bowl. Sprinkle the nuts with the spice mix and toss until well combined. Redistribute the walnuts in an even layer in the baking pan. Bake for 8 to 10 minutes, stirring occasionally. Remove from the oven and let cool completely before serving. Store in an airtight container for up to 7 days.

Quick Snack Fix

- INDIVIDUAL BOXES OF WHOLE-GRAIN CEREAL WITH SKIM MILK.

- WHOLE-GRAIN ENGLISH MUFFINS OR TORTILLAS TOPPED WITH 2 TABLESPOONS OF MILD SALSA; DICED CANADIAN BACON, COOKED CHICKEN, OR TURKEY SAUSAGE, OR YOUR FAVORITE VEGGIES; AND A SPRINKLE OF SHREDDED LOW-FAT CHEESE; THEN BAKED IN A TOASTER OVEN.

- RYE CRACKERS OR MELBA TOAST ROUNDS TOPPED WITH SALSA AND LOW-FAT CHEESE, THEN MICROWAVED FOR 30 TO 60 SECONDS ON LOW OR DEFROST SETTING UNTIL THE CHEESE MELTS.

SERVING SIZE: 2 tablespoons
EXCHANGE LIST VALUES: 1½ fat
CARBOHYDRATE CHOICES: 0
CALORIES: 91
CALORIES FROM FAT: 74

TOTAL FAT: 8 g
SATURATED FAT: 1 g
CHOLESTEROL: 0 mg
SODIUM: 37 mg
TOTAL CARBOHYDRATE: 3 g

FIBER: 1 g
TOTAL SUGARS: 2 g
PROTEIN: 2 g

Let's Do Lunch

A HEALTHY LUNCH IS AN important part of a good diabetic meal plan. A nutritious lunch helps maintain balanced glucose levels and assists with weight control. Eating a nourishing lunch also is important to hone your focus and concentration and reduce low energy levels in the afternoon.

Most people use the majority of their energy between breakfast and dinner, so lunch is necessary to be productive and energetic. Dramatic calorie highs and lows aren't good for anyone, especially those with diabetes and diet-related illnesses. Researchers at the University of Georgia studied the eating patterns of athletes. Their study determined that men and women showed higher levels of body fat if they had irregular eating patterns throughout the day, even if they were in energy balance by the end of the day. In addition, compared with athletes who ate consistently through the day (breakfast, lunch, snacks, and dinner), they had worse muscle mass, lower energy levels, and poor mental focus. This study proves that when it comes to lunch, you are what you eat.

Good sources of protein, whole grains, vegetables, and fruits will help you be more focused, productive, and energetic throughout the rest of the day. When selecting breads, look for products that list whole grains (not just whole wheat) as the first or main ingredient. Whole-grain wheat breads, rolls, pita, English muffins, or tortillas are good choices for sandwiches, burgers, and wraps. Bread products should have 3 grams of fiber per serving and, ideally, be fortified with extra fiber. Prepackaged condiments are often high in fat, sugar, salt, and additives. Recipes and suggestions for condiments, spreads, and dressings that are low in fat are included to help you make healthful choices for lunch.

The recipes in this chapter contain a variety of delicious lunch options—from sandwiches and wraps to salads and stews—that provide a balance of fruit and vegetables; high-fiber content from whole-grain breads, pasta, and beans; and protein from lean meats, poultry, and seafood. These wonderful recipes will provide you with a midday meal that you'll eagerly look forward to, and will provide you with the fuel your body needs to have a healthy and productive day.

SLIM CAESAR WITH LITE DRESSING   73

CAROLINA COLESLAW   74

SOUTHERN SALAD   75

JERK CHICKEN SALAD WITH TROPICAL FRUIT DRESSING   77

PASTA, BROCCOLI, AND LENTIL SALAD WITH GREEK DRESSING   80

ASIAN-STYLE SALMON AND CABBAGE SALAD
   WITH GINGER–SOY DRESSING   82

CALYPSO COCONUT SHRIMP SALAD WITH ISLAND VINAIGRETTE   84

PEAR AND WALNUT SALAD   86

TUNA–SUNCHOKE SALAD NIÇOISE WITH
   HONEY–MUSTARD DRESSING   88

SWEET AND SOUR WATERMELON AND CUCUMBER SALAD   91

TWO-CHICK SALAD WITH MEDITERRANEAN-STYLE DRESSING   92

BARBECUE BURGERS   93

MINI MUFFULETTAS   94

SEAFOOD BURGERS   95

ROAST BEEF SLIDERS WITH SPICY WALNUT MUSTARD   97

BROILED PIMIENTO CHEESE AND ROASTED TOMATO SANDWICHES   99

OPEN-FACED CHICKEN SALAD SANDWICHES   100

SARDINE TOASTS   101

MICROWAVE VEGGIE TORTILLA WRAPS   102

MICROWAVE EGG FOO YUNG CABBAGE WRAP   103

PUMPKIN AND TORTELLINI SOUP WITH FETA CHEESE CROUTONS   105

THREE-BEAN SOUP   107

CHINESE CABBAGE SOUP   108

FIRE-ROASTED TOMATO AND KALE SOUP   109

CREOLE CHICKEN STEW   110

SLOW-COOKER CURRY STEW   112

Slim Caesar with Lite Dressing

MAKES 2 SERVINGS

Like many others, I was under the impression that I was making a healthy choice if I ordered a Caesar salad at a restaurant. However, most Caesar salad dressings pack 18 grams of fat in just 2 tablespoons. A chicken Caesar salad at most popular dining spots averages 1,500 calories, 16 grams of saturated fat, 1,481 milligrams of sodium, and 23 grams of carbs. This "slimmer" version of a Caesar salad uses protein-packed tofu and low-fat Greek yogurt infused with garlic and spices to create a creamy, flavorful dressing. Sardines are used instead of the traditional anchovies to provide a unique flavor and additional protein.

DRESSING

¼   cup silken soft tofu

2   tablespoons low-fat Greek yogurt

½   tablespoon olive oil

½   tablespoon red wine vinegar

1   tablespoon Dijon mustard

½   teaspoon Worcestershire sauce

2   sardines, canned, packed in water, mashed

1   clove garlic, minced

1   teaspoon freshly ground black pepper

4   cups torn romaine lettuce leaves

¼   cup fat-free croutons

2   tablespoons shaved Parmesan cheese

To make the dressing, combine all the ingredients in a blender or food processor and blend until smooth.

Pour half of the dressing into a large bowl. Toss the lettuce with the dressing until the leaves are coated, adding more dressing as needed. Divide the salad between 2 serving plates. Top each with croutons and cheese and serve.

SERVING SIZE: 1 salad
EXCHANGE LIST VALUES: ½ starch, 1 vegetable, 1 medium-fat meat, ½ fat
CARBOHYDRATE CHOICES: 1

CALORIES: 190
CALORIES FROM FAT: 82
TOTAL FAT: 9 g
SATURATED FAT: 2 g
CHOLESTEROL: 22 mg

SODIUM: 575 mg
TOTAL CARBOHYDRATE: 12 g
FIBER: 2 g
TOTAL SUGARS: 3 g
PROTEIN: 13 g

Carolina Coleslaw

MAKES 6 SERVINGS

I love this coleslaw because it incorporates apples and apple cider vinegar, creating a sweet and tangy flavor base. Serve it as a side salad, or use as a topping for Barbecue Burgers (page 93) or Seafood Burgers (page 95).

1	green cabbage, cored and finely shredded, or 1 (16-ounce) package coleslaw mix
1	medium red onion, quartered and thinly sliced
1	large carrot, peeled and shredded
1	large Granny Smith, York, Rome, Gala, or Fuji apple, cored and diced
1	cucumber, thinly sliced
1	stalk celery, diced
¼	cup no-sugar-added apple cider vinegar
3	tablespoons canola oil
¼	cup stevia granulated sweetener
1	tablespoon Italian seasoning
1	teaspoon dry mustard
¼	teaspoon salt
1	teaspoon freshly ground black pepper

In a large bowl, combine the shredded cabbage or coleslaw mix, onion, carrot, apple, cucumber, and celery. In a small microwaveable bowl, combine the vinegar, oil, stevia, Italian seasoning, mustard, salt, and pepper. Microwave on high for 3 to 4 minutes until the dressing ingredients come to a boil. Pour the dressing over the cabbage to slightly wilt it. Toss to combine. Let cool, then refrigerate overnight to allow the flavors to combine. Stir before serving.

SERVING SIZE: ⅔ cup
EXCHANGE LIST VALUES: ½ fruit, 1 vegetable, 1 fat
CARBOHYDRATE CHOICES: 1
CALORIES: 132

CALORIES FROM FAT: 64
TOTAL FAT: 7 g
SATURATED FAT: 1 g
CHOLESTEROL: 0 mg
SODIUM: 129 mg

TOTAL CARBOHYDRATE: 17 g
FIBER: 4 g
TOTAL SUGARS: 8 g
PROTEIN: 2 g

Southern Salad

MAKES 4 SERVINGS

George Washington Carver popularized planting crops of black-eyed peas throughout the South. The legumes add nitrogen to the soil and have a high nutritional value. Black-eyed peas are an excellent source of calcium, are low in fat and sodium, and contain no cholesterol. They are high in potassium, iron, and fiber.

You can make this delicious salad into a vegetarian entrée by omitting the chicken, and still get the protein benefit from the black-eyed peas. One-half cup of cooked black-eyed peas has about the same amount of protein as 1 ounce of lean meat. The creamy peas provide a silky texture to the salad and are a great contrast to the crunchy vegetables. The romaine lettuce can be used as a wrap for the salad filling, if desired.

1   tablespoon olive oil

2   tablespoons fresh lemon juice

2   teaspoons poultry seasoning

⅛   teaspoon salt

1   teaspoon freshly ground black pepper

1   clove garlic, minced

1½ cups diced cooked chicken breast

1   cup peeled and diced cucumber

1   (15-ounce) can no-salt-added or low-sodium black-eyed peas, rinsed and drained

1   (16-ounce) package prewashed baby spinach

1   stalk celery, diced

⅔   cup diced red bell pepper

¼   cup slivered red onion

1   (3-ounce) bag romaine lettuce hearts

Mix the oil, lemon juice, poultry seasoning, salt, pepper, and garlic in a large bowl until combined. Add the chicken, cucumber, black-eyed peas, spinach, celery, bell pepper, and onion. Toss to coat. Serve over the lettuce at room temperature or chilled.

SERVING SIZE: 1 salad
EXCHANGE LIST VALUES: 1 starch, 2 vegetable, 2 lean meat, 1 plant-based protein, ½ fat
CARBOHYDRATE CHOICES: 2

CALORIES: 287
CALORIES FROM FAT: 62
TOTAL FAT: 7 g
SATURATED FAT: 1 g
CHOLESTEROL: 54 mg

SODIUM: 334 mg
TOTAL CARBOHYDRATE: 31 g
FIBER: 10 g
TOTAL SUGARS: 3 g
PROTEIN: 29 g

Jerk Chicken Salad with Tropical Fruit Dressing

SERVES 4

Jerk chicken is one of my signature recipes. The spices that are used to create this flavorful dish originated in the Caribbean and can be traced back to slavery times. Jerk seasoning also is delicious on fish or pork. Make extra portions of the chicken to serve as a main course or to use in wraps or sandwiches.

Adding fruit to this salad provides a hint of sweetness to cool down the spiciness of the chicken, as well as lots of nutrients. Figs are rich in fiber and are a good source of potassium, calcium, and manganese. They're also a good source of polyphenols, plant-based chemicals that help fight heart disease and cancer.

MARINADE

¼ cup no-sugar-added apple cider vinegar

3 tablespoons stevia granulated sweetener or agave syrup

2 to 3 tablespoons habanero hot sauce (or your preference)

2 teaspoons ground allspice

2 teaspoons onion powder

2 teaspoons garlic powder

2 teaspoons ground cinnamon

¼ teaspoon salt

1 teaspoon freshly ground black pepper

2 green onions, including green parts, chopped

4 (4-ounce) boneless, skinless chicken breasts

Olive oil cooking spray

1 (3- to 6-ounce) bag prewashed mixed salad greens

1½ cups chopped or shredded radicchio

8 figs, quartered, or 12 green or purple seedless grapes, halved

1 cup fresh or canned pineapple chunks in natural juices

4 tablespoons Tropical Fruit Dressing (recipe follows)

Pomegranate seeds, for garnish

SERVING SIZE: 1 salad
EXCHANGE LIST VALUES: 2 fruit, 3 lean meat
CARBOHYDRATE CHOICES: 2
CALORIES: 258

CALORIES FROM FAT: 38
TOTAL FAT: 4 g
SATURATED FAT: 2 g
CHOLESTEROL: 63 mg
SODIUM: 241 mg

TOTAL CARBOHYDRATE: 32 g
FIBER: 5 g
TOTAL SUGARS: 23 g
PROTEIN: 25 g

To make the marinade, mix together all the ingredients in a small bowl until well blended.

Spray the chicken with the olive oil cooking spray. Place the chicken in a resealable plastic bag. Pour the jerk seasoning marinade over the chicken and press and shake the bag until all the pieces are thoroughly coated. Press out any air, seal the bag, and place it in a baking pan to prevent leaks. Refrigerate for at least 8 hours or up to 24 hours.

Remove the chicken from the refrigerator. Discard the marinade and allow the chicken to come to room temperature, about 30 minutes. Spray a large skillet with the olive oil cooking spray and turn the heat to medium-high. Cook the chicken for about 6 minutes, on each side, or until browned and no longer pink. Remove the chicken from the skillet, and let it rest for 6 to 7 minutes. Thinly slice each chicken breast.

Toss together the greens, radicchio, figs or grapes, and pineapple. Divide the salad among 4 plates. Arrange the warm chicken slices on top of each salad. Drizzle each with 1 tablespoon of the tropical fruit dressing. Sprinkle with pomegranate seeds, if desired.

Tropical Fruit Dressing

MAKES ¾ CUP

This tangy dressing cools down spicy Jerk Chicken while adding a fresh citrus flavor to the salad. For a change of pace, try this dressing on other types of salads.

¼	cup nonfat Greek yogurt
¼	cup fresh squeezed pomegranate juice
1	tablespoon coconut oil or olive oil
2	teaspoons stevia granulated sweetener or agave syrup
½	teaspoon grated orange or lime zest
¼	cup fresh orange juice or lime juice

In a small bowl, mix together all the ingredients until blended. Store in an airtight container in the refrigerator for up to 7 days.

SERVING SIZE: 1 tablespoon
EXCHANGE LIST VALUES: 0
CARBOHYDRATE CHOICES: 0
CALORIES: 18
CALORIES FROM FAT: 10

TOTAL FAT: 1 g
SATURATED FAT: 1 g
CHOLESTEROL: 0 mg
SODIUM: 2 mg
TOTAL CARBOHYDRATE: 2 g

FIBER: 0 g
TOTAL SUGARS: 1 g
PROTEIN: 0 g

Pasta, Broccoli, and Lentil Salad with Greek Dressing

MAKES 6 SERVINGS

Lentils, often used as a meat substitute in north Africa and the Middle East, provide the protein in this nourishing salad. Lentils come in several colors: green, brown, yellow, and red. This legume is easy to cook, but canned varieties are a quick substitute. The Greek Dressing adds a creamy, lemony finish to the salad.

2   cups (6 ounces) small, whole-wheat shell pasta

1   (15-ounce) can lentils, rinsed and drained, or ½ cup dried lentils (see Note)

6   cherry tomatoes, halved

¾   cup chopped broccoli

¼   cup chopped red bell pepper

½   red onion, diced

1   stalk celery, diced

½   large carrot, peeled and sliced into rounds

1   tablespoon Italian seasoning

⅛   teaspoon salt

1   teaspoon freshly ground black pepper

⅛   teaspoon cayenne pepper

    Greek Dressing (recipe follows)

3   cups chopped Romaine lettuce

In a large pot of salted boiling water, cook the pasta until tender but with a slight firmness, 6 to 8 minutes. Drain and set aside. If using canned lentils, soak the drained lentils in hot water for about 10 minutes to warm them and help them absorb the seasonings; drain again.

In a large bowl, combine the drained lentils, pasta, tomatoes, broccoli, bell pepper, onion, celery, carrot, Italian seasoning, salt, pepper, and cayenne pepper. Toss to mix. Pour the dressing over the lentil mixture and toss to coat. Cover and refrigerate for at least 2 hours to allow the flavors to combine. Serve over a bed of the chopped romaine lettuce.

NOTE: To cook dried lentils, pick through the lentils and remove any rocks or debris. Rinse and drain the lentils. In a small saucepan, combine the lentils, 1½ cups of water, 1 bay leaf, and 1 teaspoon of salt. Bring to a boil, then reduce the heat to a simmer. Cover and cook for 15 to 20 minutes, or until tender. Drain the lentils and remove the bay leaf.

SERVING SIZE: 2 cups
EXCHANGE LIST VALUES: 2 starch, 1 plant-based protein, ½ fat
CARBOHYDRATE CHOICES: 2
CALORIES: 229

CALORIES FROM FAT: 30
TOTAL FAT: 3 g
SATURATED FAT: 1 g
CHOLESTEROL: 2 mg
SODIUM: 244 mg

TOTAL CARBOHYDRATE: 40 g
FIBER: 9 g
TOTAL SUGARS: 4 g
PROTEIN: 12 g

Greek Dressing

MAKES ½ CUP

½ cup low-fat Greek yogurt

1 tablespoon olive oil

2 teaspoons fresh lemon juice

1 tablespoon minced fresh flat-leaf parsley

1 teaspoon Dijon mustard

1 teaspoon stevia granulated sweetener or agave syrup

¼ teaspoon salt

½ teaspoon freshly ground black pepper

In a small bowl, combine all the ingredients and stir until well combined. Store in an airtight container in the refrigerator for up to 7 days. Stir to combine before using.

SERVING SIZE: 2 tablespoons
EXCHANGE LIST VALUES: 1 fat
CARBOHYDRATES CHOICES: 0
CALORIES: 54
CALORIES FROM FAT: 37

TOTAL FAT: 4 g
SATURATED FAT: 1 g
CHOLESTEROL: 2 mg
SODIUM: 185 mg
TOTAL CARBOHYDRATE: 2 g

FIBER: 0 g
TOTAL SUGARS: 0 g
PROTEIN: 2 g

Asian-Style Salmon and Cabbage Salad with Ginger–Soy Dressing

MAKES 4 SERVINGS

Salads are the perfect way to add new vegetables and fruits to your diet. Kohlrabi, a knobby purple or pale green member of the cabbage family, tastes like a crisp, mustard-flavored Granny Smith apple. It works beautifully with the tender salmon and the crunchy coleslaw in this dish.

1   (6-ounce) salmon fillet, poached, boned, skinned, and flaked, or 1 (15-ounce) can no-salt-added wild Alaskan salmon, drained, bones and skin removed and discarded

1   (10- to 12-ounce) bag coleslaw, or 1 small head green cabbage, cored and shredded

1   kohlrabi, peeled and cut into thin strips

1   large apple (York, Rome, Gala, or Fuji), cored and cut into thin strips

2   tablespoons finely sliced green onion, including green parts

1½ cups seeded and diced cucumber

1   jalapeño chile, seeded and minced (see Note)

2   tablespoons ground flaxseed

2   tablespoons minced fresh cilantro

    Ginger–Soy Dressing (recipe follows)

In a large bowl, combine the salmon, coleslaw or cabbage, kohlrabi, apple, onion, cucumber, and jalapeño and toss to mix. Sprinkle with the flaxseed. Divide evenly among 4 plates. Sprinkle with the cilantro and drizzle each serving with 1 tablespoon of the dressing.

SERVING SIZE: 1 salad
EXCHANGE LIST VALUES: ½ fruit, 2 vegetable, 1 lean meat, 1½ fat
CARBOHYDRATE CHOICES: 1½
CALORIES: 254

CALORIES FROM FAT: 121
TOTAL FAT: 14 g
SATURATED FAT: 2 g
CHOLESTEROL: 25 mg
SODIUM: 206 mg

TOTAL CARBOHYDRATE: 24 g
FIBER: 6 g
TOTAL SUGARS: 14 g
PROTEIN: 12 g

Ginger–Soy Dressing

MAKES ABOUT ¼ CUP

The combination of soy, ginger, sesame oil, and lime juice makes an unusual and tasty salad dressing, as well as a 30-minute marinade for chicken, pork, or fish before grilling, roasting, baking, or broiling.

2   tablespoons olive oil

3   tablespoons rice wine vinegar

2   tablespoons minced fresh ginger

2   cloves garlic, minced

1   tablespoon reduced-sodium soy sauce

½   tablespoon toasted sesame oil

1   tablespoon fresh lime juice

1   tablespoon honey or stevia granulated sweetener

In a small bowl or a jar with a tight-fitting lid, combine all the ingredients and whisk or shake until well combined. Store in an airtight container in the refrigerator for up to 2 weeks. Shake to combine before using.

NOTE: To prepare the chile, wear rubber gloves, and always wash your hands immediately afterward. If you have not used gloves, and your hands begin to burn, rub them with vinegar or alcohol immediately. Don't touch your eyes, nose, mouth, or other sensitive areas.

SERVING SIZE: 1 tablespoon
EXCHANGE LIST VALUES: 1½ fat
CARBOHYDRATE CHOICES: 0
CALORIES: 102
CALORIES FROM FAT: 78

TOTAL FAT: 9 g
SATURATED FAT: 1 g
CHOLESTEROL: 0 mg
SODIUM: 153 mg
TOTAL CARBOHYDRATE: 6 g

FIBER: 0 g
TOTAL SUGARS: 4 g
PROTEIN: 0 g

Calypso Coconut Shrimp Salad with Island Vinaigrette

MAKES 4 SERVINGS

This colorful salad is a perfect meal for a hot summer day. Shrimp, a nutritious alternative to meat, is high in omega-3 fats, is low in calories and saturated fat, and is a very good source of vitamins D and B12.

2 cups cooked (16-20 count) shrimp, shelled and deveined

1 bag (16 ounces) mixed baby greens

1 red or yellow bell pepper, seeded, deribbed, and chopped

¼ cup chopped red onion

1 cup chopped fresh pineapple, or 1 (15-ounce) can pineapple chunks, chilled and drained

   Island Vinaigrette (recipe follows)

2 tablespoons sweetened flaked coconut

In a large bowl, toss together the shrimp, greens, bell pepper, onion, and pineapple until well combined. Divide evenly among 4 plates and dress each salad with 2 tablespoons of the vinaigrette. Sprinkle with coconut and serve immediately.

SERVING SIZE: 1 salad
EXCHANGE LIST VALUES: ½ fruit, 1 vegetable, 3 lean meat, 2 fat
CARBOHYDRATE CHOICES: 1
CALORIES: 270

CALORIES FROM FAT: 112
TOTAL FAT: 13 g
SATURATED FAT: 10 g
CHOLESTEROL: 172 mg
SODIUM: 461 mg

TOTAL CARBOHYDRATE: 19 g
FIBER: 4 g
TOTAL SUGARS: 11 g
PROTEIN: 23 g

Island Vinaigrette

MAKES ½ CUP

Virgin coconut oil is extracted from fresh coconut meat without using high temperatures or chemicals to maintain many of its natural health properties. If you enjoy the flavors of coconut oil, remember to use it in moderation as many of the health claims posed by manufacturers have not been proven accurate. This vinaigrette beautifully complements shrimp, greens, and tropical fruit.

¼ cup no-sugar-added apple cider vinegar

3 tablespoons liquid virgin coconut oil or olive oil

¾ teaspoon Dijon mustard

1 tablespoon chopped fresh flat-leaf parsley

1 teaspoon honey or stevia granulated sweetener

¼ teaspoon salt

½ teaspoon freshly ground black pepper

⅛ teaspoon cayenne pepper

In a small bowl or jar with a tight-fitting lid, whisk or shake together all the ingredients until blended. Store in an airtight container for up to 7 days. Let sit at room temperature for 20 minutes and shake to recombine the ingredients before using.

SERVING SIZE: 2 tablespoons
EXCHANGE LIST VALUES: 2 fat
CARBOHYDRATE CHOICES: 0
CALORIES: 105
CALORIES FROM FAT: 90

TOTAL FAT: 11 g
SATURATED FAT: 9 g
CHOLESTEROL: 0 mg
SODIUM: 168 mg
TOTAL CARBOHYDRATE: 4 g

FIBER: 0 g
TOTAL SUGARS: 1 g
PROTEIN: 0 g

Pear and Walnut Salad

MAKES 8 SERVINGS

Pears and walnuts are a beautiful salad combination. The crisp sweetness of the pears and the toasted crunchiness of the walnuts, combined with the sweet-and-sour fruit vinaigrette, make this a simple meal to savor.

DRESSING

¼   cup orange juice

3   tablespoons seasoned rice wine vinegar

3   tablespoons olive oil

¼   teaspoon salt

½   teaspoon freshly ground black pepper

4   cups mixed salad greens

2   large pears (Anjou, Bartlett, Bosc, or Comice), cored and thinly sliced

½   small red onion, thinly sliced and separated into rings

¼   cup chopped walnuts, toasted (see Note)

For the dressing, whisk together all the ingredients in a small bowl. Set aside.

Arrange the greens on eight salad plates. Divide the pears, onion, and walnuts among the salads. Drizzle with the dressing and serve.

TOASTING NUTS: Toast nuts in a dry, heavy skillet over medium heat for 1 to 2 minutes, stirring frequently, or until golden brown. Watch closely when using this method, as it's easy to burn them. Remove from the pan to cool. Store in an airtight container in the refrigerator for up to 2 weeks, or freeze in an airtight freezer container for up to 3 months.

SERVING SIZE: 1 salad
EXCHANGE LIST VALUES: 1 fruit, 1½ fat
CARBOHYDRATE CHOICES: 1
CALORIES: 118
CALORIES FROM FAT: 70

TOTAL FAT: 8 g
SATURATED FAT: 1 g
CHOLESTEROL: 0 mg
SODIUM: 195 mg
TOTAL CARBOHYDRATE: 13 g

FIBER: 3g
TOTAL SUGARS: 8 g
PROTEIN: 1 g

Tuna–Sunchoke Salad Niçoise with Honey–Mustard Dressing

MAKES 4 SERVINGS

A traditional niçoise salad is made of tuna, olives, hard-cooked eggs, green beans, tomatoes, and potatoes. My Diva-style version uses sunchokes (also known as Jerusalem artichokes) as a potato substitute. They have a crunchy texture and taste like a cross between a russet potato and jicama. This tuber looks a bit like fresh ginger, but the thin skin doesn't need to be peeled. Like potatoes, sunchokes will turn brown when exposed to the air. It's best to soak the slices in acidulated water.

1   (6½-ounce) can tuna packed in water, drained

    Honey–Mustard Dressing (recipe follows)

2   cups thinly sliced unpeeled sunchokes (Jerusalem artichokes)

1   cup fresh green beans, trimmed, or frozen cut green beans

2   tablespoons apple cider vinegar or fresh lemon juice

⅛   teaspoon salt

1   teaspoon freshly ground black pepper

3   cups chopped romaine lettuce

1   cup torn radicchio leaves

½   cup niçoise or kalamata olives, pitted

8   tomato slices

3   hard-cooked large eggs, quartered

¼   cup fat-free croutons

In a small bowl, toss the tuna with 2 tablespoons of the dressing. Cover and refrigerate for at least 30 minutes or up to 2 hours.

In a medium microwaveable bowl, toss together the sunchokes, green beans, vinegar or lemon juice, salt, and pepper. Cover with microwave-safe plastic wrap and microwave on high for 3 minutes, or until the green beans are crisp-tender.

Arrange the lettuce and radicchio leaves on 4 plates. Arrange the tuna mixture, olives, tomato slices, and eggs on the lettuce and radicchio. Drizzle with the remaining dressing and sprinkle with the croutons.

SERVING SIZE: 1 salad
EXCHANGE LIST VALUES: 1½ starch, 1 vegetable, 1 lean meat, 1 fat
CARBOHYDRATE CHOICES: 2
CALORIES: 252

CALORIES FROM FAT: 93
TOTAL FAT: 10 g
SATURATED FAT: 2 g
CHOLESTEROL: 67 mg
SODIUM: 352 mg

TOTAL CARBOHYDRATE: 26 g
FIBER: 4 g
TOTAL SUGARS: 12 g
PROTEIN: 17 g

Honey–Mustard Dressing

MAKES ABOUT ⅓ CUP

2   tablespoons olive oil

3   tablespoons no-sugar-added apple cider vinegar

½   tablespoon honey or honey-flavored agave syrup

1   tablespoon Dijon mustard

2   cloves garlic, finely diced

1   tablespoon minced fresh flat-leaf parsley

1½ teaspoons capers plus ½ teaspoon brine

½   teaspoon freshly ground black pepper

In a small bowl or a jar with a tight-fitting lid, mix together all the ingredients and whisk or shake until well combined. Store in an airtight container in the refrigerator for up to 2 weeks. Shake to combine before using.

SERVING SIZE: 1 tablespoon
EXCHANGE LIST VALUES: 1 fat
CARBOHYDRATE CHOICES: 0
CALORIES: 83
CALORIES FROM FAT: 63

TOTAL FAT: 7 g
SATURATED FAT: 1 g
CHOLESTEROL: 0 mg
SODIUM: 130 mg
TOTAL CARBOHYDRATE: 5 g

FIBER: 0 g
TOTAL SUGARS: 2 g
PROTEIN: 0 g

Watermelons

Watermelons are classified as a fruit. However, as a member of the cucurbitaceae plant family of gourds, watermelon is related to cucumber and squash. Some prefer to call watermelon a "fregetable," a combination of a fruit and a vegetable.

Watermelons now are available all year long in various sizes, with or without seeds, and with either red or yellow flesh. To pick the perfect watermelon, select one that is firm, symmetrical, and free from bruises, cuts, or dents. A ripe watermelon should be heavy for its size and sound hollow when thumped. If it's at room temperature when you buy it, you can keep it at room temperature. If it's refrigerated, be sure to keep the watermelon cool. Whole melons will keep for 7 to 10 days at room temperature.

Sweet and Sour Watermelon and Cucumber Salad

MAKES 4 SERVINGS

Watermelon adds a refreshing sweetness to this salad. Low in fat and cholesterol free, watermelon contains high levels of the antioxidant lycopene, it is an excellent source of the important amino acid citrulline, and it is a good source of vitamins C, B1, B6, and A.

1	teaspoon grated lemon zest
½	cup fresh lemon juice
1	cup water
½	cup stevia granulated sweetener
1	tablespoon poppy seeds
¼	teaspoon salt
1	teaspoon freshly ground black pepper
1	bunch green onions, white and green parts, chopped
3	cups seedless watermelon balls or small chunks
2	cucumbers, peeled, seeded, and sliced

Mix together the lemon zest, juice, water, stevia, poppy seeds, salt, and pepper in a bowl. Stir in the green onions. Add the watermelon and cucumbers and toss gently. Cover and refrigerate for 1 hour. Stir before serving.

SERVING SIZE: 1 cup
EXCHANGE LIST VALUES: ½ fruit, 1 vegetable
CARBOHYDRATE CHOICES: 1
CALORIES: 86

CALORIES FROM FAT: 11
TOTAL FAT: 1 g
SATURATED FAT: 0 g
CHOLESTEROL: 0 mg
SODIUM: 155 mg

TOTAL CARBOHYDRATE: 19 g
FIBER: 2 g
TOTAL SUGARS: 10 g
PROTEIN: 2 g

Two-Chick Salad with Mediterranean-Style Dressing

MAKES 4 SERVINGS

Chicken and chickpeas (also called garbanzo beans) are the two "chicks" in this protein-packed salad, which is perfect for lunch or a light supper. Chickpeas are a good source of zinc, folate, and protein. They also are very high in dietary fiber, are low in fat, and are a good source of slowly digested carbohydrates for diabetics. Mediterranean-inspired ingredients, including olive oil, oregano, and olives, turn this delicious salad into a heart-healthy lunch.

MEDITERRANEAN-STYLE DRESSING

¼ cup no-sugar-added apple cider vinegar

2 tablespoons olive oil

1 tablespoon minced fresh dill, or 1 teaspoon dried

1 teaspoon dried oregano

1 teaspoon minced garlic

⅛ teaspoon salt

1 teaspoon freshly ground black pepper

1 (15-ounce) can low-sodium chickpeas, drained and rinsed

2 cups (10 ounces) chopped cooked chicken breast

6 cups chopped romaine lettuce

2 medium tomatoes, chopped

1 medium cucumber, peeled, seeded, and chopped

½ cup finely chopped red onion

½ cup sliced black olives

¼ cup crumbled reduced-fat feta cheese

To make the dressing, whisk together all the ingredients in a large bowl until smooth. Add the chickpeas to the dressing and set aside to marinate for 5 minutes.

Meanwhile, in another large bowl, toss together the chicken, lettuce, tomatoes, cucumber, onion, olives, and feta. Drizzle the chickpeas and dressing over the salad and toss to coat.

SERVING SIZE: 3 cups
EXCHANGE LIST VALUES: 1 starch, 2 vegetable, 3 lean meat, 1 plant-based protein, 1 fat
CARBOHYDRATE CHOICES: 1½

CALORIES: 335
CALORIES FROM FAT: 102
TOTAL FAT: 11 g
SATURATED FAT: 3 g
CHOLESTEROL: 63 mg

SODIUM: 365 mg
TOTAL CARBOHYDRATE: 29 g
FIBER: 10 g
TOTAL SUGARS: 4 g
PROTEIN: 31 g

Barbecue Burgers

MAKES 4 BURGERS

This is one of my favorite ways to use leftover cooked meats. The flavorful barbecue sauce is made by boosting the flavor of a store-bought low-sugar or sugar-free sauce with added ingredients, and can be used on Beefy Mini Meat Loaves (page 116) or brushed on a roasted chicken, if desired. The burger mixture can be made ahead of time, separated into serving portions, and frozen. Instead of the lettuce, pile some Carolina Coleslaw (page 74) on your burger, or serve alongside for a nutritious crunch.

2	cups shredded cooked chicken breast, pork loin, or turkey breast
¼	cup shredded carrots or broccoli slaw mix
½	yellow onion, thinly sliced
1	clove garlic, minced
¼	cup low-sugar barbecue sauce or Kickin' Barbecue Sauce (page 12)
¼	cup mild or hot salsa
1	tablespoon stevia granulated sweetener or agave syrup
1	tablespoon Dijon mustard
4	small whole-wheat sandwich buns, toasted
½	cup shredded romaine lettuce

In a large microwaveable bowl, combine the shredded meat with the carrots or broccoli slaw mix, onion, garlic, barbecue sauce, salsa, stevia or agave syrup, and mustard. Toss until well combined. Microwave on high for 4 to 5 minutes. Stir the meat mixture and place ½ cup on each of the bottom buns. Top with the lettuce and the top bun.

SERVING SIZE: 1 sandwich
EXCHANGE LIST VALUES: 2 starch, 3 lean meat
CARBOHYDRATE CHOICES: 2
CALORIES: 278

CALORIES FROM FAT: 46
TOTAL FAT: 5 g
SATURATED FAT: 1 g
CHOLESTEROL: 72 mg
SODIUM: 506 mg

TOTAL CARBOHYDRATE: 28 g
FIBER: 4 g
TOTAL SUGARS: 5 g
PROTEIN: 30 g

Mini Muffulettas

MAKES 6 SANDWICHES

These sandwiches are a "mini" tribute to the 10-inch round, ingredient-packed, sub sandwich served in New Orleans. The original muffuletta dates back to 1906, and is available only at Central Grocery on Decatur Street. The secret ingredients are the homemade sesame bread and the olive spread. My version captures the flavors of the famous New Orleans sandwich, with far fewer calories.

2	ounces fat-free cream cheese
2	tablespoons low-fat mayonnaise
½	cup Italian pickled vegetables, chopped
¼	cup sliced pimiento-stuffed olives, drained
¼	cup sliced ripe black olives, drained
1	tablespoon capers, plus 2 tablespoons brine from jar
1	tablespoon Italian seasoning
½	teaspoon hot sauce
6	(4-inch) whole-wheat Italian-style sesame rolls, halved horizontally
6	slices low-fat Swiss cheese
6	thin slices reduced-sodium deli turkey breast
6	thin slices reduced-sodium deli ham

In a medium bowl, mix together the cream cheese, mayonnaise, pickled vegetables, olives, capers, Italian seasoning, and hot sauce until smooth. Add the caper brine as needed for the desired spreading consistency. Cover and refrigerate overnight to allow the flavors to combine.

Preheat the oven to 350°F. Spread the cream cheese mixture evenly over each cut side of the roll bottoms. Top each with 1 slice of cheese, turkey, and ham. Cover with the roll tops. Wrap each sandwich in a piece of aluminum foil. Place the sandwiches on a baking sheet and bake for 14 to 16 minutes, or until the cheeses are melted.

NOTE: The aluminum-wrapped sandwiches can be frozen for up to 3 months, then baked for 12 to 15 minutes, or until warmed through before serving.

SERVING SIZE: 1 sandwich
EXCHANGE LIST VALUES: 2 starch, 3 lean meat
CARBOHYDRATE CHOICES: 2
CALORIES: 261

CALORIES FROM FAT: 62
TOTAL FAT: 7 g
SATURATED FAT: 2 g
CHOLESTEROL: 41 mg
SODIUM: 971 mg

TOTAL CARBOHYDRATE: 26 g
FIBER: 3 g
TOTAL SUGARS: 6 g
PROTEIN: 26 g

Seafood Burgers

MAKES 6 BURGERS

This burger goes far beyond the fast-food variety. Imitation crabmeat, canned tuna, or salmon all make delicious seafood burgers, and are a healthy source of omega-3 fatty acids. Try a combination of all three for a tasty treat.

1   pound imitation crabmeat, canned tuna packed in water, or canned salmon

1   large egg, lightly beaten

½   cup whole-wheat panko (Japanese bread crumbs)

¼   cup plain low-fat Greek yogurt

2   tablespoons low-fat mayonnaise

⅓   cup finely chopped celery

¼   cup finely chopped red bell pepper

2   green onions, including green parts, finely chopped

1   teaspoon Dijon mustard

1   tablespoon fresh lemon juice

1   tablespoon poultry seasoning

¼   teaspoon cayenne pepper

1   teaspoon freshly ground black pepper

6   whole-wheat hamburger buns

½   cup shredded romaine lettuce

1   avocado, peeled, pitted, and sliced

In a large bowl, combine the crabmeat, egg, bread crumbs, yogurt, mayonnaise, celery, bell pepper, green onions, mustard, lemon juice, poultry seasoning, cayenne, and black pepper. Gently form the mixture into 6 patties. Refrigerate for 30 minutes.

Spray a large nonstick skillet with cooking oil spray and heat over medium heat. Cook the patties until golden brown, about 4 minutes per side. Toast the burger buns, cut side up, on a large baking sheet for about 3 minutes, or until lightly browned. Place a seafood burger on each one of the bottom buns. Top with the lettuce, 2 slices of avocado, and the top bun.

SERVING SIZE: 1 sandwich
EXCHANGE LIST VALUES: 2 starch, 3 lean meat, 1 fat
CARBOHYDRATE CHOICES: 2
CALORIES: 330

CALORIES FROM FAT: 100
TOTAL FAT: 11 g
SATURATED FAT: 2 g
CHOLESTEROL: 119 mg
SODIUM: 560 mg

TOTAL CARBOHYDRATE: 33 g
FIBER: 7 g
TOTAL SUGARS: 5 g
PROTEIN: 26 g

Roast Beef Sliders with Spicy Walnut Mustard

MAKES 16 SERVINGS

These little sandwiches are easy to prepare using my technique for slicing the package of dinner rolls across the middle, preparing them as one large sandwich, and then separating the rolls into individual sliders. You can wrap the sliders, freeze them in plastic wrap, and defrost them in the microwave for a quick snack (see Note).

2	(9¼-ounce) packages whole-wheat dinner rolls (16 rolls)
¼	cup Spicy Walnut Mustard (recipe follows)
¾	pound thinly sliced reduced-sodium deli roast beef, chopped
½	pound thinly sliced low-fat sharp cheddar cheese
½	teaspoon freshly ground black pepper

Preheat the oven to 325°F. Without separating the rolls, cut them in half horizontally, creating 1 top and 1 bottom per package. Spread the mustard on the top half of the rolls. Place the roast beef and cheese on the bottom half of the rolls. Sprinkle with the pepper. Cover with the top halves of the rolls, mustard side down. Wrap in aluminum foil and heat in the oven until the cheese melts. Separate the rolls into individual sliders and serve immediately.

NOTE: To freeze the sliders, separate the rolls, make individual sandwiches, wrap in plastic wrap, and freeze for up to 6 months. Reheat in the microwave on the defrost setting for 6 to 8 minutes, or until warm and the cheese is melted.

SERVING SIZE: 1 sandwich
EXCHANGE LIST VALUES: 1 starch, 1 medium-fat meat
CARBOHYDRATE CHOICES: 1
CALORIES: 165

CALORIES FROM FAT: 53
TOTAL FAT: 6 g
SATURATED FAT: 3 g
CHOLESTEROL: 18 mg
SODIUM: 463 mg

TOTAL CARBOHYDRATE: 17 g
FIBER: 1 g
TOTAL SUGARS: 1 g
PROTEIN: 10 g

Spicy Walnut Mustard

MAKES ABOUT ¼ CUP

This tasty mustard adds crunch and punch to sandwiches and wraps. Mix 2 tablespoons of this fabulous mustard with ¼ cup of apple cider vinegar and 3 tablespoons of olive oil to make a unique walnut–mustard salad dressing.

¼ cup chopped walnuts

½ cup spicy brown mustard

2 tablespoons stevia granulated sweetener or agave syrup

2 tablespoons water, boiling

1 tablespoon no-sugar-added apple cider vinegar

2 tablespoons unsweetened applesauce

Toast the walnuts in a small, dry nonstick skillet over medium-low heat, stirring often, for 5 to 6 minutes, or until lightly browned. In a small bowl, combine the mustard and stevia or syrup. Add the water and stir until the stevia or syrup is dissolved. Stir in the vinegar, then the applesauce. Mix in the walnuts and blend thoroughly. Store in an airtight container in the refrigerator for up to 2 weeks.

SERVING SIZE: ¾ teaspoon
EXCHANGE LIST VALUES: 0
CARBOHYDRATE CHOICES: 0
CALORIES: 7
CALORIES FROM FAT: 4

TOTAL FAT: 0 g
SATURATED FAT: 0 g
CHOLESTEROL: 0 mg
SODIUM: 25 mg
TOTAL CARBOHYDRATE: 0 g

FIBER: 0 g
TOTAL SUGARS: 0 g
PROTEIN: 0 g

Broiled Pimiento Cheese and Roasted Tomato Sandwiches

MAKES 4 SANDWICHES

Silken soft tofu adds a smooth, creamy texture and protein to this vegetarian sandwich. Tofu can be bland, but it easily absorbs the flavor of the other ingredients. This sandwich is good at room temperature, too, so make it ahead, let it cool, and pack it for lunch.

¼   red onion

⅓   cup drained pimientos

2   cloves garlic

½   cup shredded low-fat sharp cheddar cheese

2   ounces low-fat cream cheese, softened

4   ounces silken soft tofu, drained

1   teaspoon freshly ground black pepper

⅓   cup plain low-fat Greek yogurt

2   large or 3 medium tomatoes (about 1½ pounds), sliced ½ inch thick

1½ tablespoons olive oil

8   thin slices whole-wheat bread

8   fresh basil leaves

In a blender or food processor, chop the onion, pimientos, and garlic until minced. Add the cheese, cream cheese, tofu, and ½ teaspoon of the pepper and blend until smooth. Add the yogurt and process until well blended. Transfer the mixture to an airtight container and refrigerate for at least 15 minutes or up to 3 days.

Preheat the broiler. Place the sliced tomatoes on a nonstick baking pan. Drizzle with the olive oil and sprinkle with the remaining ½ teaspoon of pepper. Broil the tomatoes for 4 to 5 minutes, or until they brown slightly around the edges. Set aside to cool.

Lay the slices of bread on a baking sheet. Spread each slice with 1 tablespoon of the pimiento cheese mixture. Toast until the cheese is slightly melted, about 1 minute. Place 1 to 2 slices of the roasted tomato and a few of the basil leaves on each of 4 slices of the toasted pimiento cheese bread. Top with the remaining slice.

SERVING SIZE: 1 sandwich

EXCHANGE LIST VALUES: 2 starch, 1 medium-fat meat

CARBOHYDRATE CHOICES: 2

CALORIES: 313

CALORIES FROM FAT: 104

TOTAL FAT: 12 g

SATURATED FAT: 6 g

CHOLESTEROL: 29 mg

SODIUM: 513 mg

TOTAL CARBOHYDRATE: 31 g

FIBER: 6 g

TOTAL SUGARS: 7 g

PROTEIN: 18 g

Open-Faced Chicken Salad Sandwiches

MAKES 4 SANDWICHES

This is one of my favorite ways to prepare and serve chicken salad. When I'm roasting a chicken, I try to plan ahead and roast an extra chicken breast. Sliced grapes may be substituted for the apple.

1	cup chopped cooked chicken breast
⅓	cup chopped apple (York, Rome, Gala, or Fuji)
½	small red onion, diced
1	clove garlic, minced
1	rib celery, diced
1	hard-cooked large egg, peeled and chopped
2	tablespoons plain low-fat Greek yogurt
2	tablespoons low-fat mayonnaise
1	tablespoon Dijon mustard
1	tablespoon poultry seasoning
¼	teaspoon salt
1	teaspoon freshly ground black pepper
4	thin slices whole-wheat bread
4	romaine lettuce leaves

In a medium bowl, stir together the chicken, apple, onion, garlic, celery, and egg. Add the yogurt, mayonnaise, mustard, poultry seasoning, salt, and pepper. Toast the bread until lightly browned. Top each slice with a lettuce leaf. Mound a few tablespoons of chicken salad on each of the lettuce leaves. Serve immediately.

SERVING SIZE: 1 open-faced sandwich
EXCHANGE LIST VALUES: 1 starch, 2 lean meat, ½ fat
CARBOHYDRATE CHOICES: 1
CALORIES: 223

CALORIES FROM FAT: 60
TOTAL FAT: 7 g
SATURATED FAT: 1 g
CHOLESTEROL: 86 mg
SODIUM: 464 mg

TOTAL CARBOHYDRATE: 19 g
FIBER: 3 g
TOTAL SUGARS: 4 g
PROTEIN: 19 g

Sardine Toasts

MAKES 4 TOASTS

This open-faced sandwich was my go-to choice when my husband wanted something different for lunch. Sardines, a budget-friendly change from deli meats, are packed with omega-3s, protein, selenium, phosphorus, and vitamins B12 and D.

1 (3¾- to 4⅜-ounce) can sardines in water, drained

¼ cup low-fat mayonnaise

3 tablespoons finely chopped onion

1 tablespoon Dijon mustard

1 clove garlic, minced

2 tablespoons chopped fresh flat-leaf parsley or dill

1½ teaspoons poultry seasoning

1 teaspoon fresh lemon juice

1 teaspoon freshly ground black pepper

8 slices whole-wheat sandwich bread, lightly toasted

Preheat the oven or toaster oven to 375°F. Mash the sardines with the mayonnaise, onion, mustard, garlic, parsley or dill, poultry seasoning, lemon juice, and pepper. Spread the mixture on each slice of bread. Bake until lightly golden, 8 to 10 minutes.

SERVING SIZE: 2 toasts
EXCHANGE LIST VALUES: 2 starch, 1 lean meat, 1 fat
CARBOHYDRATE CHOICES: 2
CALORIES: 260

CALORIES FROM FAT: 93
TOTAL FAT: 10 g
SATURATED FAT: 2 g
CHOLESTEROL: 27 mg
SODIUM: 645 mg

TOTAL CARBOHYDRATE: 26 g
FIBER: 4 g
TOTAL SUGARS: 3 g
PROTEIN: 13 g

Microwave Veggie Tortilla Wraps

MAKES 2 WRAPS

Loading these wraps with leftover roasted veggies makes good use of ingredients you may already have on hand.

2   (8-inch) whole-wheat tortillas

4   tablespoons canned diced tomatoes
     with chiles and onions, mild or hot

1   cup chopped cooked vegetables

3   tablespoons shredded low-
     fat cheddar cheese

Place the tortillas on a food-safe paper towel. Cover the tortillas with another paper towel. Sprinkle the paper towel with water and microwave for 10 seconds to soften the tortillas. Remove the top paper towel and set it aside.

Spread 2 tablespoons of the diced tomatoes on each tortilla. Place an equal amount of the vegetables and cheese in the center of each tortilla.

Fold the top end of the tortilla an inch over the filling and fold in the sides. While holding the top and sides in place, roll the tortilla until all ends are covered. Repeat with the second tortilla.

Wrap the paper towels around the wraps, making sure to fold the ends inside. Place the wraps in the microwave for 30 seconds, checking to see if the cheese is melted. Cook for an additional 10 seconds or until the cheese is melted, as needed.

SERVING SIZE: 1 wrap
EXCHANGE LIST VALUES: 1½ starch, 1 vegetable, 1 lean meat
CARBOHYDRATE CHOICES: 2
CALORIES: 190

CALORIES FROM FAT: 49
TOTAL FAT: 5 g
SATURATED FAT: 2 g
CHOLESTEROL: 2 mg
SODIUM: 520 mg

TOTAL CARBOHYDRATE: 29 g
FIBER: 7 g
TOTAL SUGARS: 4 g
PROTEIN: 7 g

Microwave Egg Foo Yung Cabbage Wrap

MAKES 2 WRAPS

Egg foo yung was a popular dish in the 1950s. Asian-American restaurants scrambled eggs with meat, vegetables, and spices in an oil-filled wok. I've created an easy-to-prepare, fat-free version of this popular dish. The microwave allows you to quickly cook the dish at home or prepare it at work for a light lunch. You can pack all of the ingredients in a microwave-safe covered bowl, and then use the same bowl to cook the dish in. A crisp napa cabbage or lettuce leaf provides a crunchy way to wrap up this delicious retro favorite!

½   cup bean sprouts, fresh
     or canned, drained

1   green onion, diced, white and
     green parts, or 2 tablespoons
     minced yellow onion

3   tablespoons sliced water chestnuts,
     fresh or canned, drained, or 3
     tablespoons thinly sliced celery

2   tablespoons water

1   tablespoon light soy sauce plus
     2 teaspoons for sprinkling

1   teaspoon sriracha or other hot sauce

3   eggs

2   large napa cabbage or romaine
     lettuce leaves, washed and dried

Using a microwave-safe bowl, cook the bean sprouts, onion, water chestnuts or celery, water, and 1 tablespoon soy sauce and ½ teaspoon sriracha or other hot sauce together on high for 2 minutes. Add the eggs to the bowl. Beat the eggs and the vegetable mixture lightly with a fork, but not enough so that bubbles form.

Microwave the egg mixture on low or on the defrost setting for 2 to 3 minutes, or until the eggs are almost set; stir. Continue to microwave on low or the defrost setting for another 2 to 3 minutes; stir. Cover the bowl and let the mixture stand for 1 to 2 minutes until set. Fill each leaf with equal portions of the mixture. Sprinkle each leaf with 1 teaspoon of the soy sauce and serve immediately.

SERVING SIZE: 1 wrap
EXCHANGE LIST VALUES: 1 vegetable, 1 medium-fat meat
CARBOHYDRATE CHOICES: ½
CALORIES: 139

CALORIES FROM FAT: 65
TOTAL FAT: 7 g
SATURATED FAT: 2 g
CHOLESTEROL: 279 mg
SODIUM: 652 mg

TOTAL CARBOHYDRATE: 7 g
FIBER: 1 g
TOTAL SUGARS: 2 g
PROTEIN: 12 g

Pumpkin and Tortellini Soup with Feta Cheese Croutons

MAKES 6 SERVINGS

Canned pumpkin purée (not the pie filling) is an easy, nutritious way to create a fabulous soup. Tortellini come with a variety of fillings, so try other kinds than cheese. Make an extra batch of feta cheese croutons to add to your favorite salad.

2 (14½-ounce) cans low-sodium chicken broth

1½ cups water

1 (9-ounce) package refrigerated whole-wheat cheese tortellini

2 (15-ounce) cans or 1 (29-ounce) can pumpkin purée

⅛ teaspoon salt

1 teaspoon freshly ground black pepper

½ teaspoon ground nutmeg

⅛ teaspoon cayenne pepper

1 tablespoon stevia granulated sweetener

1 tablespoon heart-healthy butter spread or whipped butter

Feta Cheese Croutons (recipe follows)

In a large saucepan, mix together the broth and water and bring to a boil over high heat. Add the tortellini to the broth and cook for 8 to 10 minutes, or until the tortellini float to the top of the saucepan. Stir in the pumpkin, salt, black pepper, nutmeg, and cayenne pepper until well blended. Bring to a boil and immediately reduce the heat. Simmer, uncovered, for 5 to 6 minutes, stirring occasionally. Add the stevia and spread or butter, stirring until just melted.

Ladle the soup into bowls and top with the feta croutons.

Continued on page 106

SERVING SIZE: 1½ cups
EXCHANGE LIST VALUES: 1½ starch, ½ medium-fat meat
CARBOHYDRATE CHOICES: 1½
CALORIES: 205

CALORIES FROM FAT: 66
TOTAL FAT: 7 g
SATURATED FAT: 3 g
CHOLESTEROL: 25 mg
SODIUM: 653 mg

TOTAL CARBOHYDRATE: 25 g
FIBER: 7 g
TOTAL SUGARS: 5 g
PROTEIN: 12 g

Feta Cheese Croutons

MAKES 6 SERVINGS

These breaded cheese croutons add an extra dimension to soups and salads without the calories found in traditional croutons.

½ cup whole-wheat panko (Japanese bread crumbs)

3 teaspoons minced fresh thyme, or 1 teaspoon dried thyme

1 teaspoon freshly ground black pepper

4 ounces reduced-fat feta cheese, cut into ¾-inch cubes

Cooking oil spray

In a bowl, mix together the bread crumbs, thyme, and pepper. Toast the mixture in a skillet over high heat for 2 to 3 minutes. Coat the feta cubes with cooking oil spray. Roll the cheese in the warm bread crumb mixture until covered on all sides, pressing the bread crumb mixture firmly onto the cheese cubes. Place on a plate and refrigerate for at least 15 minutes uncovered.

SERVING SIZE: 6 croutons

EXCHANGE LIST VALUES:
  ½ medium-fat meat

CARBOHYDRATE CHOICES: 0

CALORIES: 47

CALORIES FROM FAT: 21

TOTAL FAT: 2 g

SATURATED FAT: 1 g

CHOLESTEROL: 5 mg

SODIUM: 204 mg

TOTAL CARBOHYDRATE: 3 g

FIBER: 0 g

TOTAL SUGARS: 0 g

PROTEIN: 4 g

Three-Bean Soup

MAKES 6 SERVINGS

Beans, as the old song goes, are good for your heart. U.S. consumers gobble up an estimated 8 pounds of beans per person each year, with pinto beans and navy beans being the most popular. Red beans also enjoy immense popularity, particularly during colder months, as a staple ingredient in chili. Although not as popular in the States as other varieties, black beans are a main ingredient in many international dishes. This soup brings out the best of each type of bean by showcasing them in a flavorful broth.

1   tablespoon olive oil

¾   cup chopped red onion

1   tablespoon poultry seasoning

2   medium carrots, thinly sliced

2   stalks celery, chopped

2   cloves garlic, minced

2   bay leaves

¼   teaspoon salt

1   teaspoon freshly ground black pepper

½   teaspoon cayenne pepper

½   cup mild or hot salsa

2   (14-ounce) cans reduced-sodium chicken or vegetable broth

1   (14½-ounce) can no-salt-added or low-sodium cannellini beans, rinsed and drained

1   (14½-ounce) can no-salt-added or low-sodium black beans, rinsed and drained

1   (14½-ounce) can no-salt-added or low-sodium navy beans, rinsed and drained

1½ tablespoons apple cider vinegar

¼   cup shredded low-fat sharp cheddar cheese (optional)

Heat the oil in a large pot or Dutch oven. Cook the onion and poultry seasoning over medium heat for 5 minutes, or until the onion is tender, stirring occasionally. Add the carrots, celery, garlic, bay leaves, salt, and the black and cayenne pepper. Cook and stir for 1 minute more. Add the salsa and broth. Bring to a boil, then reduce the heat to a simmer, and cook, uncovered, for 5 minutes, or until the carrots are tender. Stir in the beans and vinegar. Cook until heated, about 3 minutes. Remove and discard the bay leaves. Ladle into soup bowls and sprinkle with the cheddar cheese, if desired.

SERVING SIZE: 1½ cups	**CALORIES:** 245	**SODIUM:** 580 mg
EXCHANGE LIST VALUES: 2 starch,	**CALORIES FROM FAT:** 31	**TOTAL CARBOHYDRATE:** 41 g
1 vegetable, 2 plant-based protein,	**TOTAL FAT:** 3 g	**FIBER:** 12 g
½ fat	**SATURATED FAT:** 0 g	**TOTAL SUGARS:** 3 g
CARBOHYDRATE CHOICES: 2	**CHOLESTEROL:** 0 mg	**PROTEIN:** 14 g

Chinese Cabbage Soup

MAKES 6 SERVINGS

Canadian bacon and Chinese, or napa, cabbage are the main ingredients in this unusual soup. Bacon and cabbage are a delicious duo. Shiitake mushrooms add an earthiness to the soup as well as a unique health benefit. The active component in shiitake mushrooms is called eritadenine, which researchers are studying as a potential cholesterol-lowering agent.

1	tablespoon olive oil
½	medium yellow onion, diced
1	teaspoon freshly ground black pepper
2	cloves garlic, minced
6	ounces shiitake mushrooms, sliced
2	teaspoons grated fresh ginger, or ½ teaspoon ground ginger
¼	teaspoon cayenne pepper
3	(14-ounce) cans low-sodium chicken or vegetable broth
1	tablespoon reduced-sodium soy sauce
12	ounces Canadian Bacon (page 27), cut into bite-size pieces
2	cups thinly sliced Chinese (napa) cabbage
2	tablespoons no-sugar-added apple cider vinegar
1	green onion, including green parts, thinly sliced

Heat the oil in a large pot or Dutch oven over medium heat. Add the yellow onion and black pepper and cook for 3 minutes, or until the onion is soft and translucent. Add the garlic, mushrooms, ginger, and cayenne pepper. Cook for 3 to 5 minutes, or until the vegetables soften.

Stir in the broth and soy sauce; bring to a boil. Stir in the Canadian bacon, cabbage, and 1 tablespoon of the vinegar. Cook, stirring occasionally, for 5 to 7 minutes, or until the cabbage begins to soften and is heated through. Remove from the heat and stir in the remaining tablespoon of the vinegar. Sprinkle with the green onion.

SERVING SIZE: 1½ cups
EXCHANGE LIST VALUES: ½ starch, 1 vegetable, 2 lean meat
CARBOHYDRATE CHOICES: 1
CALORIES: 184

CALORIES FROM FAT: 65
TOTAL FAT: 7 g
SATURATED FAT: 2 g
CHOLESTEROL: 43 mg
SODIUM: 441 mg

TOTAL CARBOHYDRATE: 12 g
FIBER: 2 g
TOTAL SUGARS: 3 g
PROTEIN: 17 g

Fire-Roasted Tomato and Kale Soup

MAKES 4 SERVINGS

Fire-roasted tomatoes add a smoky flavor to this soup. The richness of the tomatoes and the earthiness of the kale is a delicious combination. Kale is high in fiber, vitamin C, beta-carotene, and manganese. Like other high-fiber vegetables, it provides valuable cardiovascular support because of its cholesterol-lowering abilities.

½ tablespoon olive oil

1 large onion, chopped

2 stalks celery, chopped

2 cloves garlic, minced

¼ teaspoon salt

1 teaspoon freshly ground black pepper

1 (14½-ounce) can diced fire-roasted tomatoes, with juices

½ teaspoon ground cloves or ground nutmeg

½ teaspoon light or dark brown sugar or Splenda brown sugar blend

3 (14-ounce) cans reduced-sodium vegetable broth

4 cups coarsely shredded kale

2 medium zucchini, halved and sliced

⅛ teaspoon red pepper flakes

½ cup chopped fresh flat-leaf parsley or basil, plus 2 tablespoons for garnish

2 tablespoons apple cider vinegar

In a 5-quart Dutch oven, heat the oil over medium heat and cook the onion, celery, garlic, salt, and ½ teaspoon of the black pepper for 10 minutes, or until the vegetables soften and begin to brown. Stir in the tomatoes, cloves or nutmeg, and brown sugar. Cook for 2 to 3 minutes. Add the broth, kale, zucchini, red pepper flakes, and the remaining ½ teaspoon of black pepper. Bring to a boil and reduce the heat to low. Simmer, covered, for 5 minutes, stirring once. Stir in the ½ cup of the parsley or basil and the vinegar. Garnish with the remaining 2 tablespoons of parsley or basil.

SERVING SIZE: 1½ cups
EXCHANGE LIST VALUES: 3 vegetable
CARBOHYDRATE CHOICES: 1
CALORIES: 74
CALORIES FROM FAT: 12

TOTAL FAT: 1 g
SATURATED FAT: 0 g
CHOLESTEROL: 0 mg
SODIUM: 314 mg
TOTAL CARBOHYDRATE: 13 g

FIBER: 2 g
TOTAL SUGARS: 4 g
PROTEIN: 3 g

Creole Chicken Stew

MAKES 8 SERVINGS

This is a quick and healthy version of New Orleans–style gumbo. Using frozen vegetables is a real time-saver when making this tasty stew; it's also the perfect way to use kohlrabi when in season. Select small, tender okra pods for this recipe, and don't slice them until right before you add them to the stew.

1½ tablespoons olive oil

1 cup chopped yellow onions

1 cup coarsely chopped carrots

¼ cup chopped celery

4 cloves garlic, minced

1 bay leaf

2 teaspoons diced seeded jalapeño chile

¼ teaspoon salt

1 teaspoon freshly ground black pepper

½ teaspoon dried thyme

2 tablespoons whole-wheat flour

3 cups reduced-sodium chicken broth

1½ pounds boneless, skinless chicken breasts, cut into 1-inch-wide strips

1 cup peeled cubed Yukon Gold potatoes or kohlrabi, or a combination

1 cup diced zucchini

1 cup halved okra or frozen cut okra

4 cups cooked brown rice

2 green onions, chopped, including green parts

In a large pot, heat 1 tablespoon of the oil over medium-high heat. Add the yellow onions, carrots, celery, garlic, bay leaf, jalapeño, salt, pepper, and thyme and sauté until the onion is translucent, about 3 minutes. Using a slotted spoon, transfer the vegetables to a plate, leaving as much oil in the pot as possible. Add the remaining ½ tablespoon of oil. Stir in the flour. Cook, stirring constantly, until the flour begins to turn golden brown, about 3 minutes. Gradually whisk in the broth and cook for another 5 minutes, whisking until smooth. Bring the mixture to a boil, then reduce the heat to a simmer. Add the chicken, potatoes or kohlrabi, and zucchini. Return the sautéed vegetables to the pan. Partially cover and simmer, stirring occasionally, for 20 to 30 minutes.

Add the okra and cook for 15 to 20 minutes. Remove the bay leaf. Serve over ½ cup of rice per person and sprinkle with the green onions.

SERVING SIZE: 1½ cups stew plus ½ cup rice
EXCHANGE LIST VALUES: 1½ starch, 1 vegetable, 2 lean meat, ½ fat
CARBOHYDRATE CHOICES: 2

CALORIES: 276
CALORIES FROM FAT: 51
TOTAL FAT: 6 g
SATURATED FAT: 1 g
CHOLESTEROL: 47 mg

SODIUM: 349 mg
TOTAL CARBOHYDRATE: 33 g
FIBER: 4 g
TOTAL SUGARS: 3 g
PROTEIN: 22 g

Slow-Cooker Curry Stew

MAKES 6 SERVINGS

Coconut oil, curry, cinnamon, and ginger give a uniquely flavorful profile to this stew. And the fiber-packed split peas help slow your body's absorption of sugar and improve blood glucose levels.

2	tablespoons coconut oil or olive oil
1	medium yellow onion, chopped
2	tablespoons tomato paste
1½	tablespoons curry powder
½	teaspoon ground cinnamon
3	cloves garlic, minced
2	teaspoons grated fresh ginger
¼	teaspoon salt
1	teaspoon freshly ground black pepper
1	pound yellow split peas
2	(14-ounce) cans reduced-sodium chicken broth
3	cups water
¾	pound Yukon Gold or new potatoes, quartered

1	pound lean ground turkey
1	tablespoon rice wine vinegar or no-sugar-added apple cider vinegar
¼	cup chopped fresh cilantro, for garnish
4	teaspoons chopped dry-roasted peanuts, for garnish

In a small microwaveable bowl, combine the oil, onion, tomato paste, curry powder, cinnamon, garlic, ginger, salt, and pepper. Microwave for 2 minutes on high.

Transfer the onion mixture to a 4-quart slow cooker. Stir in the split peas, broth, water, and potatoes. Pinch off pieces of the ground turkey and drop it into the slow cooker to prevent the meat from clumping. Stir to combine.

Cook on low for 8 to 9 hours, or on high for 3 to 4 hours. Stir in the vinegar. Ladle the stew into bowls and sprinkle with the cilantro and chopped peanuts.

SERVING SIZE: 1½ cups
EXCHANGE LIST VALUES: 2½ starch, 2 lean meat, 2 plant-based protein, ½ fat
CARBOHYDRATE CHOICES: 2½

CALORIES: 375
CALORIES FROM FAT: 82
TOTAL FAT: 9 g
SATURATED FAT: 4 g
CHOLESTEROL: 33 mg

SODIUM: 401 mg
TOTAL CARBOHYDRATE: 48 g
FIBER: 19 g
TOTAL SUGARS: 3 g
PROTEIN: 27 g

Delectable

Dinners

TAKE THE TIME AT THE END of the day to enjoy a balanced meal. The Diva-licious dinners in this chapter include a variety of easy preparation techniques, from sautéing to slow cooking. The simple, healthy, and satisfying recipes range from easy-to-prepare Beefy Mini Meat Loaves, Garlic Flank Steak, and a slow-cooked Salsa Verde Pork to Chicken and Apples with Lemon Balsamic Sauce, Italian-Style Microwave Salmon, and Veggie Lasagne.

Studies show that if you eat dinner with your children, it is more likely that meals will be healthier and more balanced. This is particularly important for children with diabetes. Eating the evening meal together as a family has been shown to improve family harmony, communication, and social skills, and is a simple, effective way to raise healthier children.

Some studies suggest that eating dinner at least three hours before going to bed helps with weight maintenance and maintaining blood glucose levels. The last meal of the day should be low in sugar and fat and contain some protein to repair organs, tissues, and muscles.

Slowing down at dinner, allowing yourself to savor what you're eating and to feel full, helps with digestion and weight maintenance. Skipping dinner may cause sleep problems due to hunger and irritability, and risks putting your body into glycemic imbalance and causing weight gain.

If at all possible, gather the ones you love around the dinner table—it's one of the best things you can do to improve their health and yours.

BEEFY MINI MEAT LOAVES   116

MICROWAVE MEAT-STUFFED BELL PEPPERS   117

GARLIC FLANK STEAK   120

TEXAS-STYLE BEEF STEW   122

BEEF FAJITAS   124

FRENCH DIP SANDWICHES   125

GINGER BEEF STIR-FRY WITH SOBA NOODLES   126

SPICED LAMB SHANKS   129

GREEK-STYLE LAMB-STUFFED EGGPLANT   130

LAMB AND SWEET POTATO CASSEROLE   134

APPLE–PECAN PORK CHOPS   135

PORK AND MUSHROOM STROGANOFF   136

SALSA VERDE PORK   137

QUICK CURRIED CHICKEN   139

CRISPY ROASTED CHICKEN   140

CHICKEN AND APPLES WITH LEMON BALSAMIC SAUCE   143

SPAGHETTI AND CHICKEN MEATBALLS   144

PEPPERCORN CHICKEN   146

CHICKEN LOLLIPOPS   148

STIR-FRIED CHERRY CHICKEN WITH DIVA-STYLE
SWEET AND SOUR SAUCE   150

ASIAN-STYLE CHICKEN WRAPS   153

TURKEY SAUSAGE AND PEPPERS PASTA   154

FAST TURKEY PATTIES WITH MAPLE–ROSEMARY SAUCE   156

TURKEY ENCHILADAS   160

BAKED CATFISH WITH GREEN ONION AND BUTTER SAUCE   162

QUICK CREOLE COD   166

CRUNCHY FISH STICKS   167

FIVE-SPICE FISH   168

SHRIMP AND BULGUR RISOTTO   169

OVEN-FRIED TROUT WITH PAPAYA SAUCE   171

ITALIAN-STYLE MICROWAVE SALMON   173

ORANGE PEPPER SHRIMP AND TEXMATI RICE   175

SALMON CAKES WITH DILL SAUCE   177

JAMAICAN-STYLE FISH EN PAPILLOTE   178

BUTTERMILK PECAN-CRUSTED TILAPIA   180

DIVA-LICIOUS POTPIE   182

VEGGIE LASAGNE   184

FIESTA TACOS   188

Beefy Mini Meat Loaves

MAKES 6 SERVINGS

This healthful mini version of a traditional meat loaf is healthier and cooks quickly. Lean beef is used in this recipe, but ground turkey also would be a delicious choice.

½ cup low-sugar ketchup or Kickin' Barbecue Sauce (page 12)

¼ cup mild or hot salsa

1½ tablespoons Worcestershire sauce

½ tablespoon agave syrup

¼ teaspoon salt

1 teaspoon freshly ground black pepper

1½ pounds lean ground beef

1 large egg, beaten

½ onion, finely chopped

1 medium carrot, peeled and chopped

2 cloves garlic, minced

½ cup crushed whole-wheat crackers

Preheat the oven to 450°F. In a small bowl, stir together the ketchup or barbecue sauce, salsa, Worcestershire sauce, syrup, salt, and pepper.

In a large bowl, gently combine the beef, half of the ketchup mixture, the egg, onion, carrot, garlic, and cracker crumbs until well mixed. Spray a 13 by 9-inch pan with cooking spray. Place the meat mixture in the baking pan and pat it into a 12 by 4-inch rectangle. Using a spatula, divide the meat lengthwise down the center and then crosswise into sixths to form 12 loaves. Separate the loaves so no edges are touching. Brush the loaves with the remaining sauce mixture. Bake for 18 to 20 minutes, or until the loaves are no longer pink in the center and an instant-read thermometer inserted in the center of a loaf registers 160°F.

SERVING SIZE: 1 mini meat loaf
EXCHANGE LIST VALUES: ½ starch, 1 vegetable, 3 lean meat
CARBOHYDRATE CHOICES: 1
CALORIES: 230

CALORIES FROM FAT: 97
TOTAL FAT: 11 g
SATURATED FAT: 4 g
CHOLESTEROL: 100 mg
SODIUM: 484 mg

TOTAL CARBOHYDRATE: 17 g
FIBER: 1 g
TOTAL SUGARS: 4 g
PROTEIN: 23 g

Microwave Meat-Stuffed Bell Peppers

SERVES 6

These bell peppers are stuffed with Mini Meat Loaves, topped with sauce, and popped into the microwave for a fast and tasty meal.

6	red, yellow, or orange bell peppers
2	cups cooked brown rice, whole-wheat couscous, or orzo pasta
1	cup shredded low-fat Monterey Jack cheese
3	Mini Meat Loaves, crumbled (page 116)
½	cup low-sugar ketchup or Kickin' Barbecue Sauce (page 12)
¼	cup mild or hot salsa
1½	tablespoons Worcestershire sauce
½	tablespoon agave syrup
⅛	teaspoon salt
1	teaspoon freshly ground black pepper

Cut around the stem ends of the bell peppers and remove the tops and the seedpods. Cut out and discard the stems. Gently scrape the ribs and any seeds from the inside of the peppers. Finely chop the tops.

In a medium bowl, mix together the diced peppers; the rice, couscous, or pasta; 2 tablespoons of the cheese; and the crumbled meat loaves. Stuff the prepared peppers with this mixture. Stand the peppers upright in a lightly greased 12 by 8 by 2-inch baking dish. In a small bowl, stir together the ketchup or barbecue sauce, salsa, Worcestershire sauce, syrup, salt, and black pepper. Pour the sauce over the peppers.

Cover tightly with microwave-safe plastic wrap; fold back one corner of the plastic wrap to allow steam to escape. Microwave on high for 12 to 15 minutes, or until the filling is hot, the cheese melted, and the peppers are almost tender. Let stand for 6 to 8 minutes. Sprinkle each pepper with some of the remaining cheese and serve.

SERVING SIZE: 1 stuffed pepper
EXCHANGE LIST VALUES: 1 starch, 4 vegetable, 2 lean meat, 1 medium-fat meat
CARBOHYDRATE CHOICES: 3

CALORIES: 289
CALORIES FROM FAT: 96
TOTAL FAT: 11 g
SATURATED FAT: 5 g
CHOLESTEROL: 64 mg

SODIUM: 747 mg
TOTAL CARBOHYDRATE: 43 g
FIBER: 4 g
TOTAL SUGARS: 10 g
PROTEIN: 19 g

Microwave Magic

I've found that using my microwave oven saves hours of time and keeps my kitchen clean and cool. While most modern kitchens are equipped with a microwave, very few people know how to utilize it to make "magic" in the kitchen.

The history of the microwave oven goes back to 1946. Dr. Percy Spencer, an electronics genius and war hero, was touring one of the laboratories at the Raytheon Company. The company was testing a vacuum tube called a magnetron, the power tube that drives a radar set. As Dr. Percy stood in front of the "radar box," a candy bar in his pocket melted.

Dr. Percy designed a metal box to fit around the magnetron and tried other experiments with food, including popcorn. Engineers developed and refined the idea, and the first commercial microwave oven hit the market in 1947. However, the original response was weak, and it wasn't until 1975 that a microwave oven was created for the consumer kitchen. Now, Dr. Percy's invention has become standard kitchen equipment, but many consumers still don't fully understand how it works.

I encourage you to read the instruction book that came with your microwave oven. It's the easiest way to find out how to successfully use all of the functions on your appliance. I especially love the warming oven feature.

It cycles on and off so that I can hold dinner for my husband when he's running late, or keep a casserole dish warm during the holidays.

A microwave works by heating water molecules inside food and causing them to vibrate, which generates heat. That heat is then conducted to the outside of the food. When cooking on any power level other than high, the oven cooks by cycling power on and off, so the energy has a chance to move through the food without overcooking it. Medium and low power generally are used to soften, melt, and defrost foods, while high is usually used for cooking.

Use your microwave to prepare everything from appetizers to desserts. A microwave won't heat up your kitchen during the warm months, it uses less energy than an oven, and it also helps to retain more nutrients in your foods during the cooking process. A microwave is the best way to cook vegetables, retaining more taste and texture.

Carefully follow the recipe when using your microwave, use a plastic wrap that indicates that it's microwave safe on the packaging, and make a small slit in the plastic wrap to vent steam. Use a slightly damp food-safe paper towel to cover bread products when reheating. Placing items in round glass dishes ensures that foods cook more evenly in the microwave. Follow these tips and you'll have beautifully cooked meals in your microwave each time.

Garlic Flank Steak

MAKES 4 SERVINGS, PLUS LEFTOVERS

The garlicky, salt-free marinade in this recipe tenderizes flank steak and also makes a delicious sauce or salad dressing. This recipe makes a double batch of flank steak and sauce. Use the leftovers to make Beef Fajitas (page 124) or slice the meat to use in salads, sandwiches, or tacos, using the ¼ reserved marinade as a dressing for any of these dishes. The marinade will stay fresh in an airtight container in the refrigerator for up to 1 month. Shake the container to combine the ingredients before using.

2	(1-pound) flank steaks
1	large yellow onion, sliced
2	red bell peppers, seeded, deribbed, and sliced

MARINADE

6	cloves garlic, minced
¼	cup extra-virgin olive oil
¾	cup low-sodium beef broth
¼	cup reduced-sodium soy sauce
⅓	cup no-sugar-added apple cider vinegar
¼	cup fresh lemon juice
3	tablespoons Worcestershire sauce
1	tablespoon freshly ground black pepper
2	tablespoons Dijon mustard
1	small onion, chopped
½	teaspoon onion powder
1	teaspoon grated fresh ginger
¼	teaspoon dried basil
¼	teaspoon red pepper flakes

SERVING SIZE: 3 ounces steak and ½ cup vegetables
EXCHANGE LIST VALUES: 1 vegetable, 3 lean meat, ½ fat
CARBOHYDRATE CHOICES: ½

CALORIES: 232
CALORIES FROM FAT: 99
TOTAL FAT: 11 g
SATURATED FAT: 3 g
CHOLESTEROL: 68 mg

SODIUM: 302 mg
TOTAL CARBOHYDRATE: 7 g
FIBER: 1 g
TOTAL SUGARS: 3 g
PROTEIN: 25 g

Trim all the fat from the flank steaks. Place the steaks, onion, and bell peppers in a shallow baking dish.

To make the marinade, combine all the ingredients in a medium bowl and stir until well combined.

Reserve ½ cup of the marinade. Pour the remaining marinade over the steaks and vegetables. Cover and refrigerate for at least 30 minutes or up to 3 hours, turning often.

Preheat the broiler. Spray the grill pan with the cooking oil spray. Remove the steaks and vegetables from the marinade and discard the marinade. Place the steaks and vegetables on the grill pan and broil the steak for 6 to 7 minutes on each side, stirring the vegetables once or twice and brushing the steaks once or twice with ¼ cup of the reserved marinade.

Transfer the steaks and vegetables to a plate and cover them with a piece of aluminum foil. Let rest for 4 minutes to retain the juices and keep tender and moist. Slice against the grain of the meat and serve.

Texas-Style Beef Stew

MAKES 10 SERVINGS

If you're having trouble getting your children to eat stew, try this recipe. This version is made without carrots or potatoes, so you can serve it—with its thick, rich gravy—over a mash of potatoes and parsnips, or a mound of fluffy brown rice. Serve some crunchy raw vegetables, Carolina Coleslaw (page 74), or a crisp salad on the side, and you've got a meal that will please the pickiest eater. Reserve leftover stew for French Dip Sandwiches (page 125).

1½	tablespoons extra-virgin olive oil
2½	pounds lean beef chuck, cut into 1- to 2-inch cubes
½	teaspoon salt
1	teaspoon freshly ground black pepper
¼	teaspoon red pepper flakes
3	extra-large yellow onions, finely chopped
5	garlic cloves, smashed
½	cup unbleached all-purpose flour
4	cups reduced-sodium beef broth
2	cups water
2	tablespoons no-sugar-added apple cider vinegar
1	tablespoon tomato paste
2	sprigs fresh rosemary, or 1 teaspoon dried
2	sprigs fresh thyme, or 1 teaspoon dried

Spray a 6- to 8-quart Dutch oven with cooking oil spray. Add ½ tablespoon of the olive oil and heat over medium heat. Add half of the beef, season lightly with salt, pepper, and red pepper flakes and sauté until browned, about 8 minutes. Transfer to a plate and repeat with ½ tablespoon of the oil and the remaining beef.

Add the remaining ½ tablespoon of oil, the onions, and garlic and cook, stirring occasionally, until softened, about 6 minutes. Sprinkle the flour on top and cook, stirring constantly, until thick and lightly browned, about 2 minutes. Whisk in the broth, water, vinegar, and tomato paste. Bring the mixture to a boil.

SERVING SIZE: 1½ cups
EXCHANGE LIST VALUES: ½ starch, 1 vegetable, 3 lean meat, ½ fat
CARBOHYDRATE CHOICES: 1
CALORIES: 217

CALORIES FROM FAT: 66
TOTAL FAT: 7 g
SATURATED FAT: 2 g
CHOLESTEROL: 70 mg
SODIUM: 351 mg

TOTAL CARBOHYDRATE: 11 g
FIBER: 1 g
TOTAL SUGARS: 3 g
PROTEIN: 26 g

Return the meat to the pan, add the rosemary and thyme, and return to a boil, stirring occasionally. Reduce the heat to medium-low, cover, and simmer gently, stirring occasionally, for 1½ hours. Uncover the pot and continue simmering for 30 minutes, until the meat is nicely tender but still holds it shape.

Alternatively, prepare the meat and the sauce, and bring the sauce mixture to a boil. Transfer the meat and sauce to a 5-quart slow cooker. Add the rosemary and thyme. Cover and cook on low for 7 hours or until tender. Remove the herb sprigs before serving. This stew freezes well in a freezer bag for up to 6 months.

Beef Fajitas

MAKES 4 SERVINGS

Leftover Garlic Flank Steak and broiled vegetables are a delicious filling for fajitas. Fajitas are traditionally made with either skirt steak or chicken, but any type of meat can be used.

1	Garlic Flank Steak, sliced (page 120), plus ¼ cup leftover cooked vegetables and ¼ cup leftover marinade
8	(6-inch) whole-wheat flour tortillas
2	cups chopped romaine lettuce
½	cup shredded low-fat Monterey Jack or sharp cheddar cheese
4	tablespoons plain nonfat Greek yogurt or low-fat sour cream
2	tablespoons chopped fresh cilantro (optional)
½	cup chunky salsa or pico de gallo (optional)
1	avocado, peeled, pitted, and sliced (optional)

In a large skillet, heat the flank steak, vegetables, and marinade over medium heat. Or, microwave on low (or the defrost setting) for 1 to 2 minutes. Wrap the tortillas in microwave-safe paper towels. Sprinkle each side with 2 teaspoons of water. Warm on high in the microwave for 10 seconds.

Divide the steak and vegetables evenly among the tortillas. Divide the lettuce and cheese evenly among the tortillas and top each one with ½ tablespoon of the yogurt or sour cream; fold the tortillas in half. If desired, sprinkle with the cilantro and serve with salsa or pico de gallo and avocado.

Yogurt ONE OF THE EASIEST WAYS TO LIGHTEN A HEAVY RECIPE IS TO SUBSTITUTE A HIGH-QUALITY LOW-FAT YOGURT, SUCH AS GREEK YOGURT, FOR SOUR CREAM, MAYONNAISE, OR HEAVY CREAM. YOGURT HELPS TO KEEP BAKED GOODS MOIST AND TENDER. USING LOW-FAT GREEK YOGURT INSTEAD OF REGULAR SOUR CREAM SAVES 20 CALORIES AND 2 GRAMS OF FAT PER TABLESPOON, AND IT CAN BE SUBSTITUTED FOR MAYONNAISE IN EQUAL AMOUNTS. YOGURT ALSO IS A FLAVORFUL TOPPING ON A BAKED POTATO, OR IN STROGANOFFS AND STEWS, AND A LOW-FAT WAY TO THICKEN SAUCES.

SERVING SIZE: 2 fajitas
EXCHANGE LIST VALUES: 1½ starch, 1 vegetable, 3 lean meat, 2 fat
CARBOHYDRATE CHOICES: 2
CALORIES: 466

CALORIES FROM FAT: 174
TOTAL FAT: 19 g
SATURATED FAT: 7 g
CHOLESTEROL: 78 mg
SODIUM: 880 mg

TOTAL CARBOHYDRATE: 38 g
FIBER: 6 g
TOTAL SUGARS: 7 g
PROTEIN: 35 g

French Dip Sandwiches

MAKES 4 SERVINGS

If you're fortunate enough to have leftovers of Texas-Style Beef Stew (page 122), transform them into French Dip Sandwiches. This is the perfect way to use frozen leftover meat stew long after winter is over and the weather is warm.

2   cups Texas-Style Beef Stew, with sauce (page 122)

¼   cup water

¼   cup grated Parmesan cheese

4   whole-wheat hot dog buns or hoagie rolls

8   dill pickle slices

½   red onion, thinly sliced

Shred the beef. In a microwave, reheat the meat, sauce, and water on high for 2 to 3 minutes, or until warm. Pour the sauce into a serving dish and reserve the shredded meat.

Sprinkle some Parmesan cheese inside each bun or roll. Place the bread on a baking sheet in a toaster oven or under a broiler until the cheese starts to melt.

Pile the shredded beef in the buns or rolls and add a few dill pickles and slices of onion. Serve the reserved sauce on the side for dipping.

SERVING SIZE: 1 sandwich
EXCHANGE LIST VALUES: 2 starch, 1 lean meat
CARBOHYDRATE CHOICES: 2
CALORIES: 215

CALORIES FROM FAT: 53
TOTAL FAT: 6 g
SATURATED FAT: 2 g
CHOLESTEROL: 27 mg
SODIUM: 498 mg

TOTAL CARBOHYDRATE: 27 g
FIBER: 4 g
TOTAL SUGARS: 5 g
PROTEIN: 14 g

Ginger Beef Stir-Fry with Soba Noodles

MAKES 4 SERVINGS

Stir-frying is a quick way to get dinner on the table in a hurry. Partially defrosted meat is easier to cut for use in this recipe, and you also can use frozen stir-fry vegetables. Serve leftover stir-fried beef and vegetables wrapped in butter lettuce leaves and topped with cilantro, mint, or parsley for a quick and easy meal.

1	pound boneless beef top round steak or flank steak
1	medium yellow or green bell pepper, seeded, deribbed, and cut into bite-sized strips
2	small zucchini, cut into thin strips
½	medium red onion, cut into thin wedges
⅓	cup sugar-free ginger ale
2	tablespoons reduced-sodium soy sauce
2	cloves garlic, minced
½	teaspoon red pepper flakes or sriracha hot sauce
½	pound buckwheat (soba) noodles
2	teaspoons cornstarch
2	teaspoons minced fresh ginger
2	teaspoons canola oil
¼	cup fresh cilantro, mint, or parsley leaves, chopped (optional)

For easy slicing, wrap and freeze the beef for 30 to 45 minutes, or until firm. Trim the fat from the beef and slice the beef thinly across the grain. Place the beef on one side of a shallow ceramic bowl large enough to hold the meat and the vegetables on separate sides; place the bell pepper, zucchini, and onion on the other side of the plate. In a small bowl, combine the ginger ale, soy sauce, garlic, and red pepper flakes or hot sauce. Pour the marinade over the beef and vegetables. Let stand at room temperature for 30 minutes, or cover and refrigerate for up to 8 hours, stirring the ingredients occasionally.

SERVING SIZE: 4 ounces of meat and vegetables, 2 ounces of noodles
EXCHANGE LIST VALUES: 3 starch, 1 vegetable, 4 lean meat, ½ fat
CARBOHYDRATE CHOICES: 3½

CALORIES: 432
CALORIES FROM FAT: 75
TOTAL FAT: 8 g
SATURATED FAT: 2 g
CHOLESTEROL: 77 mg

SODIUM: 204 mg
TOTAL CARBOHYDRATE: 51 g
FIBER: 4 g
TOTAL SUGARS: 4 g
PROTEIN: 38 g

In a large pot of boiling water, cook the noodles for 4 to 7 minutes, or until tender. Drain, reserving 1 cup of the water to use in the stir-fry sauce. Set the noodles aside.

Drain the marinade from the meat and vegetables into a small bowl. Add the reserved water and the cornstarch, whisking until smooth. Set aside.

Spray a large nonstick wok or extra-large nonstick skillet with cooking oil spray. Heat the wok or skillet over medium-high heat. Add the ginger and stir-fry for 15 seconds. Turn the heat to high and add the vegetables and stir-fry for 3 to 5 minutes, or until crisp-tender. Transfer the vegetables to a plate. Add 1 teaspoon of the canola oil to the pan. Add half the beef and stir-fry for 2 to 3 minutes, or until the beef is browned but still slightly pink in the center. Transfer the beef to a plate. Repeat with the remaining 1 teaspoon of oil and the remaining beef.

Return all the ingredients to the wok or skillet, making a hole in the center and pushing the mixture to the sides. Stir the marinade mixture into the center of the wok. Cook until bubbly. Toss the beef and vegetables to coat with the sauce. Serve on a bed of soba noodles. Sprinkle with the cilantro, mint, or parsley, if desired.

Soba Noodles

SOBA NOODLES ARE A TRADITIONAL JAPANESE COMFORT FOOD, THIN AND LIGHT BROWN, WITH A SLIGHTLY NUTTY FLAVOR. THEY'RE MADE FROM BUCKWHEAT AND SOLD FRESH OR DRIED, PLAIN OR FLAVORED. THE NOODLES ARE DELICIOUS HOT, AT ROOM TEMPERATURE, OR COLD. BUCKWHEAT IS HIGH IN PROTEIN AND ABUNDANT IN VITAMIN B2, MINERALS, FIBER, AMINO ACIDS, AND IMPORTANT ANTIOXIDANTS. THE FLAVONOIDS IN BUCKWHEAT MAY HELP TO LOWER CHOLESTEROL AND BLOOD PRESSURE AND INCREASE BLOOD CIRCULATION.

Spiced Lamb Shanks

MAKES 4 SERVINGS

Shanks are one of the most flavorful cuts of lamb. The exterior fat can easily be removed, and only a small amount of fat marbles the meat, unlike most cuts of beef. Lamb also is high in B vitamins, zinc, and absorbable iron. Serve these shanks over whole-wheat noodles, couscous, or brown rice.

MARINADE

2	tablespoons poultry seasoning
1	tablespoon ground cumin
1	tablespoon ground coriander
½	tablespoon curry powder
¼	teaspoon salt
1	teaspoon freshly ground black pepper
¼	teaspoon cayenne pepper
2	tablespoons olive oil
4	(12-ounce) lamb shanks
1	large onion, sliced
4	cloves garlic, smashed
2	cups canned low-sodium chicken broth
1	(15-ounce) can medium-hot diced tomatoes with chiles
2	tablespoons apple cider vinegar
2	tablespoons agave syrup

To make the marinade, in a small bowl mix together the poultry seasoning, cumin, coriander, curry powder, salt, black pepper, and cayenne pepper. Add the oil and stir to make a paste. Rub the paste all over the shanks. Place the shanks in a large, heavy resealable plastic bag in a baking dish and refrigerate for at least 1 hour or overnight, turning occasionally.

Preheat the oven to 350°F. Spray a medium Dutch oven with cooking oil spray. Heat the pan over high heat and sear the shanks until golden brown, about 4 minutes per side. Transfer to a plate. Add the onion and garlic and cook until caramelized, about 5 minutes. Add the chicken broth, tomatoes, vinegar, and agave syrup and bring to a boil. Turn off the heat and add the lamb shanks. Cover and bake in the oven for about 2 hours, or until tender.

Transfer the shanks to a platter. On the stovetop, bring the sauce to a boil over high heat and cook to reduce the liquid by half. Serve the sauce over the lamb shanks.

SLOW-COOKER LAMB SHANKS: Place the marinated lamb shanks, onion, and garlic in a 5-quart slow cooker. Pour in 1 (15-ounce) can of low-sodium chicken broth. Add the tomatoes, vinegar, and agave syrup. Cook on low for 8 to 10 hours, or until tender.

SERVING SIZE: 1 lamb shank	**CALORIES:** 482	**SODIUM:** 388 mg
EXCHANGE LIST VALUES:	**CALORIES FROM FAT:** 187	**TOTAL CARBOHYDRATE:** 21 g
½ carbohydrate, 2 vegetable,	**TOTAL FAT:** 21 g	**FIBER:** 3 g
7 lean meat, 1½ fat	**SATURATED FAT:** 6 g	**TOTAL SUGARS:** 13 g
CARBOHYDRATE CHOICES: 1½	**CHOLESTEROL:** 144 mg	**PROTEIN:** 50 g

Greek-Style Lamb-Stuffed Eggplant

MAKES 6 SERVINGS

Lamb and eggplant have been part of Greek cuisine for centuries. This dish is called "Little Shoes" in Greek, because when the eggplant is cut in half, it resembles traditional Greek slippers.

The texture of eggplant improves as it cooks. An undercooked eggplant will have a chewy texture, but an eggplant cooked for a long period of time will just become softer. Do not use a carbon-blade knife or aluminum cookware when preparing or cooking eggplant because it may discolor the vegetable and the cookware.

	Cooking oil spray	1	tablespoon Italian seasoning
6	large Japanese eggplants	¼	teaspoon red pepper flakes
½	teaspoon salt	1	(8-ounce) can tomato sauce
1	teaspoon freshly ground black pepper	½	teaspoon ground nutmeg
1	pound lean ground lamb	¼	cup whipped butter
½	large onion, finely chopped	¼	cup all-purpose flour
2	cloves garlic, minced	1¼	cups 1 percent low-fat milk
1	large red bell pepper, diced	½	cup grated Parmesan cheese

SERVING SIZE: 2 stuffed eggplant halves with sauce
EXCHANGE LIST VALUES: 4 vegetable, 2 medium-fat meat, 1 fat
CARBOHYDRATE CHOICES: 1½

CALORIES: 378
CALORIES FROM FAT: 181
TOTAL FAT: 20 g
SATURATED FAT: 10 g
CHOLESTEROL: 77 mg

SODIUM: 589 mg
TOTAL CARBOHYDRATE: 29 g
FIBER: 11 g
TOTAL SUGARS: 12 g
PROTEIN: 23 g

Preheat the oven to 400°F. Spray a 13 by 9-inch baking dish with cooking oil spray. Cut the eggplants in half lengthwise. Scoop out the pulp, leaving a ½-inch shell. Reserve the pulp aside to use in the stuffing. Sprinkle the insides with ¼ teaspoon of the salt and ½ teaspoon of the pepper. Arrange in a baking dish, cut side down. Spray with the cooking oil spray. Bake for 5 minutes, or until the shells are slightly tender.

Spray a large nonstick skillet with cooking oil spray and heat over medium-high heat. Add the reserved eggplant pulp, the ground lamb, onion, garlic, bell pepper, Italian seasoning, the remaining ¼ teaspoon of salt, the remaining ½ teaspoon of pepper, and the red pepper flakes and stir. Add the tomato sauce and ¼ teaspoon of the nutmeg and simmer for 10 minutes. Stuff the eggplant halves with the lamb filling.

Preheat the oven to 350°F. Wipe out the skillet with a paper towel. Melt the butter over medium-high heat. Add the flour and cook, stirring, for 2 minutes. Add the milk and stir until thick, about 5 minutes. Add the cheese and the remaining ¼ teaspoon of nutmeg, stirring well. Pour the sauce over the stuffed eggplants and bake for 30 minutes.

Eggplant

The National Diabetes Education Program, the Mayo Clinic, and the American Diabetes Association all recommend a diet containing abundant vegetables as a choice for management of type 2 diabetes. Eggplant is one of the best choices, since it is a low-carb, high-fiber vegetable that is meaty enough to use as a main course. Eggplant also has lots of chlorogenic acid, an antioxidant that may help fight cancer and prevent heart disease.

Eggplant ranks with spinach and sweet potatoes as the highest plant sources of antioxidants. It also is rich in potassium, a mineral needed to balance sodium and prevent hypertension. As a good source of soluble fiber, eggplant can lower blood glucose levels. The purple skin of eggplant comes from anthocyanins, which help to protect the heart and blood vessels. Eggplant skin also contains nasunin, a potent antioxidant that protects cell membranes from damage from free radicals.

When selecting an eggplant, look for a symmetrical vegetable with smooth, uniformly colored skin. Tan patches, scars, or bruises, and wrinkled or flabby-looking skin indicate decay. Oversized purple eggplants, usually more than 6 inches in diameter, may be tough and bitter. An eggplant should feel heavy; one that feels light for its size may not have a good flavor. When you press gently on an eggplant, the finger mark will disappear quickly if the eggplant is fresh. The stem and cap should be bright green.

Store eggplant uncut and unwashed in a plastic bag in the crisper section of the refrigerator. Wash eggplant just before using it, and cut off the cap and stem. Use a stainless-steel knife, because carbon blades will discolor the eggplant.

Eggplant should not be eaten raw. Steaming or baking brings out the flavor and avoids adding fat and calories to your diet. Eggplant has a spongelike texture and tends to soak up water and oil. When salting eggplant to remove bitterness, wipe off the salt after allowing it to sit for 30 minutes to 1 hour. Do not wash the salt off because the eggplant will absorb the water.

Lamb and Sweet Potato Casserole

MAKES 8 SERVINGS

The rich flavor of lamb combined with creamy sweet potatoes makes this casserole a comforting and highly nutritious dish. Sweet potatoes are an excellent source of beta-carotene and vitamins A, B, and C. Both beta-carotene and vitamin C are powerful antioxidants that help to eliminate free radicals.

1	large onion, diced
2	cloves garlic, minced
1	tablespoon Italian seasoning
½	teaspoon salt
1	teaspoon freshly ground black pepper
2	teaspoons olive oil
2	pounds lean lamb shoulder, cut into 1-inch cubes
2	large sprigs rosemary
1	tablespoon Worcestershire sauce
⅛	teaspoon cayenne pepper
1	(13¾-ounce) can low-sodium chicken broth
3	medium sweet potatoes, peeled and cut into 1-inch cubes
3	cups chopped fresh or frozen broccoli
1	tablespoon and 1 teaspoon cornstarch
2	tablespoons water

Spray a 2½-quart baking dish with cooking oil spray and set aside. Spray a large skillet with cooking oil spray and set over medium heat. Add the onion, garlic, Italian seasoning, ¼ teaspoon of the salt, and ½ teaspoon of the pepper. Sauté until the onion is translucent, about 3 minutes. Using a slotted spoon, transfer the vegetables to the baking dish. Add the olive oil to the same pan and increase the heat to medium-high. Add the lamb cubes, rosemary, Worcestershire sauce, the remaining ¼ teaspoon of salt, the remaining ½ teaspoon of pepper, and the cayenne.

Working in batches, brown the lamb on all sides, placing the finished batch in the baking dish. Drain the fat from the skillet. Stir in the chicken broth and bring it to a boil. Pour the broth into the baking dish. Add the sweet potato cubes and broccoli and stir. Cover and let stand for 30 minutes.

Preheat the oven to 350°F. Bake the stew for 1½ hours, or until the meat is tender. Place the cornstarch and water in a small bowl, stir until combined, and add it to the stew, stirring constantly. Bake, uncovered, stirring once, for 8 to 10 minutes longer, or until the gravy is thickened.

SERVING SIZE: 2 cups

EXCHANGE LIST VALUES: ½ starch, 1 vegetable, 3 medium-fat meat

CARBOHYDRATE CHOICES: 1

CALORIES: 312

CALORIES FROM FAT: 153

TOTAL FAT: 17 g

SATURATED FAT: 7 g

CHOLESTEROL: 83 mg

SODIUM: 290 mg

TOTAL CARBOHYDRATE: 15 g

FIBER: 3 g

TOTAL SUGARS: 5 g

PROTEIN: 24 g

Apple–Pecan Pork Chops

MAKES 4 SERVINGS

This simple recipe is a great way to involve the whole family in preparing dinner. One person can prepare the pork chops while the rest of the family assembles and measures ingredients or tosses a salad. In less than 45 minutes, the whole family can sit down to a delicious meal.

1	pound thin center-cut boneless pork loin chops
1	tablespoon olive oil
1	tablespoon poultry seasoning
½	teaspoon salt
1	teaspoon freshly ground black pepper
1	(16-ounce) can no-sugar-added sliced apples, drained
2	tablespoons firmly packed Splenda brown sugar blend
½	teaspoon ground cinnamon
¼	cup chopped pecans

Trim the fat from the pork. Heat the oil in a large skillet over medium-high heat until shimmering. Reduce the heat to medium. Sprinkle both sides of the pork with the poultry seasoning, salt, and black pepper.

Place the pork chops in the skillet. Cook for 2 minutes, then turn over the chops. Combine the apples, brown sugar blend, cinnamon, and pecans in a small bowl. Spoon the fruit mixture over the pork. Cover the skillet and cook for 8 to 10 minutes more, until the chops are tender.

SERVING SIZE: 2 pork chops plus 4 tablespoons sauce
EXCHANGE LIST VALUES: ½ carbohydrate, ½ fruit, 3 lean meat, 1½ fat
CARBOHYDRATE CHOICES: 1

CALORIES: 305
CALORIES FROM FAT: 132
TOTAL FAT: 15 g
SATURATED FAT: 3 g
CHOLESTEROL: 60 mg

SODIUM: 349 mg
TOTAL CARBOHYDRATE: 19 g
FIBER: 2 g
TOTAL SUGARS: 6 g
PROTEIN: 23 g

Pork and Mushroom Stroganoff

MAKES 6 SERVINGS

This dish is usually made with beef. Using lean pork and low-fat ingredients lightens this traditionally calorie-laden dish, while retaining all the rich flavors. Mushrooms, which are rich in the antioxidant selenium and in B vitamins, add a healthful component to this recipe. Serve this dish over whole-wheat noodles.

1½ pounds pork tenderloin, cut into 1-inch cubes

1 tablespoon poultry seasoning

½ teaspoon salt

1 teaspoon freshly ground black pepper

6 ounces button, cremini, portobello, or chanterelle mushrooms, sliced

1 large yellow onion, sliced

2 cloves garlic, minced

⅛ teaspoon cayenne pepper

2 teaspoons Dijon mustard

¼ cup reduced-sodium chicken broth

1 tablespoon Worcestershire sauce

1 (8-ounce) container low-fat sour cream or plain Greek yogurt

3 tablespoons chopped fresh flat-leaf parsley

Spray a large skillet with cooking oil spray and place it over medium-high heat. Add the pork and sprinkle it with the poultry seasoning, ¼ teaspoon of the salt, and ½ teaspoon of the black pepper. Brown on all sides, 4 to 5 minutes. Transfer the pork to a plate. Add the mushrooms, onion, garlic, the remaining ¼ teaspoon of salt, the remaining ½ teaspoon of black pepper, and the cayenne pepper. Sauté until tender but slightly firm, about 5 minutes.

Add the cooked pork to the pan and stir. Increase the heat to high. Add the mustard, chicken broth, and Worcestershire sauce and bring to a boil for 30 seconds. Turn the heat to low. Cover and simmer for 45 to 50 minutes. Serve topped with the sour cream or yogurt and the parsley.

SERVING SIZE: 4 ounces meat and sauce
EXCHANGE LIST VALUES: 1 vegetable, 4 lean meat, ½ fat
CARBOHYDRATE CHOICES: ½
CALORIES: 197

CALORIES FROM FAT: 54
TOTAL FAT: 6 g
SATURATED FAT: 3 g
CHOLESTEROL: 86 mg
SODIUM: 360 mg

TOTAL CARBOHYDRATE: 7 g
FIBER: 1 g
TOTAL SUGARS: 4 g
PROTEIN: 27 g

Salsa Verde Pork

MAKES 6 SERVINGS

I created this saucy slow-cooked pork dish to feed my family without a lot of effort on my part. The beauty of this recipe is the number of ways you can transform one roast for use. You may want to serve the dish as a dinner entrée with rice and vegetables. Or, you can shred the meat and use it to make quesadillas, nachos, or soft tacos; as a hearty filling for a baked potato; to stuff in a whole-wheat pita; or to combine it with the Kickin' Barbecue Sauce (page 12) as a pulled-pork sandwich on a hamburger bun.

1	tablespoon chili powder
2	teaspoons ground cumin
1	teaspoon ground cinnamon
½	teaspoon salt
1	teaspoon freshly ground black pepper
	Cooking oil spray
1	(1½-pound) boneless pork shoulder (pork butt), trimmed of fat and cut into 1-inch pieces
1	(8-ounce) jar salsa verde
1	pound fresh tomatillos, husked, rinsed, and chopped
1	large yellow onion, chopped
3	teaspoons grated lime zest
2	tablespoons fresh lime juice
4	cloves garlic, chopped
2	tablespoons snipped fresh cilantro (optional)

In a small bowl, combine the chili powder, cumin, cinnamon, salt, and pepper. Spray the pork with the cooking oil spray. Sprinkle the chili mixture over the pork and toss to coat. Place the pork in a 3½- or 4-quart slow cooker. Add the salsa verde, tomatillos, onion, 1 teaspoon of the lime zest, the lime juice, and garlic and stir to combine.

Cover and cook on low for 6 hours, or on high for 3 to 4 hours. Alternatively, spray a 13 by 9-inch baking pan with cooking oil spray and add the seasoned pork and the other ingredients. Cover with aluminum foil and bake in a preheated 350°F oven for 2½ to 3 hours, until the pork is tender.

To serve, sprinkle the pork with the remaining 2 teaspoons of lime zest and the cilantro, if desired.

SERVING SIZE: 4 ounces of meat and sauce
EXCHANGE LIST VALUES: 2 vegetable, 3 lean meat
CARBOHYDRATE CHOICES: ½

CALORIES: 222
CALORIES FROM FAT: 84
TOTAL FAT: 9 g
SATURATED FAT: 3 g
CHOLESTEROL: 76 mg

SODIUM: 478 mg
TOTAL CARBOHYDRATE: 10 g
SUGARS: 4 g
PROTEIN: 24 g

Rotisserie Chicken

I love using rotisserie chicken in my recipes when I'm pressed for time. Reasonably priced, convenient, and seasoned in a variety of ways, it can be transformed into a multitude of quick-and-easy main dishes. Best of all, you can use the bones to make a rich, homemade chicken stock or enhance the flavors of commercial stocks or broths, so nothing goes to waste.

Most rotisserie chickens are large enough to serve 4 people as a main course. Or, the meat can be pulled from the bones and shredded to use in a range of dishes, from salads, sandwiches, and soups to enchiladas or chicken potpies.

Using a precooked chicken gives you the opportunity to explore new and unusual recipes that would ordinarily take a lot of time to prepare, such as Quick Curried Chicken (page 139), which is reminiscent of an exotic Moroccan tagine. A tagine is both a type of heavy clay pot with a domed lid and the dish that is cooked in it. Traditional tagines combine lamb, chicken, or beef with a variety of ingredients and seasonings, including citrus fruits, nuts, honey, and pungent spices.

Quick Curried Chicken

MAKES 6 SERVINGS

You can create all the exotic flavors of the traditional dish in half the time by using a rotisserie chicken already seasoned with lemon pepper from the grocery store. Toasting the curry powder in the oil first gives the dish an authentic taste and brings out the flavors of the spice. A blend of spicy salsa and curry powder adds a hint of sweetness by incorporating agave syrup and raisins. Serve with whole-wheat couscous, bulgur, or brown rice to make the most of the savory sauce.

1   tablespoon olive oil

2   teaspoons curry powder

1   (15½-ounce) can diced tomatoes
     with chiles, mild or hot

½   cup reduced-sodium chicken broth

¼   cup golden raisins

¼   cup agave syrup

2   tablespoons chopped
     green or black olives

1   (10-ounce) package frozen
     peas and carrots

1   rotisserie chicken (2 to 2½ pounds),
     cut into 6 to 8 pieces and skinned

In a large nonstick skillet, heat the oil over medium heat. Add the curry powder and cook for 1 minute, stirring constantly. Add the diced tomatoes, chicken broth, raisins, agave syrup, and olives. Cook for 2 minutes. Add the vegetables and chicken, stirring to coat with the sauce. Cover and cook over medium-high heat for 5 to 6 minutes, turning the chicken occasionally, until the sauce is bubbly and the chicken is thoroughly heated.

SERVING SIZE: 2 pieces chicken plus 4 tablespoons sauce
EXCHANGE LIST VALUES: 1 carbohydrate, 1 vegetable, 6 lean meat, ½ fat
CARBOHYDRATE CHOICES: 1½

CALORIES: 409
CALORIES FROM FAT: 127
TOTAL FAT: 14 g
SATURATED FAT: 3 g
CHOLESTEROL: 128 mg

SODIUM: 301 mg
TOTAL CARBOHYDRATE: 24 g
FIBER: 3 g
TOTAL SUGARS: 16 g
PROTEIN: 45 g

Crispy Roasted Chicken

MAKES 10 SERVINGS

This is one of my family's favorite chicken dishes. I usually prepare it for Sunday dinner after church and for birthday celebrations. Sprinkling the skin with baking powder helps draw out the moisture, so the skin gets crackling crisp in the oven. You can cut the recipe in half and only prepare one chicken, but by preparing two, you can use the leftover chicken in a salad, or with leftover vegetables to make a quick chicken soup.

2	chickens (3½ to 4 pounds)
½	tablespoon baking powder
	Cooking oil spray
1	tablespoon olive oil
2	tablespoons garlic powder
2	tablespoons poultry seasoning
1½	teaspoons salt
1½	teaspoons freshly ground black pepper
1	small onion, halved
1	lemon, halved
8	sprigs rosemary
4	cloves garlic, smashed
3	teaspoons minced fresh thyme

Remove the neck and giblets and any pieces of fat inside the birds. Rinse the birds with cold water inside and out. Remove any excess fat and leftover pin feathers. Pat the chickens dry with paper towels. Sprinkle the chicken skin (breast side only) with the baking powder. Place the chickens on a roasting rack in a large baking pan and let them air-dry in the refrigerator for 30 minutes. Pat the chickens dry with more paper towels.

Spray two large baking pans with cooking oil spray. Rub the olive oil all over the chickens. Turn the chickens breast side up, twist the wing tips, and tuck them behind the birds. Sprinkle the chickens inside and out with the garlic powder, poultry seasoning, salt, and pepper. Rub the spices inside and on the outside of the birds. Stuff the cavities with the onion, lemon, rosemary, garlic, and thyme.

SERVING SIZE: 5 ounces light and dark meat with skin	**CALORIES:** 306	**SODIUM:** 468 mg
	CALORIES FROM FAT: 159	**TOTAL CARBOHYDRATE:** 2 g
EXCHANGE LIST VALUES:	**TOTAL FAT:** 18 g	**FIBER:** 0 g
5 medium-fat meat	**SATURATED FAT:** 5 g	**TOTAL SUGARS:** 0 g
CARBOHYDRATE CHOICES: 0	**CHOLESTEROL:** 104 mg	**PROTEIN:** 33 g

Preheat the oven to 425°F. Place the chickens in the upper half of the oven and cook, uncovered, for 20 minutes to brown and crisp the skin. Lower the oven temperature to 350°F. Spray the chickens with the cooking oil spray. Roast the chickens for an additional 35 to 40 minutes, or until the juices run clear when a thigh is pierced with a knife, or an instant-read thermometer inserted in the thigh and not touching bone registers 165°F.

Remove the chickens from the oven and allow them to rest, uncovered, for at least 10 minutes prior to carving. Do not cover the meat, because it will steam and soften the crispy skin.

Chicken and Apples with Lemon Balsamic Sauce

MAKES 4 SERVINGS

Chicken breast meat is a healthy but rather bland source of protein. Pairing it with apples and a flavorful lemon–balsamic sauce showcases each ingredient. Serve this dish with whole-wheat pasta or couscous, or brown rice.

4   boneless, skin-on chicken breast halves (about 1¼ pounds)

1½   tablespoons poultry seasoning

½   teaspoon salt

1   teaspoon freshly ground black pepper

¼   cup balsamic vinegar

1   teaspoon grated lemon zest

2   tablespoons fresh lemon juice

2   cloves garlic, minced

1   cup reduced-sodium chicken broth

½   teaspoon agave syrup

1   tablespoon whipped butter

1   large Jonagold or Mutsu apple (8 ounces), halved, cored, and thinly sliced

Season the chicken on both sides with 1 tablespoon of the poultry seasoning, the salt, and pepper. Spray a large skillet with cooking oil spray and heat over high heat until hot; reduce the heat to medium-high and add the chicken breasts, skin side down. Sauté for 6 minutes, or until the skin is nicely browned. Using tongs, transfer to a plate and loosely cover with aluminum foil.

Turn the heat to high. Add the remaining ½ tablespoon of poultry seasoning, the vinegar, lemon zest, lemon juice, garlic, broth, and syrup and stir until well blended. Bring the sauce to a boil. Turn the heat to low and add the butter, stirring until it melts. Stir in the apples. Simmer for 6 to 8 minutes, or until the apples soften and the sauce slightly reduces.

Return the chicken, skin side up, along with any juices from the plate, to the pan. Cook for 12 to 14 minutes over medium heat, or until the chicken is just cooked through. Divide the chicken among 4 plates and top each serving with some of the sauce.

SERVING SIZE: 1 chicken breast half plus 3 tablespoons sauce
EXCHANGE LIST VALUES: 1 fruit, 4 lean meat, ½ fat
CARBOHYDRATE CHOICES: 1

CALORIES: 322
CALORIES FROM FAT: 141
TOTAL FAT: 16 g
SATURATED FAT: 5 g
CHOLESTEROL: 96 mg

SODIUM: 540 mg
TOTAL CARBOHYDRATE: 13 g
FIBER: 2 g
TOTAL SUGARS: 9 g
PROTEIN: 31 g

Spaghetti and Chicken Meatballs

MAKES 6 SERVINGS

Spaghetti and meatballs always are a hit with both children and adults. Here, this dish has been reinvented to provide a healthier alternative to the traditional favorite by reducing the carbs and increasing the amount of vegetables used in the dish. Bulgur, used to bind the lean chicken meatballs, adds fiber and has a lower glycemic index than white rice. This hearty grain is made from wheat that has been cleaned, parboiled, dried, ground into particles, and sifted into distinct sizes. The result is a nutritious, versatile food with a pleasant, nutlike flavor.

Another delicious way to use these power-packed chicken meatballs is in a sub or hoagie roll or as a filling for tortillas or pita bread.

½	cup bulgur wheat	½	teaspoon red pepper flakes
¾	cup hot water	½	teaspoon ground nutmeg
1½	pounds lean ground chicken	2	cups reduced-sodium pasta sauce
1	medium yellow onion, finely chopped	1	(28-ounce) can stewed tomatoes
1	large egg, lightly beaten	12	ounces frozen Italian- or Mediterranean-style vegetables
3	cloves garlic, minced		
2	tablespoons Italian seasoning	1	tablespoon Worcestershire sauce
1	teaspoon Hungarian or sweet paprika	8	ounces whole-wheat spaghetti
1½	teaspoons freshly ground black pepper	½	cup grated Parmesan or Romano cheese
1	teaspoon Liquid Smoke	½	cup torn fresh basil leaves or chopped fresh flat-leaf parsley
1	teaspoon stevia granulated sweetener		

SERVING SIZE: 3 meatballs, plus 1 cup sauce and vegetables, 1¼ ounces pasta

EXCHANGE LIST VALUES: 2 starch, 2 vegetable, 3 lean meat

CARBOHYDRATE CHOICES: 3

CALORIES: 434
CALORIES FROM FAT: 66
TOTAL FAT: 7 g
SATURATED FAT: 2 g
CHOLESTEROL: 100 mg
SODIUM: 620 mg

TOTAL CARBOHYDRATE: 54 g
FIBER: 12 g
TOTAL SUGARS: 9 g
PROTEIN: 37 g

Combine the bulgur and hot water in a small bowl. Let stand until the bulgur is tender and the liquid is absorbed, about 30 minutes. Drain any excess liquid from the bulgur and set aside.

Preheat the oven to 350°F. Coat a wire rack with cooking spray and place it in a baking pan lined with aluminum foil. In a large bowl, combine the ground chicken, onion, egg, garlic, 1 tablespoon of the Italian seasoning, the paprika, 1 teaspoon of the black pepper, Liquid Smoke, stevia, red pepper flakes, nutmeg, and the soaked bulgur. Mix well until all the ingredients are combined. Form the mixture into 18 meatballs. Place the meatballs on the oiled rack and bake for 25 minutes. Remove from the oven and blot any excess oil from the meatballs with a paper towel.

Bring the pasta sauce and the stewed tomatoes to a simmer in a Dutch oven. Add the frozen vegetables, the remaining 1 tablespoon of Italian seasoning, the remaining ½ teaspoon of the pepper, the Worcestershire sauce, and meatballs to the sauce. Cover and simmer for 20 minutes.

In a large pot of salted boiling water, cook the spaghetti until al dente, 8 to 10 minutes. Drain the spaghetti and place it in a serving bowl. Top with the sauce and meatballs. Sprinkle with the cheese and the basil or parsley.

Nutritious and Delicious Chicken CHICKEN IS A GOOD SOURCE OF NIACIN AND VITAMIN B$_6$. A 4-OUNCE SERVING SUPPLIES 72 PERCENT OF THE DAILY VALUE FOR NIACIN AND 32 PERCENT OF THE DAILY VALUE FOR VITAMIN B$_6$, WHICH IS ESSENTIAL FOR THE BODY'S PROCESSING OF CARBOHYDRATES (SUGAR AND STARCH), ESPECIALLY THE BREAKDOWN OF GLYCOGEN, THE FORM IN WHICH GLUCOSE IS STORED IN MUSCLE AND LIVER CELLS.

Peppercorn Chicken

MAKES 6 SERVINGS

Whenever I'm thinking about ways to add variety to chicken recipes, my spice rack always provides inspiration. Freshly ground or crushed peppercorns add a much-needed boost to the mild flavors of chicken, pork, and fish. Here, they are combined with a bottled light ranch dressing to make a flavorful coating for baked chicken. Ranch dressing has been one of America's favorite condiments for more than forty years. It's used on everything from salads to pizza to potato chips.

	Cooking oil spray
1½	pounds (4 to 6 pieces) boneless, skinless chicken breasts
2	tablespoons poultry seasoning
2	teaspoons black or mixed peppercorns, freshly ground or finely crushed
1	cup light ranch dressing
1	small yellow onion, chopped
2	cloves garlic, minced
½	teaspoon cayenne pepper
1	cup whole-wheat panko (Japanese bread crumbs)
¼	cup grated Parmesan cheese

Preheat the oven to 375°F. Spray a 13 by 9-inch baking dish with cooking oil spray.

Rinse and pat the chicken breasts dry with paper towels. Season both sides of the chicken with 1 tablespoon of the poultry seasoning. Set aside.

In a large bowl, combine the black pepper or mixed peppercorns, ranch dressing, onion, garlic, and cayenne. Mix well. Pour the panko, Parmesan cheese, and the remaining tablespoon of poultry seasoning onto a large plate and mix well.

SERVING SIZE: 1 chicken breast
EXCHANGE LIST VALUES:
    ½ carbohydrate, ½ starch,
    3 lean meat, 1 fat
CARBOHYDRATE CHOICES: 1

CALORIES: 281
CALORIES FROM FAT: 81
TOTAL FAT: 9 g
SATURATED FAT: 2 g
CHOLESTEROL: 72 mg

SODIUM: 621 mg
TOTAL CARBOHYDRATE: 20 g
FIBER: 1 g
TOTAL SUGARS: 4 g
PROTEIN: 27 g

Dip the chicken in the ranch dressing mixture, coating each piece on both sides. Roll the chicken in the panko mixture until coated on both sides. Place the chicken in the prepared baking dish. Spray the chicken with cooking oil spray.

Place the chicken in the oven and bake for 25 to 35 minutes or until golden brown on the outside and opaque throughout, or until an instant-read thermometer inserted in the center of a piece registers 165°F. Serve immediately.

Varieties of Peppercorns
PEPPERCORNS, THE SEED OF THE PIPER *NIGRUM* PLANT, COME IN WHITE, GREEN, AND BLACK. GREEN PEPPERCORNS ARE IMMATURE SEEDS, WHILE WHITE PEPPERCORNS ARE BLACK PEPPERCORNS WITH THE SKINS REMOVED. PINK PEPPERCORNS ARE NOT REALLY PEPPERCORNS; INSTEAD, THEY ARE THE DRIED BERRIES OF THE BAIES ROSE, ALSO KNOWN AS THE PERUVIAN PEPPER TREE.

Chicken Lollipops

MAKES 4 SERVINGS

I enjoy making fun, tactile food for children that adults also enjoy eating. Here, using a simple frenching technique, the meat is pushed into lollipop shapes with a sharp knife. This leaves the bones clean to represent the lollipop sticks. These crunchy chicken lollipops also are great appetizers for an adult gathering.

8   (1½- to 2-pound) chicken drumsticks, skinned

1   tablespoon poultry seasoning

1   teaspoon freshly ground black pepper

1   tablespoon agave syrup

½   cup whole-grain mustard

2   tablespoons apple cider vinegar

2   cups whole wheat panko bread crumbs

1   tablespoon chili powder

Cooking oil spray

Cut around the thinner, joint end of the drumstick with a sharp knife. Scrape the meat with a knife down toward the large end of the drumstick, shaping each like a lollipop. Rinse the drumsticks and pat them dry with paper towels. Season the drumsticks with ½ tablespoon of the poultry seasoning and the black pepper and set them aside.

Combine the agave syrup, mustard, and cider vinegar in a small bowl. Mix together the bread crumbs, the remaining ½ tablespoon of the poultry seasoning, and the chili powder. Coat the drumsticks with the mustard mixture, shaking off any excess, then coat each drumstick with the bread crumbs, shaking off any excess.

Preheat the oven to 425°F. Place a baking pan on the lowest rack of the oven to heat for 5 minutes. Carefully remove the hot baking pan from the oven and spray it with the cooking oil spray. Place the chicken lollipops on the hot baking pan. Spray with the cooking oil spray. Roast for 15 minutes and turn over the lollipops. Spray with the cooking oil spray. Cook for an additional 8 to 10 minutes until the lollipops are crispy and brown. Serve immediately.

SERVING SIZE: 2 drumsticks
EXCHANGE LIST VALUES: 2 starch, 4 lean meat
CARBOHYDRATE CHOICES: 2
CALORIES: 320

CALORIES FROM FAT: 62
TOTAL FAT: 7 g
SATURATED FAT: 1 g
CHOLESTEROL: 82 mg
SODIUM: 520 mg

TOTAL CARBOHYDRATE: 33 g
FIBER: 4 g
TOTAL SUGARS: 5 g
PROTEIN: 31 g

With Cheesy Broccoli and Noodles, page 203.

Stir-Fried Cherry Chicken with Diva-Style Sweet and Sour Sauce

MAKES 6 SERVINGS

Stir-frying is an easy way to get dinner on the table in a hurry. Prepping the ingredients in advance and making the Diva-Style Sweet and Sour Sauce ahead of time cut down on cooking time even more. This dish contains a healthy mix of vegetables and fruit. Whether fresh or frozen, cherries make a delicious addition to this recipe. It's simple to prepare and showcases cherries to perfection. Serve over brown rice or soba noodles.

1   tablespoon canola oil

1   pound boneless, skinless chicken breasts, cut into ½-inch strips

1   teaspoon garlic powder

¼   teaspoon salt

½   teaspoon ground ginger

1   yellow or orange bell pepper, seeded, deribbed, and chopped

2   green onions, including green parts, chopped

1½ cups pitted dark cherries or frozen unsweetened sweet cherries

¾   cup Diva-Style Sweet and Sour Sauce (recipe follows)

Heat the oil in a large nonstick skillet over medium heat until shimmering. Season the chicken with the garlic powder, salt, and ginger and add the chicken to the pan. Stir for 4 to 5 minutes, or until the chicken is no longer pink. Add the bell pepper and green onions to the pan.

Turn the heat to low and simmer for 4 to 5 minutes, or until the pepper is crisp-tender. Stir in the cherries and the sweet and sour sauce. Cook and stir until the sauce is thoroughly heated, 3 to 5 minutes.

SERVING SIZE: 3 ounces chicken, with ½ cup sauce, cherries, and vegetables
EXCHANGE LIST VALUES: 1 carbohydrate, ½ fruit, 3 lean meat, ½ fat
CARBOHYDRATE CHOICES: 1

CALORIES: 182
CALORIES FROM FAT: 37
TOTAL FAT: 4 g
SATURATED FAT: 1 g
CHOLESTEROL: 45 mg

SODIUM: 225 mg
TOTAL CARBOHYDRATE: 20 g
FIBER: 1 g
TOTAL SUGARS: 13 g
PROTEIN: 18 g

Diva-Style Sweet and Sour Sauce

ABOUT 2/3 CUP

Many bottled sweet and sour sauces contain too much sugar. My version is delicious but uses ingredients that keep blood glucose levels in balance. This sauce can be used in Asian recipes and as a dipping sauce.

4	teaspoons cornstarch
4	teaspoons water
1/3	cup rice vinegar
3	tablespoons agave syrup
1	tablespoon low-sugar ketchup
2	teaspoons reduced-sodium soy sauce

In a small bowl, mix together the cornstarch and water. In a small saucepan, combine the vinegar, agave syrup, ketchup, and soy sauce and bring to a boil over high heat. Add the cornstarch mixture and stir to thicken. Store in an airtight container in the refrigerator for up to 10 days.

Cherries CHERRIES HAVE BEEN CALLED A "SUPERFRUIT" BECAUSE THEY HAVE SO MANY NUTRITIONAL BENEFITS. RESEARCH SUGGESTS THAT THE RED COMPOUNDS IN CHERRIES MAY HELP EASE THE PAIN OF ARTHRITIS AND GOUT AND THAT THEY HAVE HEART-HEALTH BENEFITS RELATED TO REDUCING INFLAMMATION, TOTAL CHOLESTEROL, AND BELLY FAT. SCIENTISTS BELIEVE IT'S THE FRUIT'S POWERFUL ANTHOCYANINS—ALSO RESPONSIBLE FOR ITS VIBRANT RED COLOR—THAT ARE RESPONSIBLE FOR THIS ANTIINFLAMMATORY BENEFIT.

SELECT CHERRIES FREE OF SPOTS AND BRUISES. THE STEM SHOULD BE FIRMLY ATTACHED TO THE FRUIT, WHICH SHOULD LOOK PLUMP AND FEEL FIRM AND HEAVY FOR ITS SIZE. WHEN NOT IN SEASON, CHERRIES ARE AVAILABLE DRIED, FROZEN, AND CANNED.

SERVING SIZE: 2 tablespoons	**CALORIES FROM FAT:** 0	**TOTAL CARBOHYDRATE:** 11 g
EXCHANGE LIST VALUES:	**TOTAL FAT:** 0 g	**FIBER:** 0 g
1 carbohydrate	**SATURATED FAT:** 0 g	**TOTAL SUGARS:** 8 g
CARBOHYDRATE CHOICES: 1	**CHOLESTEROL:** 0 mg	**PROTEIN:** 0 g
CALORIES: 38	**SODIUM:** 90 mg	

Asian-Style Chicken Wraps

MAKES 6 SERVINGS

This is one of my favorite make-ahead meals. The ground meat can be combined with fresh or frozen stir-fry veggies, or you can use lean ground chicken or turkey and whatever leftover fresh or cooked vegetables you may have on hand. Chinese five-spice powder often contains a combination of cinnamon, star anise, nutmeg, ginger, and Szechuan peppercorns. You can prepare the turkey and rice filling ahead of time, place serving portions in a resealable plastic bag, freeze them, and reheat them for use in wraps at a later time, stuffed into a whole-wheat pita, or over brown rice for a delicious dinner.

1	tablespoon canola or vegetable oil
8	ounces lean ground chicken or turkey
1½	tablespoons Chinese five-spice powder
¼	cup water or low-sodium chicken broth
3	cloves garlic, peeled and minced
3	tablespoons reduced-sodium soy sauce
1	(8-ounce) package fresh or frozen Asian stir-fry vegetables, thawed
3	tablespoons rice vinegar, plain or seasoned
3	tablespoons hoisin sauce
½	teaspoon sriracha sauce or other hot sauce (optional)
6	large romaine or butter lettuce leaves
2	green onions, white and green parts, chopped

Heat the oil in a large skillet over medium-high heat; add the chicken and the five-spice powder. Break the chicken into small pieces with a fork or a potato masher. Add the water or broth, garlic, and 2 tablespoons soy sauce. Stir in the frozen vegetables. Stir for 4 to 5 minutes or until the chicken is brown and cooked through and any liquid has evaporated. Stir in the remaining 1 tablespoon soy sauce, the rice vinegar, and the hoisin sauce. Reduce the heat and simmer about 4 to 5 minutes to the blend flavors. Add the sriracha or other hot sauce, if desired.

Place a lettuce leaf on each plate. Spoon ½ cup of the filling into each lettuce leaf, and sprinkle with the green onion. Wrap lettuce around the filling to enclose, or serve filled lettuce leaves open faced on a plate.

SERVING SIZE: 1 stuffed lettuce leaf
EXCHANGE LIST VALUES: 2 vegetable, 1 lean meat, ½ fat
CARBOHYDRATE CHOICES: 1
CALORIES: 124

CALORIES FROM FAT: 53
TOTAL FAT: 6 g
SATURATED FAT: 1 g
CHOLESTEROL: 33 mg
SODIUM: 448 mg

TOTAL CARBOHYDRATE: 10 g
FIBER: 2 g
TOTAL SUGARS: 4 g
PROTEIN: 9 g

Turkey Sausage and Peppers Pasta

MAKES 6 SERVINGS

This versatile dish is a comfort food favorite made healthier by using turkey sausage. Cook a few extra sausages and peppers separately to use as a stuffing for pita bread or whole-wheat tortillas. You also can pair this dish with other types of whole-wheat pasta such as a farfalle (bow ties), fusilli (corkscrews), wagon wheels, or ribbon pastas, as well as brown rice, bulgur, or whole-wheat couscous. This is a great dish to make ahead and freeze for lunch or dinner on busy days.

1   (12-ounce) package whole-wheat penne pasta

6   turkey sausage links (about 1½ pounds)

¼   cup water

2   teaspoons olive oil

2   cloves garlic, minced

4   medium red, green, or yellow sweet peppers, seeded, deribbed, and cut into thin strips

1   large yellow onion, thinly sliced and separated into rings

1½ tablespoons Italian seasoning

1   teaspoon freshly ground black pepper

½   teaspoon red pepper flakes

2   (14½-ounce) cans no-salt-added diced tomatoes

½   cup low-sodium chicken broth

1   (10-ounce) package frozen chopped spinach, thawed and drained

½   teaspoon agave syrup

½   teaspoon ground nutmeg or cloves

¼   cup grated Parmesan cheese

SERVING SIZE: 4 ounces meat, vegetables, and sauce
EXCHANGE LIST VALUES: 2 starch, 2 vegetable, 3 lean meat
CARBOHYDRATE CHOICES: 3

CALORIES: 495
CALORIES FROM FAT: 145
TOTAL FAT: 16 g
SATURATED FAT: 2 g
CHOLESTEROL: 71 mg

SODIUM: 893 mg
TOTAL CARBOHYDRATE: 52 g
FIBER: 10 g
TOTAL SUGARS: 10 g
PROTEIN: 33 g

In a large pot of salted boiling water, cook the pasta until al dente, about 11 minutes.

Meanwhile, prick the sausages all over to prevent them from bursting. Spray a large nonstick skillet with cooking oil spray. Cook the sausage over medium heat, turning frequently, for 5 to 8 minutes, or until browned. Reduce the heat to medium-low. Add the water to the pan, cover, and cook for about 10 minutes, or until the juices run clear. Transfer the sausage to a cutting board and slice into thin coins.

Add the olive oil to the same skillet. Increase the heat to medium. Add the garlic and cook for 30 seconds. Add the bell peppers, onion, 1 tablespoon of the Italian seasoning, the black pepper, and ¼ teaspoon of the red pepper flakes. Cook, stirring occasionally, for about 5 minutes, or until the bell peppers are crisp-tender.

Add the sausage slices, the tomatoes, chicken broth, spinach, syrup, nutmeg or cloves, the remaining ½ tablespoon of the Italian seasoning, and the remaining ¼ teaspoon of the red pepper flakes. Bring to a boil, then reduce the heat and simmer, uncovered, for 5 minutes.

Drain the pasta and place it in a serving bowl. Top with the sausage and vegetables. Sprinkle with the Parmesan cheese and serve.

Fast Turkey Patties with Maple–Rosemary Sauce

MAKES 20 PATTIES

These patties are delicious when topped with Maple–Rosemary Sauce (page 157). They're also great for a quick burger or to stuff in pita bread. You can serve some of the cooked patties right away and freeze the rest.

¼ cup plain low-fat Greek yogurt

4 large eggs. lightly beaten

2 tablespoons Italian seasoning

½ teaspoon salt

1 teaspoon freshly ground black pepper

2½ tablespoons canola oil

3 tablespoons minced garlic

1 large yellow onion, finely chopped

5 pounds lean ground turkey

1 tablespoon Worcestershire sauce

½ teaspoon cayenne pepper

½ cup chopped fresh flat-leaf parsley

1½ cups whole-wheat panko
(Japanese bread crumbs)

Maple–Rosemary Sauce
(recipe follows), optional

In a large bowl, mix together the yogurt, eggs, 1 tablespoon of the Italian seasoning, ¼ teaspoon of the salt, and ½ teaspoon of the pepper. Cover and refrigerate for 10 minutes.

In a large skillet, heat ½ tablespoon of the oil over medium heat. Sauté the garlic and onion in the oil until the onion is translucent, about 3 minutes. Remove from the heat and let cool.

Add the turkey, the remaining tablespoon of the Italian seasoning, the remaining ¼ teaspoon of the salt, the remaining ½ teaspoon of the pepper, Worcestershire sauce, cayenne pepper, parsley, and the cooled vegetables to the yogurt mixture and combine well. Gradually add the bread crumbs; don't overmix. Divide into 20 3-inch-wide patties, each ½ inch thick.

Heat the remaining 2 tablespoons of the canola oil in a large skillet over medium-high heat. Working in batches, cook the patties for 5 minutes on each side, or until no longer pink in the center. Serve immediately, with 2 tablespoons of sauce per patty. Or, let cool completely, wrap individually in plastic wrap, and place in a large freezer bag and freeze for up to 3 months.

SERVING SIZE: 1 patty
EXCHANGE LIST VALUES: ½ starch, 3 lean meat
CARBOHYDRATE CHOICES: ½
CALORIES: 212

CALORIES FROM FAT: 90
TOTAL FAT: 10 g
SATURATED FAT: 3 g
CHOLESTEROL: 103 mg
SODIUM: 168 mg

TOTAL CARBOHYDRATE: 6 g
FIBER: 1 g
TOTAL SUGARS: 1 g

Maple–Rosemary Sauce

MAKES ABOUT ¼ CUP

2	teaspoons olive oil
3	green onions, including green parts, finely chopped
2	cloves garlic, minced
½	cup nonfat reduced-sodium chicken broth
1	tablespoon maple agave syrup
½	tablespoon Dijon mustard
1	tablespoon poultry seasoning
1	tablespoon minced fresh rosemary
¼	teaspoon salt
½	teaspoon freshly ground black pepper

Heat the olive oil in a small saucepan over medium-high heat. Add the green onions and garlic and sauté for 1 minute. Stir in the chicken broth, syrup, mustard, and poultry seasoning and bring to a boil. Cook until reduced to ¼ cup, about 5 minutes, stirring occasionally. Add the rosemary, salt, and black pepper and remove from the heat. Let sit for 2 minutes to infuse the rosemary into the sauce. Serve immediately.

SERVING SIZE: 1 tablespoon
EXCHANGE LIST VALUES:
   ½ carbohydrate, ½ fat
CARBOHYDRATE CHOICES: ½
CALORIES: 51

CALORIES FROM FAT: 22
TOTAL FAT: 2 g
SATURATED FAT: 0 g
CHOLESTEROL: 0 mg
SODIUM: 262 mg

TOTAL CARBOHYDRATE: 7 g
FIBER: 1 g
TOTAL SUGARS: 4 g
PROTEIN: 1 g

Fast Food from the Freezer

Let's face it, after a long day at work (or play), most of us don't want to prepare a meal. With just a little planning, your freezer can become your favorite "fast food" place. Filling your freezer with prepared meals saves time and money. It also ensures that you'll be eating something healthier than the typical fast-food meal. When you freeze meals in advance, you control the quality of the ingredients and the amount of salt. Almost everything from appetizers for dinner parties to desserts can be frozen with the proper planning and preparation.

I usually prepare all of my family's meals for the week on either Saturday or Monday. Then all I have to do is prepare some vegetables or a salad and dinner is served. I also prepare a few extra meals, using some of the same meats and other ingredients I have on hand, and freeze them. Here are some tips for doing the same thing:

- Do all your food shopping on one day and the cooking the next. Preparing meals in advance means that you'll have large amounts of food to shop for and to put away. Plan your meals and make a list. Take advantage of any sales you may find on meats or vegetables while at the grocery store.

- Use recipes with similar ingredients or cooking times so that you can chop all the vegetables you need at one time, or bake more than one dish in the oven. Serve one dish and stock your freezer with the other. You also can stock your freezer by doubling the meals that you make during the week.

- Use freezer- and microwave-safe divided plates to store individual frozen dinners. Leftovers are the perfect choice for these dinners. Divided plates make meals easy to defrost and reheat in the microwave.

- Securely wrap and seal your make-ahead meals to prevent freezer burn. Write the name of the dish and the date on a label or on the plastic freezer bag to make the dishes easy to identify. Most properly wrapped and stored foods can be stored for up to 6 months in the freezer.

Turkey Enchiladas

MAKES 12 SERVINGS

A chilly day is the perfect time to serve something spicy for dinner, such as this healthier version of traditional enchiladas. Cooked turkey breast that has been shredded and combined with Mexican spices is a delicious and lower-calorie alternative to beef.

2   cups shredded cooked turkey breast

1   (15-ounce) can no-salt-added black beans, rinsed and drained

1   cup low-fat sour cream or plain Greek yogurt

½   cup chunky salsa, medium or hot

1½   cups shredded low-fat cheddar cheese

1   tablespoon chili powder

1   teaspoon freshly ground black pepper

1   teaspoon ground cumin

½   teaspoon cayenne pepper

12   (8-inch) corn or whole-wheat flour tortillas

    Enchilada Sauce (recipe follows)

Preheat the oven to 350°F. In a large bowl, combine the turkey, black beans, sour cream or yogurt, salsa, 1 cup of the cheese, the chili powder, black pepper, cumin, and cayenne pepper. Wrap the tortillas in a microwave-safe paper towel and sprinkle both sides with a little water. Microwave for 10 to 15 seconds to warm and to soften the tortillas.

Lightly oil a 13 by 9-inch baking pan with cooking spray. Place a tortilla on a flat surface. Spoon about ½ cup of the filling in a line in the center of the tortilla. Fold the bottom edge of the tortilla up and over the filling. Fold the opposite sides in and over the filling. Roll the tortilla from the bottom. Place the filled tortilla, seam side down, on the prepared pan. Repeat with the remaining tortillas, placing them side by side until the pan is full.

Pour the sauce over the enchiladas, carefully covering the ends to keep them moist. Bake, uncovered, for about 25 minutes, or until hot and bubbly. Sprinkle with the remaining ½ cup of cheese. Bake for another 5 minutes. Remove from the oven and let stand for 5 to 10 minutes before serving.

SERVING SIZE: 1 enchilada plus 2 tablespoons sauce
EXCHANGE LIST VALUES: 1½ starch, 1 vegetable, 1 lean meat
CARBOHYDRATE CHOICES: 2

CALORIES: 304
CALORIES FROM FAT: 76
TOTAL FAT: 8 g
SATURATED FAT: 3 g
CHOLESTEROL: 33 mg

SODIUM: 754 mg
TOTAL CARBOHYDRATE: 36 g
FIBER: 8 g
TOTAL SUGARS: 6 g
PROTEIN: 21 g

Enchilada Sauce

MAKES ABOUT 3 CUPS

If you don't have time to make this sauce from scratch, use a good-quality low-sodium commercially made sauce and add the spices and the salsa from this recipe to give it a homemade taste.

2	teaspoons olive oil
1	large onion, chopped
2	cloves garlic, minced
1	tablespoon chili powder
1	teaspoon ground cumin
1	teaspoon freshly ground black pepper
2	(15-ounce) cans diced tomatoes with chiles, medium or hot
½	teaspoon agave syrup
½	cup salsa
¼	cup water

In a medium saucepan, heat the oil over medium heat and sauté the onion until translucent, about 3 minutes. Add the garlic, chili powder, cumin, and pepper and sauté for another minute. Add the tomatoes and agave syrup and sauté for 3 to 4 minutes. Add the salsa and water. Increase the heat to high and bring the sauce to a rolling boil. Then decrease the heat to low and simmer until slightly thickened, about 10 minutes.

SERVING SIZE: ¼ cup
EXCHANGE LIST VALUES: 0
CARBOHYDRATE CHOICES: 0
CALORIES: 30
CALORIES FROM FAT: 8

TOTAL FAT: 1 g
SATURATED FAT: 0 g
CHOLESTEROL: 0 mg
SODIUM: 131 mg
TOTAL CARBOHYDRATE: 5 g

FIBER: 1 g
TOTAL SUGARS: 3 g
PROTEIN: 1 g

Baked Catfish with Green Onion and Butter Sauce

MAKES 4 SERVINGS

Most of the students who attend my cooking classes express a fear of cooking fish because they can't tell when it's done. This is a great dish for beginners, as baking the fish in the sauce keeps it moist while it cooks, and it's easy to check for doneness. Select U.S. farm-raised catfish for the best quality.

4	small whole catfish (2 pounds), dressed and rinsed
½	tablespoon olive oil
1	tablespoon poultry seasoning
¼	teaspoon salt
1	teaspoon freshly ground black pepper
8	green onions, green parts only (reserve white parts for sauce)
1	small yellow onion, thinly sliced
1	large bunch rosemary
4	cloves garlic, smashed
1	large lemon, cut into 8 slices
½	tablespoon Hungarian paprika
	Green Onion and Butter Sauce (recipe follows)

Preheat the oven to 350°F. Coat a 13 by 9-inch baking pan with cooking spray. Place the fish in the baking dish. Pour the olive oil over the fish and rub it inside and out to coat. Sprinkle the poultry seasoning, salt, and pepper inside and outside of the fish.

Stuff each fish with an equal amount of the green onion tops, yellow onion slices, and rosemary sprigs, plus a quarter of the smashed garlic and 1 lemon slice. Sprinkle the paprika on the fish. Place one of the remaining slices of lemon on top of each fish. Pour the green onion and butter sauce around the fish.

Place the fish, uncovered, in the oven and bake for 20 to 25 minutes, or until the fish flakes easily with a fork.

SERVING SIZE: 1 fish and ⅓ cup sauce
EXCHANGE LIST VALUES: ½ starch, 3 lean meat, 1½ fat
CARBOHYDRATE CHOICES: ½
CALORIES: 249

CALORIES FROM FAT: 134
TOTAL FAT: 15 g
SATURATED FAT: 4 g
CHOLESTEROL: 67 mg
SODIUM: 418 mg

TOTAL CARBOHYDRATE: 9 g
FIBER: 2 g
TOTAL SUGARS: 1 g
PROTEIN: 20 g

Green Onion and Butter Sauce

MAKES ABOUT 1¼ CUPS

1	tablespoon olive oil
2	tablespoons flour
1	tablespoon poultry seasoning
1	teaspoon freshly ground black pepper
¼	teaspoon cayenne pepper
8	green onions, white parts only, diced
1	cup reduced-sodium vegetable broth or water
1	tablespoon fresh lemon juice
1	tablespoon whipped butter

In a medium saucepan, heat the olive oil over medium-high heat. Add the flour, poultry seasoning,, black pepper, and cayenne pepper, stirring for a minute to combine the spices and cook the flour. Add the onions and stir for another minute. Increase the heat to high. Add the vegetable broth or water and lemon juice. Stir constantly until the sauce thickens and bubbles. Stir in the butter.

SERVING SIZE: ⅓ cup
EXCHANGE LIST VALUES: ½ starch, 1 fat
CARBOHYDRATE CHOICES: ½
CALORIES: 78

CALORIES FROM FAT: 51
TOTAL FAT: 6 g
SATURATED FAT: 2 g
CHOLESTEROL: 5 mg
SODIUM: 158 mg

TOTAL CARBOHYDRATE: 6 g
FIBER: 1 g
TOTAL SUGARS: 1 g
PROTEIN: 2 g

Why Fish Is a Good Choice, and How to Cook It

Fish is easy to prepare and cooks in minutes rather than hours. Eating fish is an excellent way to add a low-fat quality protein, omega-3 fatty acids, minerals, and vitamins to your diet and to improve your health. A recent Harvard University study recommended eating up to two portions of fish a week. Other studies have shown that fish consumption lowers the risk of death from heart disease by 36 percent.

The omega-3 fatty acids found in oily fish such as mackerel, trout, herring, sardines, tuna, and salmon are thought to raise the level of the brain chemical serotonin, which aids in reducing depression.

Here are some tips for selecting fish fillets:

• Fish fillets should be moist, with no drying or browning around the edges.

• Fresh fish should be used within 2 days of purchase.

• Fish should be kept wrapped and stored in the coldest part of the refrigerator.

- Frozen-fish packages should be undamaged, and the fish should have no freezer burn, any off color, or be covered with ice crystals.

- To thaw frozen fish, thaw in the refrigerator or seal in a bag and submerge in cold water for up to 1 hour. Never thaw at room temperature.

- When grilling, broiling, poaching, and steaming fish, or baking at 400° to 450°F, use the 10-minute rule: Measure the fish at its thickest point. If the fish is stuffed or rolled, measure after stuffing or rolling. Cook the fish for about 10 minutes per inch, turning it halfway through the cooking time. For example, cook a 1-inch fish steak for 5 minutes on each side, for a total of 10 minutes. Pieces less than ½ inch thick do not have to be turned over. Test for doneness: The fish is done when it flakes easily with a fork. Fish should reach an internal temperature of 145°F. Add 5 minutes to the total cooking time for fish cooked in foil or in a sauce. Double the cooking time for frozen fish that has not been defrosted. Use this rule as a general guideline, since fillets often do not have uniform thickness.

- For any cooking method, fish is done when the flesh is opaque and flakes easily.

Quick Creole Cod

MAKES 4 SERVINGS

Sometimes, using a microwave is the best way to cook fish and vegetables, because the nutrients are retained and the dish has a better taste and texture. The microwave method used in this recipe steams the fish and leaves it moist and tender. The citrus juice and cayenne add piquancy.

1	(1-pound) cod fillet, skinned
1	tablespoon poultry seasoning
l	tablespoon fresh lime or lemon juice
2	teaspoons olive oil
1	onion, finely chopped
2	cloves garlic, minced
1	red bell pepper, seeded, deribbed, and sliced
¼	teaspoon salt
½	teaspoon freshly ground black pepper
½	teaspoon cayenne pepper
1	(15-ounce) can diced fire-roasted tomatoes

Cut the cod fillet into bite-sized chunks. Sprinkle with the poultry seasoning and lime or lemon juice.

Place the olive oil, onion, garlic, bell pepper, salt, black pepper, and cayenne pepper in a large microwaveable bowl. Cover with microwave-safe plastic wrap and microwave on high for 3 minutes, stirring once.

Add the cod and diced tomatoes. Cover and microwave on high for 8 minutes, stirring twice, until the fish flakes easily.

SERVING SIZE: 3 ounces fish and 3 tablespoons sauce
EXCHANGE LIST VALUES: 2 vegetable, 3 lean meat, ½ fat
CARBOHYDRATE CHOICES: 1

CALORIES: 152
CALORIES FROM FAT: 29
TOTAL FAT: 3 g
SATURATED FAT: 1 g
CHOLESTEROL: 43 mg

SODIUM: 462 mg
TOTAL CARBOHYDRATE: 11 g
FIBER: 2 g
TOTAL SUGARS: 5 g
PROTEIN: 20 g

Crunchy Fish Sticks

MAKES 4 SERVINGS

Children love fish sticks, and so do I. Commercially prepared varieties usually are high in sodium and fried. Here's a recipe for this childhood favorite that's full of flavor and much healthier because it's baked to crunchy perfection in the oven. Leftover Crunchy Fish Sticks are the perfect filling for wraps or in a whole-wheat roll topped with Carolina Coleslaw (page 74).

1½ pounds fish fillets, such as trout, tilapia, cod, or catfish, cut into ½-inch strips

3 tablespoons poultry seasoning

1 tablespoon freshly ground black pepper

½ teaspoon cayenne pepper

½ tablespoon agave syrup

½ cup whole-grain mustard

2 tablespoons no-sugar-added apple cider vinegar

1 cup cornmeal

2 cups whole-wheat panko (Japanese bread crumbs)

1½ tablespoons chili powder

Cooking oil spray

Rinse the fillets and pat them dry with paper towels. Season with 1 tablespoon of the poultry seasoning, the black pepper, and cayenne pepper.

Combine the agave syrup, mustard, and vinegar in a small bowl. In a pie plate, combine the cornmeal, panko, the remaining 2 tablespoons of the poultry seasoning, and chili powder. Stir to blend. Dip the fish in the mustard mixture, coating it completely, and then allow the excess to drip off. Coat each piece of fish with the cornmeal crumb mixture by pressing the fish lightly into the mixture and shaking off the excess.

Preheat the oven to 350°F. Place a baking pan on the lowest rack of the oven to heat for 5 minutes. Carefully remove the hot pan from the oven and spray it with the cooking oil spray. Place the fish in the pan and bake for 5 to 8 minutes. Turn the fish over and spray with cooking oil spray. Cook for another 5 minutes, or until the fish sticks are crispy and brown. Serve immediately.

SERVING SIZE: 4 fish sticks
EXCHANGE LIST VALUES: 1½ starch, 4 lean meat
CARBOHYDRATE CHOICES: 1½
CALORIES: 332

CALORIES FROM FAT: 104
TOTAL FAT: 12 g
SATURATED FAT: 2 g
CHOLESTEROL: 86 mg
SODIUM: 298 mg

TOTAL CARBOHYDRATE: 22 g
FIBER: 3 g
TOTAL SUGARS: 2 g
PROTEIN: 35 g

Five-Spice Fish

MAKES 4 SERVINGS

Chinese five-spice powder is a tasty mixture of spicy, sweet, and sharp flavors. The spices work beautifully with the mild flavor of firm white-fleshed fish. Be careful not to overcook the fish in the aromatic sauce, or the delicate pieces will fall apart. Serve with whole-wheat udon noodles or brown rice.

1¼ pounds white fish fillets, such as cod, haddock, or tilapia

2 tablespoons canola oil

2 teaspoons Chinese five-spice powder

¼ cup unbleached all-purpose flour

1 (12-ounce) package fresh or frozen stir-fry vegetables

½ small yellow onion, diced

1 clove garlic, minced

I teaspoon minced fresh ginger

¼ teaspoon salt

1 teaspoon freshly ground black pepper

2 tablespoons reduced-sodium soy sauce

2 tablespoons unsweetened apple juice

1 tablespoon apple cider vinegar

1 teaspoon Dijon mustard

½ teaspoon agave syrup

Coat the fish on both sides with 1 tablespoon of the oil. Mix together the five-spice powder and flour on a plate. Press the fish into the spice mixture until coated on both sides.

Place the remaining 1 tablespoon of oil in a shallow microwaveable dish with the vegetables, onion, garlic, ginger, salt, and pepper. Stir well to combine. Cover with microwave-safe plastic wrap. Microwave on high for 4 minutes, stirring once. Place the fish on the vegetables. Cover and microwave on high for 4 to 6 minutes.

Mix together the soy sauce, apple juice, vinegar, mustard, and agave syrup. Pour the sauce over the fish. Cover and microwave on high for 2 to 3 minutes.

SERVING SIZE: 4 ounces fish and 1 tablespoon sauce
EXCHANGE LIST VALUES: ½ starch, 1 vegetable, 3 lean meat, 1 fat
CARBOHYDRATE CHOICES: 1

CALORIES: 243
CALORIES FROM FAT: 73
TOTAL FAT: 8 g
SATURATED FAT: 1 g
CHOLESTEROL: 54 mg

SODIUM: 570 mg
TOTAL CARBOHYDRATE: 18 g
FIBER: 3 g
TOTAL SUGARS: 4 g
PROTEIN: 26 g

Shrimp and Bulgur Risotto

MAKES 4 SERVINGS

This beautiful and unusual risotto makes a great weekday dinner or an elegant dish for entertaining. The fiber-rich bulgur and protein-packed shrimp will keep you full for hours, but the dish takes only minutes to make.

1	cup bulgur wheat
1½	cups low-sodium vegetable broth
1	tablespoon olive oil
3	cloves garlic, minced
1	teaspoon freshly ground black pepper
2	cups fresh or frozen corn kernels
1	medium red bell pepper, seeded, deribbed, and chopped
1	pound thawed frozen shrimp, shelled and deveined
2	limes, 1 juiced, 1 cut into wedges
¼	teaspoon red pepper flakes
¼	cup chopped fresh cilantro
1	teaspoon grated lime zest

In a large, heavy, dry pot, toast the bulgur over medium-high heat, stirring occasionally, for 5 to 10 minutes, or until the grain makes popping sounds and is lightly browned. Transfer to a bowl and let cool.

In a small saucepan over high heat or in the microwave on high, heat the vegetable broth until boiling. Meanwhile, in the same pot used to toast the bulgur, heat the oil over medium heat. Cook the garlic, stirring, for 30 seconds. Add the bulgur and black pepper; stir 1 minute more.

Gradually stir ½ cup of the hot broth into the bulgur, and cook, stirring occasionally, for 3 to 5 minutes as the bulgur absorbs most of the liquid. Continue to add ½ cup of broth at a time, stirring occasionally, until the bulgur is slightly soupy, about 6 minutes. Add the corn and bell pepper. Cook, stirring, for 3 minutes.

Add the shrimp and sauté, stirring constantly, until it turns pink, 2 to 3 minutes. Add the lime juice, red pepper flakes, and any remaining broth as needed to keep the bulgur creamy. Add the cilantro and lime zest. Serve with the lime wedges.

SERVING SIZE: about 2¼ cups

EXCHANGE LIST VALUES: 3 starch, 3 lean meat, ½ fat

CARBOHYDRATE CHOICES: 3

CALORIES: 339

CALORIES FROM FAT: 59

TOTAL FAT: 7 g

SATURATED FAT: 1 g

CHOLESTEROL: 182 mg

SODIUM: 887 mg

TOTAL CARBOHYDRATE: 46 g

FIBER: 9 g

TOTAL SUGARS: 6 g

PROTEIN: 27 g

Eating a Rainbow

Rainbow trout is an excellent lean protein. It also is a good source of many important nutrients, such as vitamins B_6 and B_{12}, thiamin, and niacin. A 3-ounce serving of cooked rainbow trout contains 22 grams of protein and only 130 calories, 4 grams of fat, 1 gram of saturated fat, and 30 milligrams of sodium.

Rainbow trout are sold fresh in many seafood markets. About 95 percent of the rainbow trout consumed in the United States is farm raised. Because of their small size, trout are usually sold whole, butterflied, or filleted.

When purchasing rainbow trout or any fish, check for the following points for freshness:

- Clear and bulging eyes
- Light pink or white firm flesh
- Shiny skin
- No brown or yellow on edges
- Fresh, ammonia-free odor
- Moist red gills

NOTE: Fresh or thawed fish will keep fresh no longer than 36 hours.

Oven-Fried Trout
with Papaya Sauce

MAKES 4 SERVINGS

Rainbow trout are a delightful addition to any meal, and an excellent source of protein and other nutrients. Leave the skin on the fish, as it permits you to easily bread or coat it. Leave the tail on while cooking to minimize skin breakage.

1 cup whole-wheat panko
   (Japanese bread crumbs)

2 tablespoons poultry seasoning

¼ teaspoon red pepper flakes

1 tablespoon grated lemon zest

½ teaspoon salt

1 teaspoon freshly ground black pepper

3 tablespoons Dijon mustard

2 tablespoons fresh lemon juice

4 (10- to 12-ounce) whole trout,
   boned, rinsed, and patted dry

2 tablespoons Papaya Sauce (recipe follows)

Preheat the oven to 400°F. Place a large baking pan in the oven to heat to create a crisper bottom crust on the fish. Combine the panko, 1 tablespoon of the poultry seasoning, the red pepper flakes, lemon zest, salt, and black pepper in a large pie plate. Combine the remaining 1 tablespoon of poultry seasoning, the mustard, and lemon juice in a small bowl. Brush both sides of the trout with the mustard mixture. Press the fish firmly into the bread crumbs, coating both sides.

Carefully remove the hot baking pan from the oven. Spray the pan with cooking oil spray. Carefully arrange the fish in a single layer on the baking pan. Bake, uncovered, for 10 minutes, without turning the fish. The fish should flake easily when tested with a fork. Carefully transfer the fish to a serving platter. Drizzle each piece with ½ tablespoon of the papaya sauce and serve.

Continued on page 172

SERVING SIZE: 1 trout and ½ tablespoon sauce
EXCHANGE LIST VALUES: 1 starch, 1 fruit, 5 lean meat
CARBOHYDRATE CHOICES: 2

CALORIES: 391
CALORIES FROM FAT: 118
TOTAL FAT: 13 g
SATURATED FAT: 2 g
CHOLESTEROL: 89 mg

SODIUM: 453 mg
TOTAL CARBOHYDRATE: 33 g
FIBER: 4 g
TOTAL SUGARS: 7 g
PROTEIN: 37 g

Papaya Sauce

MAKES ABOUT ¾ CUP

The sweet taste and butterlike consistency of the papaya sauce adds a unique layer of flavor to pan-fried trout. Papaya contains vitamins C and E and beta-carotenes. It's high in fiber, which, along with the antioxidants in the fruit, can help lower cholesterol. Papaya also contains papain, a proteolytic enzyme that breaks down proteins in food, allowing for better digestion.

2	ripe papayas, peeled, seeded, and coarsely chopped
1	tablespoon canola oil
1	large onion, coarsely chopped
1	clove garlic, chopped
1	jalapeño chile, minced
¼	teaspoon salt
1	teaspoon freshly ground black pepper
2	tablespoons apple cider vinegar
½	tablespoon agave syrup
2	tablespoons fresh lime or lemon juice
2	tablespoons coarsely chopped fresh cilantro

Place the papayas, oil, onion, garlic, jalapeño, salt, and pepper in a large microwaveable bowl. Microwave on high until soft, 5 to 7 minutes. Stir, add the vinegar, and cook on high for another 3 minutes. Add the agave syrup and stir.

Carefully place the sauce in a blender. Start the blender on low speed, with the lid slightly ajar to vent any steam. Cover the top of the blender with a kitchen towel to prevent any accidents. After the sauce is partially blended, seal the lid and increase the blending speed to high until smooth. Pour the sauce into a bowl and add the lime or lemon juice and cilantro, stirring to combine.

SERVING SIZE: ½ tablespoon
EXCHANGE LIST VALUES: 1 fruit
CARBOHYDRATE CHOICES: 1
CALORIES: 66
CALORIES FROM FAT: 16

TOTAL FAT: 2 g
SATURATED FAT: 0 g
CHOLESTEROL: 0 mg
SODIUM: 79 mg
TOTAL CARBOHYDRATE: 13 g

FIBER: 1 g
TOTAL SUGARS: 6 g
PROTEIN: 0 g

Italian-Style Microwave Salmon

MAKES 6 SERVINGS

You can vary the flavor of this recipe by changing the type of olive oil–based salad dressing you use. Try an Asian, citrus-flavored, or honey- and mustard-based dressing to create a flavorful new fish dish. You also can use rainbow trout in this recipe.

2	pounds salmon fillets, pin bones removed, rinsed and patted dry
1	tablespoon poultry seasoning
⅛	teaspoon salt
1	teaspoon freshly ground black pepper
½	cup reduced-fat Italian salad dressing
½	cup reduced-sodium chicken broth
2	bay leaves
3	green onions, including green parts, chopped
¼	cup diced green or red bell peppers, or a combination
1	tablespoon fresh orange juice or lemon juice

Season both sides of the fillets with the poultry seasoning, salt, and pepper. Place the fillets in a shallow microwaveable dish. Fold and tuck under the narrow ends of the fillets to make the pieces uniform in shape. This will help the fish to cook evenly. Place the thickest pieces near the edge of the dish.

Combine the Italian dressing, broth, bay leaves, green onions, bell peppers, and orange or lemon juice in a small bowl. Pour the sauce over the fillets. Cover with microwave-safe plastic wrap. Fold back a small (1-inch) section of the plastic wrap at the corner of the dish to allow the steam to vent.

Place a small, microwaveable saucer upside down on the turntable in the microwave. Place the dish containing the fillets on top of the saucer. This method elevates the dish and ensures that the fish cooks evenly. Microwave on high for 4 to 5 minutes. Remove and discard the bay leaves. The fish should be moist and flake easily. Serve the fish drizzled with the sauce.

SERVING SIZE: 1 salmon fillet plus 2 tablespoons sauce
EXCHANGE LIST VALUES: 5 lean meat, ½ fat
CARBOHYDRATE CHOICES: 0

CALORIES: 285
CALORIES FROM FAT: 123
TOTAL FAT: 14 g
SATURATED FAT: 2 g
CHOLESTEROL: 96 mg

SODIUM: 418 mg
TOTAL CARBOHYDRATE: 3 g
FIBER: 1 g
TOTAL SUGARS: 1 g
PROTEIN: 35 g

Orange Pepper Shrimp with Texmati Rice

MAKES 8 SERVINGS

Sweet oranges and spicy black pepper create a fantastic marinade for shrimp. It's a fairly simple dish that looks like it took hours to prepare. You can prepare the Texmati Rice (page 176) ahead of time and reheat it in the same pan you used to sauté the shrimp.

Texmati Rice (recipe follows)

2 pounds (16 to 20 count) shrimp, raw, peeled, and deveined

1 teaspoon freshly ground black pepper

1 teaspoon balsamic vinegar

2 fresh oranges, juiced and zest removed from 1 orange, reserving the orange halves

6 cloves garlic, peeled and finely minced

2 tablespoons canola oil

Prepare the Texmati Rice (recipe follows).

Meanwhile, rinse the shrimp in cold water. Place the shrimp in a glass bowl. Add the pepper, vinegar, orange juice, and 1 tablespoon of the zest (reserve 1 teaspoon of the zest for the Texmati Rice), minced garlic, and juiced orange halves. Stir mixture to combine. Cover, refrigerate, and let marinate for 20 minutes. Remove the shrimp from the marinade and discard the marinade.

Heat the oil in the skillet over medium-high heat. Sauté the shrimp until they're cooked, about 1 to 2 minutes on each side.

Fluff the rice by raking through it with a fork. Place 1/3 cup of the Texmati Rice on each plate. Top with 4 to 5 pieces of the shrimp.

Continued on page 176

SERVING SIZE: 4 to 5 shrimp with 1/3 cup rice
EXCHANGE LIST VALUES: 1 starch, 3 lean meat, 2 fat
CARBOHYDRATE CHOICES: 1

CALORIES: 230
CALORIES FROM FAT: 60
TOTAL FAT: 7 g
SATURATED FAT: 1 g
CHOLESTEROL: 184 mg

SODIUM: 953 mg
TOTAL CARBOHYDRATE: 20 g
FIBER: 1 g
TOTAL SUGARS: 1 g
PROTEIN: 22 g

Texmati Rice

MAKES ABOUT 3 CUPS

I love the bold, nutty flavor and perfume of Texmati rice. Texmati is an aromatic rice that's a blend of American long-grain and basmati rice. You also can buy Texmati rice blends with Thailand jasmine, Louisiana wild pecan rice, Asian red rice, wild rice, or brown rice.

1	cup uncooked long-grain brown Texmati or basmati rice
1¾	cups reduced-sodium chicken broth or water
⅛	teaspoon salt
1	tablespoon unsalted, whipped butter
1	teaspoon orange zest (reserved from Orange Pepper Shrimp recipe)
1	teaspoon freshly ground black pepper

Bring the rice, the broth or water, salt, and butter to a boil over high heat in a small heavy-bottomed saucepan. Stir the boiling rice. Cover and reduce the heat to low. Simmer, covered tightly, for 15 minutes. Turn off the heat and allow it to sit, covered, for 5 to 10 minutes. Sprinkle with the black pepper. Fluff with a fork and serve warm.

SERVING SIZE: ⅓ cup
EXCHANGE LIST VALUES: 1 starch
CARBOHYDRATE CHOICES: 1
CALORIES: 90
CALORIES FROM FAT: 16

TOTAL FAT: 2 g
SATURATED FAT: 1 g
CHOLESTEROL: 3 mg
SODIUM: 246 mg
TOTAL CARBOHYDRATE: 17 g

FIBER: 1 g
TOTAL SUGARS: 0 g
PROTEIN: 2 g

Salmon Cakes with Dill Sauce

MAKES 4 SERVINGS

Salmon that is caught wild and canned on-site is a nutritious source of omega-3 fatty acids and a great pantry staple. Salmon cakes typically are made using mashed potatoes to bind together the ingredients. I sometimes substitute bulgur, a healthy binder that adds fiber and flavor to these tender fish cakes.

If using potatoes, you have a few choices. Use leftover mashed potatoes, purchase shredded potatoes in most dairy cases at the grocery store, or microwave 2 large baking potatoes or 4 medium Yukon Gold potatoes for 10 minutes on high until soft. Scrape out the insides of the potato, let cool, and proceed with the recipe.

2	(6- to 7-ounce) cans boneless, skinless wild Alaskan salmon, drained and flaked
2	large eggs, lightly beaten
1	tablespoon poultry seasoning
1	tablespoon whole-grain mustard
3	teaspoons dried dill
1	green onion, including green parts, chopped
½	teaspoon salt
1	teaspoon freshly ground black pepper
1	(12-ounce) bag refrigerated shredded potatoes, or 1½ cups cooked or mashed potatoes, or 1½ cups cooked bulgur
1	tablespoon canola oil
⅓	cup reduced-fat sour cream or plain Greek yogurt
1	teaspoon fresh lemon juice

Combine the salmon, eggs, poultry seasoning, mustard, 2 teaspoons of the dill, the green onion, ¼ teaspoon of the salt, and ½ teaspoon of the pepper in a large bowl. Add the potatoes or bulgur and stir to combine.

Preheat the oven to 200°F. Heat ½ tablespoon of the oil in a large nonstick skillet over medium heat until shimmering. Pat ⅔ cup of the salmon mixture into 8 3-inch cakes. Add 4 cakes to the pan. Cover and cook until browned on the bottom, 3 to 5 minutes. Gently turn over the cakes and cook, covered, until crispy on the other side, 3 to 5 minutes more. Transfer the cakes to a baking dish and keep warm in the oven. Wipe out the skillet with a paper towel and repeat to cook the remaining 4 cakes with the remaining ½ tablespoon of oil.

Combine the sour cream or yogurt, lemon juice, the remaining 1 teaspoon of dill, the remaining ½ teaspoon of pepper, and the remaining ¼ teaspoon of salt in a small bowl. Serve the salmon cakes with the dill sauce.

SERVING SIZE: 2 salmon cakes and 1 tablespoon sauce	**CALORIES:** 345	**SODIUM:** 590 mg
	CALORIES FROM FAT: 104	**TOTAL CARBOHYDRATE:** 32 g
EXCHANGE LIST VALUES: 2 starch, 3 lean meat, 2 fat	**TOTAL FAT:** 12 g	**FIBER:** 6 g
	SATURATED FAT: 2 g	**TOTAL SUGARS:** 2 g
CARBOHYDRATE CHOICES: 2	**CHOLESTEROL:** 165 mg	**PROTEIN:** 31 g

Jamaican-Style Fish en Papillote

MAKES 4 SERVINGS

If you've been timid about preparing fish, try the steaming method. Cooking en papillote, meaning "in paper" in French, means sealing the food in a pouch and baking it. The food essentially steams in its own juices. It's a beautiful dinner party dish because it's easy to prepare and cooks quickly. If you don't have parchment paper, you can steam the fish in aluminum foil.

1   tablespoon olive oil

1   small yellow onion, sliced into rings

¼   teaspoon salt

1½ teaspoons freshly ground black pepper

1   teaspoon ground allspice

½   teaspoon cayenne pepper

4   cloves garlic, coarsely chopped

¼   teaspoon minced fresh ginger

4   (5-ounce) fish fillets (such as red snapper, tilapia, trout, salmon, catfish, perch, whiting, or whitefish)

12 cherry tomatoes, sliced

12 white button mushrooms, sliced

2   cups broccoli florets

1   small red bell pepper, seeded, deribbed, and diced

    Leaves from 4 sprigs fresh thyme

    Grated zest and juice of 1 lemon

½   cup water

1   tablespoon reduced-sodium soy sauce

Heat the oil in a medium skillet over medium heat. Add the onion and season with the salt, 1 teaspoon of the black pepper, ½ teaspoon of the allspice, and the cayenne pepper. Add the garlic and ginger and continue cooking until the onion is slightly wilted.

Preheat the oven to 350°F. Cut four 12 by 14-inch rectangles of parchment paper. Fold each piece in half. Cut each folded sheet into half of a heart shape, staying close to the outside edges of the paper when cutting out the shape. Open the cut-out heart shapes and place them on a rimmed baking sheet. Place each fillet on one side of the heart-shaped parchment, at least 2 inches from the paper's edge. Place one-quarter of

SERVING SIZE: 1 packet

EXCHANGE LIST VALUES: 2 vegetable, 4 lean meat, 1 fat

CARBOHYDRATE CHOICES: 1

CALORIES: 220

CALORIES FROM FAT: 53

TOTAL FAT: 6 g

SATURATED FAT: 1 g

CHOLESTEROL: 50 mg

SODIUM: 374 mg

TOTAL CARBOHYDRATE: 11 g

FIBER: 3 g

TOTAL SUGARS: 4 g

PROTEIN: 31 g

the onion and any remaining liquid on top of each fillet. Sprinkle some of the remaining ½ teaspoon black pepper and the remaining ½ teaspoon allspice on each fillet. Divide the cherry tomatoes, mushrooms, and broccoli florets among the fillets. Sprinkle equal amounts of the bell pepper, thyme leaves, and lemon zest over each serving of vegetables.

Fold the top half of one of the pieces of parchment paper over the fish and vegetables to enclose. Starting at the top of the heart shape, fold about ½ inch of the edge toward the center. Seal the paper closed by rolling, pinching, and flattening the edges of the paper to form a "hem." When the hem reaches the bottom tip of the heart, leave a small opening so you can add the steaming liquid. Repeat with the remaining pieces of parchment.

Mix the lemon juice, water, and soy sauce in a small bowl. Pour about 2 tablespoons into each packet and twist the bottom inch or two of the packet to seal it; fold it underneath to complete the seal.

Bake for 11 to 12 minutes, or until the packets have puffed up. Remove from the oven and let the fish rest for 2 minutes, and check one of the fish packets for doneness.

The fish should be opaque and flake easily in the center. If the fish is not fully cooked, bake all of the packets an additional 2 to 3 minutes. Serve immediately by presenting each diner with their own aromatic packet of steamed fish and beautifully cooked vegetables in a delicious sauce.

Buttermilk Pecan-Crusted Tilapia

MAKES 6 SERVINGS

Tilapia, or "St. Peter's fish," is a living relic. References to it and drawings of a tilapia-like species date back to the time of the Egyptian pharaohs. It's one of my favorite types of fish to prepare. Tilapia is available year-round and can be grilled, broiled, fried, baked, or steamed in the microwave. Cod or catfish fillets also work well in this recipe.

The buttermilk in this recipe helps the coating to adhere to the fish. Make a substitute by combining 1 tablespoon of lemon juice or vinegar with 1 cup of milk. Stir and set aside for 5 minutes before proceeding with the rest of the recipe.

1	cup low-fat buttermilk
1	large egg, lightly beaten
1	tablespoon poultry seasoning
½	teaspoon salt
1	teaspoon freshly ground black pepper
½	tablespoon hot sauce
1	cup whole-wheat panko (Japanese bread crumbs) or finely crushed cornflakes
¼	cup pecan pieces
1	tablespoon Hungarian paprika
¼	teaspoon cayenne pepper
	Cooking oil spray
6	(5-ounce) tilapia fillets

Place the buttermilk, egg, ½ tablespoon of the poultry seasoning, ¼ teaspoon of the salt, ½ teaspoon of the black pepper, and the hot sauce in a medium bowl and mix well.

In a pie plate, mix together the bread crumbs, pecans, paprika, the remaining ½ tablespoon of poultry seasoning, the remaining ¼ teaspoon of salt, the remaining ½ teaspoon of black pepper, and the cayenne pepper. Dip the fish fillets in the buttermilk mixture, then into the seasoned crumbs to coat evenly.

Spray a large nonstick skillet with the cooking spray and place it over medium-high heat. Brown the fillets in batches, 2 to 3 at a time. Do not crowd the pan. Cook for 3 minutes on each side or until the fish flakes easily when tested with a fork. Repeat the process with the cooking oil spray and fillets. Serve immediately.

SERVING SIZE: 1 fillet
EXCHANGE LIST VALUES: 1 starch, 4 lean meat, ½ fat
CARBOHYDRATE CHOICES: 1
CALORIES: 259

CALORIES FROM FAT: 79
TOTAL FAT: 9 g
SATURATED FAT: 2 g
CHOLESTEROL: 128 mg
SODIUM: 336 mg

TOTAL CARBOHYDRATE: 14 g
FIBER: 2 g
TOTAL SUGARS: 3 g
PROTEIN: 33 g

Meatless Monday

Americans consume 98 grams of protein a day, about 45 grams more than we really need, according to the U.S. Department of Agriculture. Eating a vegetarian meal once a week is a good way to consume less saturated fat, which has been linked to heart disease, stroke, and diabetes. Studies suggest we are more likely to maintain behaviors begun on Monday throughout the week, according to the Healthy Monday public-health campaign, which started in 2003 in association with Johns Hopkins University. Research compiled by the initiative suggests that going meatless conserves water, reduces carbon footprints, and lowers intake of saturated fats.

Joining the Meatless Monday movement and decreasing your meat intake can lower the risk of heart disease by reducing your consumption of artery-clogging animal fats. A recent study showed that test subjects who ate red meat and processed meat every day gained four more pounds over five years than those who did not. Since buying meat is the largest part of your food bill, reducing the amount you purchase will not only decrease your waistline and improve your health, it also will lower your grocery bill.

Diva-licious Potpie

MAKES 8 SERVINGS

This meatless potpie uses sweet potatoes to provide a hearty and nutritious filling and increases the amount of vegetables typically used in the dish. Buttermilk, combined with heart-healthy baking mix, creates a light, easy-to-prepare topping far lower in calories but just as flavorful as the traditional pie crust. Leftover vegetables work fine in this dish.

1	tablespoon heart-healthy butter spread
½	cup chopped onion
2	cloves garlic, minced
2	tablespoons poultry seasoning
¼	teaspoon salt
1	teaspoon freshly ground black pepper
1	teaspoon coarse whole-grain mustard
½	cup all-purpose or whole-wheat flour
2	cups low-sodium vegetable broth
2	cups water

1   teaspoon vegetarian or regular Worcestershire sauce

3   cups ½-inch diced sweet potatoes

2   cups cooked vegetables (peas, carrots, green beans, chopped broccoli, or cauliflower)

2   cups reduced-fat all-purpose baking mix

1   cup low-fat buttermilk

1   large egg, lightly beaten

SERVING SIZE: ⅛ of pie
EXCHANGE LIST VALUES: 3 starch
CARBOHYDRATE CHOICES: 3
CALORIES: 238
CALORIES FROM FAT: 42

TOTAL FAT: 5 g
SATURATED FAT: 1 g
CHOLESTEROL: 27 mg
SODIUM: 540 mg
TOTAL CARBOHYDRATE: 43 g

FIBER: 3 g
TOTAL SUGARS: 7 g
PROTEIN: 6 g

Preheat the oven to 400°F. In a large saucepan, melt the butter spread over medium heat. Add the onion, garlic, 1 tablespoon of the poultry seasoning, 1/8 teaspoon of the salt, 1/2 teaspoon of the black pepper, and the mustard. Stir to combine and cook for 3 minutes until the onions soften. Add the flour and cook, stirring constantly, for 2 minutes. Gradually whisk in the vegetable broth, water, and Worcestershire sauce until smooth.

Bring the sauce to a boil and add the sweet potatoes. Decrease the heat to low and cook, stirring frequently, until the sweet potatoes are tender, 6 to 10 minutes. Stir in the vegetables and remove from the heat.

Spray an 8 by 11-inch (2-quart) baking dish with butter-flavored cooking spray. Pour the vegetable filling into the pan.

Place the baking mix, buttermilk, egg, the remaining 1 tablespoon of poultry seasoning, the remaining 1/8 teaspoon of salt, and the remaining 1/2 teaspoon of pepper in a large bowl and whisk until blended. Spoon the batter over the vegetables. Bake for 30 minutes, or until the top is golden brown and the juices bubble around the edges of the pan.

Veggie Lasagne

MAKES 12 SERVINGS

The sauce for this delicious lasagne contains Soyrizo, a vegetarian chorizo. Soyrizo is available in the vegetable section of many grocery stores along with tofu and other soy-based products. You also can order it online. It's so flavorful and hearty that you'll never miss the meat. This dish tastes even better the next day and also freezes well.

8	ounces Soyrizo, casing removed	1	(32-ounce) jar low-sodium pasta sauce
½	cup finely chopped onion	1	(16-ounce) package frozen Mediterranean or Italian vegetables, thawed
2	cloves garlic, minced		
½	cup water	½	teaspoon honey or agave syrup
1	tablespoon vegetarian or regular Worcestershire sauce	1	cup (8 ounces) low-fat ricotta cheese
		1	large egg, lightly beaten
2	teaspoons freshly ground black pepper	14 to 16	oven-ready, no-boil lasagna noodles, whole-wheat or plain
2	tablespoons Italian seasoning		
½	teaspoon ground nutmeg	½	pound low-fat mozzarella cheese, thinly sliced
½	teaspoon cayenne pepper	½	cup grated Parmesan cheese

SERVING SIZE: 3 inch by 3¼ inch square
EXCHANGE LIST VALUES: 1½ starch, 2 vegetable, 1 medium-fat meat, ½ plant-based protein
CARBOHYDRATE CHOICES: 2½

CALORIES: 412
CALORIES FROM FAT: 146
TOTAL FAT: 16 g
SATURATED FAT: 6 g
CHOLESTEROL: 52 mg

SODIUM: 818 mg
TOTAL CARBOHYDRATE: 43 g
FIBER: 6 g
TOTAL SUGARS: 10 g
PROTEIN: 23 g

Preheat the oven to 375°F. Place the Soyrizo, onion, garlic, water, Worcestershire sauce, black pepper, 1 tablespoon of the Italian seasoning, the nutmeg, and cayenne pepper in a large microwaveable bowl. Mix with a fork to combine. Microwave on medium-high for 7 minutes, breaking up the Soyrizo with a fork after 3 minutes.

Add the pasta sauce, vegetables, honey, and ½ tablespoon of the remaining Italian seasoning and stir. Cover with a plate or with microwave-safe plastic wrap and microwave on medium-low to low heat for about 10 minutes, stirring after 5 minutes.

Combine the ricotta cheese with the egg and the remaining ½ tablespoon of Italian seasoning in a medium bowl.

To assemble, spread ½ cup of the sauce in the bottom of a 9 by 13-inch baking dish. Arrange 4 noodles lengthwise over the sauce and break one noodle to fit sideways across the ends of the noodles, along with any remaining pieces of the noodle. Spread the noodles with one-third of the ricotta cheese mixture. Top with one-third of the mozzarella slices. Spoon ½ cup of the sauce over the cheeses. Repeat all the layers, topping the last layer with the rest of the sauce. Reserve any remaining mozzarella.

Cover the pan with aluminum foil and bake in the preheated oven for 35 minutes. Remove the foil and top with any remaining mozzarella and the Parmesan cheese. Bake, uncovered, for 10 to 15 minutes, or until the lasagna is tender when pierced with a fork and the sauce bubbles around the edges. Remove from the oven and let cool for 15 minutes before serving.

Quinoa: Gold of the Incas

I love discovering healthful ingredients and then adding them to my favorite recipes. Lately I've been experimenting with quinoa. This grain is a complete protein that contains all nine essential amino acids, making it a perfect protein source for vegans. It looks like small, grayish pearls, and has a nutty flavor and a light, creamy texture. I love combining quinoa with rice or couscous.

Native to South America, quinoa is referred to as a grain, but it's actually the seed of the gooseplant, a relative of spinach and Swiss chard. It has a long and ancient history and is called the "gold of the Incas," who recognized its protein-packed potential as a source of energy for their warriors.

Quinoa contains lysine, an amino acid that helps to promote tissue growth and repair. It's also a good source of magnesium, iron, copper, and phosphorus. Eating quinoa has been found to be beneficial to some people who suffer with migraine headaches. It is thought that the magnesium in quinoa helps relax blood vessels, which prevents the pain, constriction, and rebound dilation characteristic of migraines, and reduces their frequency.

To prepare quinoa, place it in a fine-mesh strainer, a coffee filter, or a piece of cheesecloth. Soak it for several hours, changing the soaking water or running it under cold water to remove the saponins, a coating that has a laxative effect. Some brands of quinoa come prerinsed for convenience.

To cook, use 2 cups of liquid (water or broth) to 1 cup of quinoa, bring it to a boil, then cover and simmer for 14 to 18 minutes. The quinoa germ will curl and separate from the seed when it is fully cooked.

You can also serve quinoa for breakfast, mixed with berries, yogurt, honey, and almonds. It also can be purchased as a dry, flaked product that can be eaten like a breakfast cereal.

Fiesta Tacos

MAKES 10 TACOS

These vegetarian tacos are perfect for dinner with a salad or steamed green vegetables. The quinoa and the brown rice can be made ahead of time and refrigerated.

1   tablespoon canola oil

1   medium yellow onion, chopped

4   cloves garlic, minced

½   cup cooked quinoa

½   cup cooked brown rice

1   cup no-salt-added black beans, rinsed and drained

½   cup water or low-sodium vegetable broth

1   teaspoon freshly ground black pepper

1   teaspoon chili powder

1   teaspoon ground cumin

1   (14-ounce) can diced tomatoes with chiles

½   cup frozen corn or no-salt-added canned corn (optional)

10 (6-inch) whole-wheat tortillas

½   cup shredded low-fat cheddar cheese (optional)

¼   cup sliced pitted green or black olives (optional)

Heat the canola oil in a large skillet over medium heat. Add the onion and stir until translucent, about 3 minutes. Add the garlic and cook until the garlic turns golden, about 2 minutes. Add the quinoa, brown rice, black beans, and the water or broth. Add the pepper, chili powder, cumin, and tomatoes and stir to combine. Turn the heat to high and cook, stirring occasionally, until the mixture begins to boil. Add the corn, if desired. Cover and reduce the heat to low, stirring occasionally, for 5 minutes.

Wrap the tortillas in microwave-safe paper towels. Sprinkle the paper towels with water on both sides. Microwave on low or defrost setting for 30 seconds, or until warm and pliable.

Place 2 to 3 heaping tablespoons of filling in the center of each tortilla. Add the cheese and olives, if desired, fold the tortilla in half, and serve immediately. You also can prepare the tortillas in advance, wrap them in individual pieces of microwave-safe plastic wrap, and refrigerate or freeze them for reheating in the microwave.

SERVING SIZE: 2 tacos
EXCHANGE LIST VALUES: 2½ starch, 1 vegetable
CARBOHYDRATE CHOICES: 2½
CALORIES: 276

CALORIES FROM FAT: 42
TOTAL FAT: 5 g
SATURATED FAT: 0 g
CHOLESTEROL: 0 mg
SODIUM: 527 mg

TOTAL CARBOHYDRATE: 46 g
FIBER: 21 g
TOTAL SUGARS: 3 g
PROTEIN: 11 g

Sensational Side Dishes

CREATING HEALTHY SIDE DISHES IS EASY when you use fresh vegetables, whole-wheat grains and pastas, and nutritious ingredients such as beans, seeds, and nuts. Maintaining a well-balanced eating plan is much easier when you eat foods that are not only good for you but taste great, too.

Balancing a healthy amount of lean proteins (about 46 grams per day for women and 56 grams for men) while increasing fruits, whole grains, and vegetables ensures that you're receiving the beneficial nutrients you need. Most vegetables are low in calories and provide essential vitamins and minerals, fiber, and other substances important for good health and weight loss. Increasing the amount of healthy ingredients in a recipe, while reducing higher-calorie ingredients, reduces calories without impacting flavor.

For the best nutrients, taste, and prices, eat vegetables that are in season. Frozen vegetables or low-sodium or no-salt-added canned vegetables are good options when seasonal or fresh produce is not available. Select products without added sugars, cream sauces, or other ingredients that add calories.

The best way to get your children to eat vegetables is to set a good example by eating vegetables with your meals and as snacks. Allowing them to help you shop for, select, prepare, and serve vegetables is another good way to get your children to eat them.

The recipes in this chapter provide a variety of delicious ingredients, cooking techniques, and unique ways to incorporate more vegetables, fiber, and nutrients into your daily diet. Expand your side dish repertoire by trying a recipe from this chapter each week. Eating a rainbow of vegetables is one of the best ways to ensure you maintain a healthy and balanced diet.

HASHED BRUSSELS SPROUTS   191

ROASTED BRUSSELS SPROUTS   192

MICROWAVE ASPARAGUS WITH LEMON BUTTER   193

ASIAN-STYLE ASPARAGUS WITH WALNUTS   196

BLACK-EYED PEA CAKES   197

SMOKY RED BEANS AND RICE   198

CREAMY VEGGIE RICE   200

BROCCOLI AND CARROTS WITH ORANGE–MUSTARD SAUCE   202

CHEESY BROCCOLI AND NOODLES   203

SOUTHERN-STYLE DRESSING   204

GRILLED EGGPLANT AND PEPPERS   206

ROASTED TOMATOES STUFFED WITH LEMON
AND HERB CAULIFLOWER COUSCOUS   209

HOLIDAY GREEN BEAN CASSEROLE   211

MICROWAVE LEMON AND GARLIC GREEN BEANS   214

SUNFLOWER GREEN BEANS   215

MIXED GREENS WITH OKRA AND BULGUR   216

KOHLRABI CAKES   218

CRISPY OVEN-FRIED ONION RINGS   220

SAUTÉED SUNCHOKES WITH SAGE BUTTER SAUCE   223

KALE WITH GARLIC AND LEMON   224

MOROCCAN-STYLE SLOW-COOKED VEGETABLES   225

TOMATO, SQUASH, AND ZUCCHINI GRATIN   226

HERB-ROASTED VEGETABLES   228

Hashed Brussels Sprouts

MAKES 6 SERVINGS

Brussels sprouts, when properly selected, stored, and cooked, have a crisp texture and a delicious flavor. Brussels sprouts also have cancer-fighting phytochemicals, are high in vitamin C, and are a good source of folate, vitamin A, and potassium. When selecting the vegetable, look for small, compact, bright green sprouts for the best flavor. Use sprouts that are about the same size to ensure that they will cook quickly and evenly.

2	tablespoons fresh lemon juice
2	pounds Brussels sprouts
¼	cup whipped butter
1	clove garlic, minced
2	tablespoons Italian seasoning
½	teaspoon salt
1	teaspoon freshly ground black pepper
¼	cup water or low-sodium chicken broth
½	cup whole-wheat panko (Japanese bread crumbs)
2	teaspoons grated lemon zest

Add the lemon juice to a large bowl. Halve the sprouts lengthwise and slice them thinly, cutting around and discarding the firm core. Separate the leaves as much as possible, and immediately toss them with the lemon juice to retain the color.

Melt the butter over high heat in a skillet large enough to hold all the sprouts. When the bubbles in the butter begin to subside, add the sprouts, garlic, ½ tablespoon of the Italian seasoning, and the salt and pepper. Cook, stirring often, until the sprouts are wilted and lightly cooked, but still green and crisp, 3 minutes. Some leaves might brown slightly.

Add the water or broth, and cook, stirring occasionally, for 2 minutes. Sprinkle the sprouts with the bread crumbs and the remaining 1½ tablespoons of Italian seasoning. Cook, stirring, 2 minutes more. Turn off the heat and stir in 1 teaspoon of the lemon zest. Transfer to a serving bowl, sprinkle with the remaining 1 teaspoon of zest, and serve.

SERVING SIZE: ⅓ cup
EXCHANGE LIST VALUES: 2 vegetable, 1 fat
CARBOHYDRATE CHOICES: 1
CALORIES: 132

CALORIES FROM FAT: 52
TOTAL FAT: 6 g
SATURATED FAT: 3 g
CHOLESTEROL: 13 mg
SODIUM: 236 mg

TOTAL CARBOHYDRATE: 18 g
FIBER: 6 g
TOTAL SUGARS: 3 g
PROTEIN: 6 g

Roasted Brussels Sprouts

MAKES 4 SERVINGS

Brussels sprouts are wonderful when roasted with balsamic vinegar because it helps the sprouts caramelize and brings out the natural sugars.

1½ pounds Brussels sprouts

1 tablespoon olive oil

3 tablespoons balsamic vinegar

1 tablespoon poultry seasoning

½ teaspoon kosher salt

1 teaspoon freshly ground black pepper

1 teaspoon garlic powder

1 teaspoon onion powder

Cooking oil spray

Preheat the oven to 350°F. Place a large, rimmed baking sheet in the oven to heat. Halve the sprouts lengthwise. Cut out and discard the firm core.

In a large bowl, mix together the olive oil, balsamic vinegar, poultry seasoning, ¼ teaspoon of the kosher salt, the pepper, garlic powder, and onion powder. Add the Brussels sprouts and mix until the sprouts are coated.

Remove the heated baking sheet from the oven. Carefully spray the hot pan with the cooking oil spray. Pour the sprouts in the pan and spread them out in an even layer.

Roast for 30 minutes, shaking the pan every 10 minutes for even browning, or until lightly browned and tender. Adjust the seasoning, as needed, by sprinkling with the remaining ¼ teaspoon of the kosher salt. Serve immediately.

SERVING SIZE: ⅓ cup
EXCHANGE LIST VALUES: 2 vegetable, ½ fat
CARBOHYDRATE CHOICES: 1
CALORIES: 121

CALORIES FROM FAT: 40
TOTAL FAT: 4 g
SATURATED FAT: 1 g
CHOLESTEROL: 0 mg
SODIUM: 182 mg

TOTAL CARBOHYDRATE: 18 g
FIBER: 6 g
TOTAL SUGARS: 5 g
PROTEIN: 6 g

Microwave Asparagus with Lemon Butter

MAKES 4 SERVINGS

Steaming asparagus in the microwave is the perfect way to retain its nutrients while creating a delicious, crisp-tender side dish. Pairing fresh asparagus with lemon butter sauce gives this dish a fresh burst of citrus flavor.

1   **pound fresh asparagus**

½   **teaspoon grated lemon zest**

3   **tablespoons fresh lemon juice**

½   **tablespoon whipped butter**

½   **tablespoon olive oil**

¼   **teaspoon salt**

1   **teaspoon freshly ground black pepper**

1   **teaspoon onion powder**

1   **teaspoon garlic powder**

Break or cut thinner asparagus stalks at the point where the stem naturally snaps. For thicker stalks, trim and peel the ends with a paring knife or a vegetable peeler to remove any woody stems. Preparation can be done up to 2 hours before cooking.

In a microwaveable bowl, mix the lemon zest, lemon juice, butter, and olive oil. Cut the asparagus spears into 2-inch lengths. Place the asparagus in the bowl and sprinkle it with the salt, pepper, onion powder, and garlic powder. Add the lemon sauce and mix until the asparagus is coated.

Cover with microwave-safe plastic wrap. Turn back one corner of the plastic wrap to vent the steam. Microwave on high for 2 to 3 minutes. Stir to distribute the seasonings. Cook another 2 to 3 minutes, until the asparagus is tender. Stir once more before serving.

SERVING SIZE: 1 serving
EXCHANGE LIST VALUES: 1 vegetable
CARBOHYDRATE CHOICES: ½
CALORIES: 46
CALORIES FROM FAT: 25

TOTAL FAT: 3 g
SATURATED FAT: 1 g
CHOLESTEROL: 3 mg
SODIUM: 156 mg
TOTAL CARBOHYDRATE: 5 g

FIBER: 2 g
TOTAL SUGARS: 1 g
PROTEIN: 2 g

Fabulous Asparagus!

While asparagus is available year-round, it's much better when purchased locally. Asparagus is easy to select and to prepare and comes in a variety of vibrant colors, including green, violet, purple, and white. Asparagus also grows wild and is commercially available fresh, frozen, and canned. The stalks range in size from colossal to small.

Asparagus is a nutritional powerhouse, abundant in minerals, vitamin K, and folate, which is essential for a healthy cardiovascular system. It's also a good source of potassium, is low in sodium, and acts as a natural diuretic. Some people have found that eating asparagus may help relieve irritability, fatigue, and depression. Like sunchokes, asparagus contains inulin, a carbohydrate that the body cannot digest. Inulin also helps maintain healthy bacteria that are beneficial for the digestive system.

Asparagus should be crisp and firm, with tightly closed tips. Dull color and ridges in the stems are an indication of a lack of freshness. The stalks should be of uniform thickness and not dry at the cut end.

If you're planning to use the asparagus on the same day, rinse it under cool water, and pat dry the stalks with a paper towel. Smaller stalks can be broken or cut at the point where the stem naturally snaps. Peeling the end of thicker stalks with a paring knife or a vegetable peeler removes any woody stems and can be done up to 2 hours before cooking. Place the prepared asparagus in a plastic bag in the refrigerator to stay crisp until ready to cook.

Fresh asparagus should never be washed or soaked before storing. If the asparagus is bound with a rubber band, remove it as it will pinch and bruise the stalks. Asparagus can be stored for up to two days if the stalks are trimmed and placed upright in a jar with about an inch of water in the bottom. Cover the asparagus with a plastic bag and store the spears in the refrigerator.

This versatile vegetable works well as a room-temperature appetizer, blended into a soup, as the main ingredient in a colorful salad, as a flavorful side dish, or as part of a main course. Preparing asparagus is a delicious and nutritious way to celebrate spring.

Asian-Style Asparagus with Walnuts

MAKES 4 SERVINGS

Using spices, flavorings, and cooking techniques from other cultures is a great way to add another dimension to a familiar dish. The seasoned rice wine vinegar and soy sauce are typical Asian ingredients that add a unique flavor to the asparagus. Walnuts add a crunchy texture and omega-3 fatty acids to this dish.

1	pound asparagus
1	tablespoon olive oil
2	tablespoons plain or seasoned rice wine vinegar
2	tablespoons walnut pieces
2	tablespoons reduced-sodium soy sauce
½	tablespoon agave syrup
½	teaspoon freshly ground black pepper
¼	teaspoon red pepper flakes (optional)

Break or cut thin asparagus stalks at the point where the stem naturally snaps. For thicker stalks, trim and peel the ends with a paring knife or a vegetable peeler to remove any woody stems. Preparation can be done up to 2 hours before cooking.

Preheat the oven to 350°F. Spread the prepared asparagus spears on a rimmed baking sheet. Drizzle the oil on the asparagus. Sprinkle the spears with the vinegar and toss to combine. Bake the asparagus for 5 minutes. Sprinkle the walnuts over the asparagus and cook for another 5 to 7 minutes. Check after 5 minutes so that the walnuts don't burn, and shake the pan to mix the ingredients. Cook for another 1 to 2 minutes, until the asparagus is crisp-tender.

Place the soy sauce, agave syrup, black pepper, and the optional red pepper flakes in a small bowl. Mix until smooth. Arrange the cooked asparagus on a serving dish and drizzle with 1 to 2 tablespoons of the sauce.

SERVING SIZE: 1 serving
EXCHANGE LIST VALUES: 1 vegetable, 1 fat
CARBOHYDRATE CHOICES: ½
CALORIES: 91

CALORIES FROM FAT: 54
TOTAL FAT: 6 g
SATURATED FAT: 1 g
CHOLESTEROL: 0 mg
SODIUM: 305 mg

TOTAL CARBOHYDRATE: 8 g
FIBER: 3 g
TOTAL SUGARS: 4 g
PROTEIN: 4 g

Black-Eyed Pea Cakes

MAKES 6 SERVINGS

I love using black-eyed peas in these panfried cakes. It's a nice twist on a side dish that harkens back to Africa. Black-eyed peas are a West African crop made popular in America by George Washington Carver. They are an excellent source of calcium, folate, and vitamin A.

2	cups thawed frozen black-eyed peas
2	green onions, including green parts, finely sliced
1	red bell pepper, seeded, deribbed, and diced
2	cloves garlic, minced
2	teaspoons Hungarian paprika
1	teaspoon ground cumin
¼	teaspoon cayenne pepper
½	teaspoon salt
1	teaspoon freshly ground black pepper
1	large egg, lightly beaten
1	cup whole-wheat panko (Japanese bread crumbs)
¼	cup all-purpose flour
1	tablespoon olive oil

Place the black-eyed peas in a large bowl. Using a slotted spoon or a potato masher, smash the peas, leaving a few whole. Add the green onions, bell pepper, garlic, 1 teaspoon of the paprika, ½ teaspoon of the cumin, the cayenne pepper, salt, black pepper, and egg. Mix thoroughly. Add ½ cup of the bread crumbs and mix well.

Divide the mixture into 6 balls. Flatten into patties 2½ inches in diameter and about ½ inch thick. Place the flour in a pie plate and mix it with the remaining ½ cup bread crumbs, the remaining 1 teaspoon of paprika, and the remaining ½ teaspoon of cumin. Lightly dust both sides of the cakes with the seasoned flour. Place the cakes on a plate, cover with plastic wrap, and refrigerate for at least 30 minutes or overnight.

Heat the oil over medium heat in a large, nonstick skillet. Place the cakes in the skillet, leaving room between the cakes to flip them over. Panfry for 4 to 5 minutes per side, until brown. Serve immediately.

SERVING SIZE: 1 cake
EXCHANGE LIST VALUES: 2 starch, ½ plant-based protein, ½ fat
CARBOHYDRATE CHOICES: 2
CALORIES: 192

CALORIES FROM FAT: 37
TOTAL FAT: 4 g
SATURATED FAT: 1 g
CHOLESTEROL: 31 mg
SODIUM: 237 mg

TOTAL CARBOHYDRATE: 31 g
FIBER: 6 g
TOTAL SUGARS: 1 g
PROTEIN: 9 g

Smoky Red Beans and Rice

MAKES 8 SERVINGS

This is a traditional Southern recipe with an untraditional addition of smoked turkey wings. A friend of mine from Ghana introduced me to the many wonderful ways to use smoked turkey wings. She uses them instead of pork in her traditional African soups and stews and in vegetable dishes. Smoked turkey wings are a healthy and tasty substitute for smoked ham hocks, ham bones, and bacon.

½ pound dried red kidney beans	1 smoked turkey wing, or 1 smoked turkey thigh and drumstick
1 tablespoon olive oil	2 cups low-sodium chicken broth
1 medium yellow onion, chopped	1 cup water
1 medium red bell pepper, seeded, deribbed, and chopped	½ cup tomato sauce
1 stalk celery, chopped	½ teaspoon salt
2 bay leaves	1 teaspoon freshly ground black pepper
2 cloves garlic, minced	1 teaspoon no-sugar-added apple cider vinegar
1 tablespoon Italian seasoning	2 cups hot cooked brown rice
1 tablespoon sweet paprika	2 green onions, including green parts, thinly sliced on the diagonal
1 tablespoon ground cumin	
1 teaspoon cayenne pepper	

SERVING SIZE: ⅓ cup beans plus ¼ cup rice
EXCHANGE LIST VALUES: 2 starch, 1 plant-based protein
CARBOHYDRATE CHOICES: 2

CALORIES: 198
CALORIES FROM FAT: 30
TOTAL FAT: 3 g
SATURATED FAT: 1 g
CHOLESTEROL: 9 mg

SODIUM: 269 mg
TOTAL CARBOHYDRATE: 32 g
FIBER: 7 g
TOTAL SUGARS: 2 g
PROTEIN: 11 g

Sort through the beans and discard any debris. Rinse the beans thoroughly with cold water and drain. In a large Dutch oven, combine the beans and water to cover by 2 inches and bring to a boil. Reduce the heat and simmer for 2 minutes. Remove from the heat. Cover and let stand for 1 hour. Alternatively, place the beans in water to cover by 2 inches in a Dutch oven or large, heavy pot. Cover and let soak in a cool place for 6 to 8 hours or overnight. Drain and rinse the beans; set aside.

Heat the olive oil in a Dutch oven over medium-high heat. Stir in the onion, bell pepper, celery, bay leaves, garlic, Italian seasoning, paprika, cumin, and cayenne pepper. Return the beans to the pot. Add the turkey parts, the chicken broth, water, and tomato sauce and bring to a boil. Reduce the heat, cover, and simmer, stirring occasionally, for about 1½ hours, or until the beans are tender. Add additional water during cooking, if necessary.

Simmer, uncovered, for 30 to 40 minutes or until a thick gravy forms, stirring occasionally. Remove the turkey parts. When cool enough to handle, cut the turkey meat off the bone. Coarsely chop the meat and discard the skin and bones. Return the chopped meat to the pot. Discard the bay leaves. Stir in the salt, black pepper, and vinegar. Serve the beans and the rice and sprinkle with the green onions. This dish freezes well and can be stored in an airtight container for up to 6 months.

Beans BEANS HAVE A HIGH PROTEIN AND FIBER CONTENT AND ALSO ARE RICH IN CARBOHYDRATES, FOLATE, AND CALCIUM. FLAVONOIDS, OR PLANT PIGMENTS, WHICH ARE FOUND IN THE SKIN OF TWELVE COMMON VARIETIES OF DRIED BEANS, PROVIDE ANTIOXIDANT HEALTH BENEFITS SIMILAR TO THOSE OF CRANBERRIES, APPLES, AND GRAPES. BLACK BEANS ARE PARTICULARLY HIGH IN ANTIOXIDANTS.

ANTIOXIDANTS DESTROY FREE RADICALS, WHICH ARE HIGHLY ACTIVE CHEMICALS THAT HAVE BEEN LINKED TO HEART DISEASE, CANCER, AND AGING.

Creamy Veggie Rice

MAKES 8 SERVINGS

Asiago cheese adds a creamy texture to this nutritionally packed rice dish. Only small amounts of flavorful, aged cheeses such as extra-sharp or sharp cheddar, Gorgonzola, Asiago, and Parmesan are needed to add flavor to dishes without adding too many calories.

1	tablespoon olive oil
1	medium yellow onion, diced
½	teaspoon salt
2	cups instant basmati or brown rice
4	cloves garlic, chopped
2½	cups low-sodium chicken broth
1	pound asparagus, trimmed and cut into ¼-inch pieces
1	red bell pepper, seeded, deribbed, and finely diced
1	cup frozen peas and carrots, thawed
4	ounces reduced-fat cream cheese, preferably Neufchâtel
½	cup grated Asiago cheese
¼	cup finely chopped green onion, including green parts

Heat the olive oil in a large nonstick skillet over medium-low heat. Add the onion and salt and cook, stirring often, until the onion is golden, 4 to 6 minutes. Add the rice and garlic and cook until the garlic is fragrant, about 1 minute. Add the broth and bring it to a boil. Cover, reduce the heat to a simmer, and cook for 5 minutes.

Uncover the skillet, and spread the asparagus and bell pepper on top of the simmering rice to steam. Do not stir the vegetables into the rice. Cover and continue simmering, adjusting the heat if necessary, until the liquid is almost absorbed and the asparagus is bright green and crisp-tender, about 5 minutes.

Add the peas and carrots and the cream cheese. Stir until the cheese is incorporated. Return to a simmer and continue cooking until the liquid has evaporated and the asparagus is tender, about 5 minutes more. Stir in ¼ cup of the Asiago cheese. Serve topped with the remaining ¼ cup Asiago and the green onion.

SERVING SIZE: 1½ cups
EXCHANGE LIST VALUES: 1 starch, 1 vegetable, 1 fat
CARBOHYDRATE CHOICES: 1½
CALORIES: 200

CALORIES FROM FAT: 73
TOTAL FAT: 8 g
SATURATED FAT: 4 g
CHOLESTEROL: 18 mg
SODIUM: 339 mg

TOTAL CARBOHYDRATE: 24 g
FIBER: 3 g
TOTAL SUGARS: 3 g
PROTEIN: 8 g

Broccoli and Carrots with Orange–Mustard Sauce

MAKES 6 SERVINGS

The flavors of the broccoli and carrots blend beautifully with the zesty orange-flavored mustard sauce. Select firm heads of broccoli that are tightly packed, with leaves that are crisp and not wilted. One small head of broccoli will yield about 1¼ cups of florets.

2½ cups broccoli florets

1 large carrot, peeled and sliced into rounds

1 medium red bell pepper, seeded, deribbed, and cut into 1-inch pieces

2 tablespoons finely chopped yellow onion

1 clove garlic, minced

½ cup water

½ teaspoon salt

1 teaspoon freshly ground black pepper

1 tablespoon whipped butter

1½ teaspoons cornstarch

⅔ cup orange juice

½ teaspoon grated orange zest

2 teaspoons Dijon mustard

In a microwaveable bowl, mix the broccoli, carrot, bell pepper, onion, garlic, water, ¼ teaspoon of the salt and ½ teaspoon of the pepper. Cover with microwave-safe plastic wrap. Turn back one corner of the plastic wrap to vent the steam. Microwave on high for 3 to 5 minutes, or until the broccoli is crisp-tender. Drain and cover the bowl with plastic wrap to keep the vegetables warm.

To make the sauce, add the butter to a small saucepan and melt over medium heat. Stir in the cornstarch. Add the orange juice, orange zest, mustard, the remaining ¼ teaspoon of salt, and the remaining ½ teaspoon of pepper. Cook and stir until the sauce begins to thicken and bubble. Cook and stir for 2 minutes more. Pour the sauce over the broccoli and carrots and toss gently to coat.

SERVING SIZE: ½ cup
EXCHANGE LIST VALUES: 1 vegetable
CARBOHYDRATE CHOICES: ½
CALORIES: 49
CALORIES FROM FAT: 14

TOTAL FAT: 2 g
SATURATED FAT: 1 g
CHOLESTEROL: 3 mg
SODIUM: 214 mg
TOTAL CARBOHYDRATE: 8 g

FIBER: 2 g
TOTAL SUGARS: 4 g
PROTEIN: 1 g

Cheesy Broccoli and Noodles

MAKES 6 SERVINGS

This healthful version of macaroni and cheese is a kid-pleasing favorite and a wonderful side dish. To make this a main-course meal with more protein, add 8 ounces of drained, silken soft tofu when you add the cheeses.

2   cups (8 ounces) whole-wheat elbow noodles

1   (10-ounce) package frozen chopped broccoli

1¾ cups low-fat evaporated milk

3   tablespoons all-purpose flour

½   tablespoon poultry seasoning

¼   teaspoon salt

1   teaspoon freshly ground black pepper

¾   cup shredded low-fat extra-sharp cheddar cheese

¼   cup shredded Parmesan cheese

1   teaspoon Dijon mustard

In a large pot of salted boiling water, cook the pasta for 4 minutes, stirring occasionally. Add the frozen broccoli and cook until the pasta is al dente and the broccoli is tender, 4 to 5 minutes more. Drain and set aside.

In a small saucepan, heat 1½ cups of the evaporated milk over medium-high heat until just simmering. In a small bowl, whisk the remaining ¼ cup of milk, the flour, poultry seasoning, salt, and pepper until combined. Add the flour mixture to the simmering milk, whisking constantly for 2 to 3 minutes, until the sauce is smooth. Remove the pan from the heat and whisk in the cheddar, parmesan, and mustard until the cheese is melted.

Add the pasta and broccoli to the cheese sauce. Return to the heat and cook, stirring, over medium-low heat, until heated through, 1 to 2 minutes. Serve immediately.

SERVING SIZE: ½ cup
EXCHANGE LIST VALUES: 2 starch, ½ reduced-fat milk
CARBOHYDRATE CHOICES: 2½
CALORIES: 269

CALORIES FROM FAT: 52
TOTAL FAT: 6 g
SATURATED FAT: 3 g
CHOLESTEROL: 25 mg
SODIUM: 453 mg

TOTAL CARBOHYDRATE: 39 g
FIBER: 4 g
TOTAL SUGARS: 8 g
PROTEIN: 16 g

Southern-Style Dressing

MAKES 12 SERVINGS

I love to make this healthful version of traditional Southern corn bread dressing to serve with baked pork chops, chicken, and holiday dinners. By using olive oil and whipped butter, I've reduced the calories as compared with more traditional versions. Throughout the year, I freeze leftover whole-wheat bread ends, pieces of Buttermilk Corn Bread (page 246), whole-wheat rolls and buns, and the juices from baked or roasted chicken, to use in this flavor-packed dressing.

8	slices whole-wheat bread, cut into cubes
	Buttermilk Corn Bread (page 246), crumbled
2	(14½-ounce) cans low-sodium chicken broth
	Reserved juices from baked turkey or chicken (optional)
2	tablespoons poultry seasoning
1	tablespoon whipped butter
1	tablespoon olive oil
1	large yellow onion, chopped
2	stalks celery, chopped
2	cloves garlic, minced
2	red bell peppers, seeded, deribbed, and chopped
½	teaspoon salt
1	teaspoon freshly ground black pepper

Preheat the oven to 350°F. Arrange the bread cubes and corn bread crumbs on a rimmed baking sheet and toast in the oven for 10 to 15 minutes, until the bread is lightly browned. Stir after 5 minutes and carefully watch the bread to prevent burning. Remove from the oven and set aside to cool.

In a large saucepan, combine the chicken broth, any juices from the baked turkey or chicken, 1 tablespoon of the poultry seasoning, and ½ tablespoon of the butter and simmer for 5 minutes. Remove from the heat.

Place the olive oil and the remaining ½ tablespoon of butter in a large nonstick frying pan over medium-high heat. After the butter has melted, turn the heat to low. Add the onion, celery, garlic, bell peppers, the remaining 1 tablespoon of poultry seasoning, the salt, and pepper. Sauté for about 10 minutes, stirring a few times, until the vegetables are soft and lightly brown.

SERVING SIZE: 1 serving, 3 inch by 3¼ inch square
EXCHANGE LIST VALUES: 2 starch
CARBOHYDRATE CHOICES: 2
CALORIES: 209

CALORIES FROM FAT: 49
TOTAL FAT: 6 g
SATURATED FAT: 3 g
CHOLESTEROL: 27 mg
SODIUM: 325 mg

TOTAL CARBOHYDRATE: 33 g
FIBER: 3 g
TOTAL SUGARS: 5 g
PROTEIN: 8 g

Turn the vegetables into a large bowl and add the toasted bread and corn bread. Gently stir the broth into the bread and vegetables ½ cup at a time, mixing gently for 1 minute each time to allow the dressing to absorb the broth. Continue adding the broth ½ cup at a time until the dressing is moist but no excess broth is visible. Reserve any remaining broth to moisten the baked dressing if it seems dry.

Spray a 13 by 9-inch baking pan with nonstick spray. Put the dressing into the baking pan and cover the dressing with aluminum foil. Bake, covered, for about 20 minutes, then uncover the dressing and bake 10 minutes longer, or until the dressing is lightly browned around the edges of the pan but still moist. Serve immediately.

Grilled Eggplant and Peppers

MAKES 12 SERVINGS

You can serve grilled eggplant in a variety of ways: as thick slices along with grilled bell red peppers or mushrooms as a main dish, or as a side dish. I've also cut it into cubes as part of a veggie kebab, piled it on grilled slices of bread to make panini, and tossed it with hot or cold pasta. Any way you serve grilled eggplant, it's delicious!

3   large, globe eggplants, sliced lengthwise and salted (see page 207)

2   medium red bell peppers, halved lengthwise, seeded, and deribbed

2   medium yellow bell peppers, halved lengthwise, seeded, and deribbed

2   tablespoons olive oil

2   tablespoons Italian seasoning

1   teaspoon salt

1   teaspoon freshly ground black pepper

1   teaspoon garlic powder

1   teaspoon onion powder

Heat a charcoal or gas grill to medium-high. The grill is ready when you can hold your hand about 1 inch above the grate for 3 to 4 seconds. Clean the grill grate and lightly oil with a food-safe paper towel.

Drain the eggplants and pat dry with paper towels or a clean kitchen towel. Lay the eggplants and bell peppers on a large baking sheet or tray. Brush both sides of the eggplants and peppers with the olive oil and sprinkle both sides with the Italian seasoning, salt, black pepper, garlic powder, and onion powder.

Transfer the vegetables to the grill. Close the lid and cook until grill marks appear, 3 to 5 minutes.

Turn the slices over and cook until grill marks appear on the second side and the vegetables are tender, 2 to 3 minutes. Serve hot or at room temperature.

SERVING SIZE: ⅓ cup
EXCHANGE LIST VALUES: 2 vegetable
CARBOHYDRATE CHOICES: 1
CALORIES: 70
CALORIES FROM FAT: 25

TOTAL FAT: 3 g
SATURATED FAT: 0 g
CHOLESTEROL: 0 mg
SODIUM: 198 mg
TOTAL CARBOHYDRATE: 11 g

FIBER: 5 g
TOTAL SUGARS: 4 g
PROTEIN: 2 g

Preparing Eggplant

Eggplant can create a great side dish or main course for your vegetarian guests. It's high in dietary fiber, magnesium, potassium, and many antioxidants. I like to prep the eggplant first using salt to remove any bitterness. Using salt to prepare the eggplant guarantees that it will be crispy and brown on the outside and creamy and sweet on the inside.

First of all, cut the eggplant into slices or cubes as called for in the recipe. Layer the eggplant in a colander and salt it generously. Place the colander on top of another bowl to catch the liquid the eggplant will give off.

Next, place paper towels on top of the eggplant. Then, weigh everything down to extract as much liquid as possible. You can use heavy cans wrapped in foil, or a heavy pot with a few cans inside it. Let the eggplant drain for about an hour. Pat dry with paper towels.

Roasted Tomatoes Stuffed with Lemon and Herb Cauliflower Couscous

MAKES 8 SERVINGS

This is the perfect way to showcase large, multicolored seasonal tomatoes. Roasting the tomatoes brings out their sweetness. Stuffing them with the Lemon and Herb Cauliflower Couscous adds another dimension of flavor and creates a unique and beautiful side dish or a lovely light lunch on a bed of salad greens.

8   large, ripe tomatoes (red, green, yellow, or color of choice)

8   cloves garlic, peeled and smashed

1   teaspoon kosher salt

1   teaspoon freshly ground black pepper

1½ tablespoons fresh, chopped basil or Italian (flat-leaf) parsley

2   tablespoons olive oil

    Lemon and Herb Cauliflower Couscous (recipe follows)

Cut a ¾-inch slice off the bottom of each tomato, reserving them for lids. Scoop out the seeds and the center pulpy flesh and set it aside. Inside each tomato place a smashed clove of garlic and sprinkle a pinch of the salt and pepper, and a pinch of the basil or parsley. Drizzle some of the oil inside each tomato. Place the sliced tomato lids on top of each tomato and roast at 325°F for 10 to 12 minutes or until the tomatoes just begin to soften, but not so long that they lose their shape.

Meanwhile, prepare the Lemon and Herb Cauliflower Couscous (recipe follows). Combine the couscous with the reserved tomato pulp until they are thoroughly incorporated. Spoon the warm cauliflower mixture into the hot tomatoes and top with the lids. Serve immediately.

Continued on page 210

SERVING SIZE: 1 stuffed tomato
EXCHANGE LIST VALUES: ½ starch, 2 vegetable, 1½ fat
CARBOHYDRATE CHOICES: 1½
CALORIES: 177

CALORIES FROM FAT: 71
TOTAL FAT: 8 g
SATURATED FAT: 1 g
CHOLESTEROL: 0 mg
SODIUM: 315 mg

TOTAL CARBOHYDRATE: 25 g
FIBER: 6 g
TOTAL SUGARS: 7 g
PROTEIN: 5 g

Lemon and Herb Cauliflower Couscous

MAKES 8 SERVINGS

I enjoy turning a familiar vegetable such as cauliflower into a new and exciting look-alike dish. You'll be surprised how pulsing it finely in a food processor and flavoring it with lemon and herbs makes it resemble couscous. It makes a great stuffing for tomatoes, and the lemon and herb flavors pair well with chicken, pork, and fish.

4	cups bite-sized cauliflower florets (about 1 small head)
1	cup water or reduced-sodium chicken broth
2	tablespoons olive oil
1	clove garlic, minced
1	teaspoon poultry seasoning
½	teaspoon salt
½	cup fresh or frozen corn
1	teaspoon finely grated lemon zest
2	tablespoons fresh lemon juice
1	teaspoon freshly ground black pepper
2	tablespoons minced basil or Italian (flat-leaf) parsley
¼	cup peeled cucumber, finely diced

Working in batches, process the cauliflower in a food processor until minced into small pieces resembling couscous or rice.

Place the water or broth, olive oil, garlic, poultry seasoning, and salt in a medium saucepan. Bring to a boil over high heat, then decrease the heat to low. Add the cauliflower and corn and simmer, stirring occasionally, until tender and most of the water has evaporated, about 5 minutes. Remove the "couscous" with a slotted spoon and toss it with the lemon zest and juice, the black pepper, basil or parsley, and cucumber.

SERVING SIZE: ¾ cup
EXCHANGE LIST VALUES: 1 vegetable, 1 fat
CARBOHYDRATE CHOICES: 1
CALORIES: 57

CALORIES FROM FAT: 34
TOTAL FAT: 4 g
SATURATED FAT: 1 g
CHOLESTEROL: 0 mg
SODIUM: 164 mg

TOTAL CARBOHYDRATE: 5 g
FIBER: 2 g
TOTAL SUGARS: 2 g
PROTEIN: 1 g

Holiday Green Bean Casserole

MAKES 6 SERVINGS

This green bean casserole is a holiday side dish I've transformed into a healthier choice perfect for any occasion. Using whipped butter, nonfat yogurt, and homemade Crispy Oven-Fried Onion Rings (page 220) for the topping reduces the calories without reducing the flavor. Green beans are a low-calorie way to add nutrients to your diet, including folate, manganese, potassium, calcium, vitamins A and K, and beta-carotene.

2 (9-ounce) packages frozen French-style green beans

2 teaspoons whipped butter

⅓ cup chopped yellow onion

3 tablespoons whole-wheat panko (Japanese bread crumbs)

1 cup Cream Sauce (recipe follows) or 1 (10-ounce) can low-sodium cream of mushroom soup

¼ cup plain nonfat yogurt

¼ cup chopped pimiento

½ teaspoon salt

1 teaspoon freshly ground black pepper

1 cup Crispy Oven-Fried Onion Rings (page 220), prepared up to baking

Preheat the oven to 375°F. Cook the green beans according to the package directions, except omit the salt. Drain well.

Meanwhile, melt the butter in a small saucepan over medium heat. Add the onion and cook, stirring occasionally, until the onion is tender, 3 to 4 minutes. Stir in the bread crumbs and remove from the heat.

In a large bowl, stir together the cream sauce or soup, yogurt, pimiento, salt, and pepper. Stir in the green beans. Transfer the mixture to a 4-cup casserole.

Bake the onion rings and the green bean casserole in the preheated oven for 25 to 30 minutes, or until the green beans are heated through and the onion rings are golden brown. Garnish the casserole with the onion rings.

Continued on page 212

SERVING SIZE: ½ cup

EXCHANGE LIST VALUES: 1½ starch, 1 vegetable

CARBOHYDRATE CHOICES: 2

CALORIES: 188

CALORIES FROM FAT: 39

TOTAL FAT: 4 g

SATURATED FAT: 1 g

CHOLESTEROL: 22 mg

SODIUM: 407 mg

TOTAL CARBOHYDRATE: 30 g

FIBER: 5 g

TOTAL SUGARS: 7 g

PROTEIN: 7 g

Cream Sauce

MAKES ABOUT 1 CUP

Canned cream soups have been popular since the thirties; however, making your own sauces allows you to control the freshness and quality of the ingredients and reduce the calories. Best of all, you can use this recipe as the base for a wide range of sauces to complement your favorite dishes.

1	tablespoon whipped butter
2	tablespoons olive oil
3	tablespoons all-purpose flour
1	tablespoon poultry seasoning
¼	teaspoon salt
½	teaspoon freshly ground black pepper
½	cup low-sodium chicken or vegetable broth
½	cup evaporated low-fat milk

In a small saucepan, melt the butter with the oil over medium-low heat. Add the flour, poultry seasoning, salt, and pepper and stir until smooth and bubbly. Remove from the heat and gradually whisk in the chicken broth and milk, a little at a time, stirring to keep the sauce smooth. Place the pan over medium heat. Bring the sauce to a simmer and cook, stirring constantly, until the sauce thickens.

SERVING SIZE: 2½ tablespoons
EXCHANGE LIST VALUES: ½ starch, 1 fat
CARBOHYDRATE CHOICES: ½
CALORIES: 89

CALORIES FROM FAT: 58
TOTAL FAT: 6 g
SATURATED FAT: 2 g
CHOLESTEROL: 7 mg
SODIUM: 178 mg

TOTAL CARBOHYDRATE: 6 g
FIBER: 0 g
TOTAL SUGARS: 2 g
PROTEIN: 2 g

Variation: Awesome Cream Sauces

Making your own cream sauces provides you with a delicious way to add flavor to a variety of dishes, select and control your ingredients, and reduce calories. These sauces also are a wonderful base for soups and stews.

CREAMY MUSHROOM SAUCE

Add ½ cup chopped mushrooms and 1 clove of minced garlic to the oil and butter mixture. Simmer for 2 to 3 minutes to soften the vegetables. Proceed with the recipe.

CREAMY CELERY SAUCE

Add ½ cup chopped celery and 1 clove of minced garlic to the oil and butter mixture. Simmer for 2 to 3 minutes to soften the vegetables. Proceed with the recipe.

Power-Packed Green Beans FOR THOSE STRUGGLING WITH

DIABETIC HEART DISEASE, FEW FOODS ARE AS HIGH IN HELPFUL NUTRIENTS AS GREEN BEANS.

LOW IN CALORIES AND HIGH IN FIBER, THEY ALSO ARE A GOOD SOURCE OF MINERALS, OMEGA-3

FATTY ACIDS, AND VITAMINS C, K, AND A. FROZEN GREEN BEANS ARE A GOOD OPTION IF YOU

CAN'T FIND FRESH, AS THEY'RE TYPICALLY PROCESSED IMMEDIATELY AFTER THEY'RE PICKED. EAT

LARGER PORTIONS OF VEGETABLE DISHES SUCH AS GREEN BEANS AND SCALE DOWN SERVINGS OF

MEATS AND STARCHES FOR AN EASY WAY TO MAINTAIN A HEALTHY WEIGHT.

Microwave Lemon and Garlic Green Beans

MAKES 4 SERVINGS

This easy microwave recipe uses steam to bring out the best flavors in fresh green beans. Tossing the beans in garlic-infused oil, lemon juice, and basil is a delicious way to finish the dish.

1   pound fresh green beans, preferably thin French haricots, trimmed, or frozen cut green beans

2   tablespoons water or reduced-sodium chicken broth

1   tablespoon Italian seasoning

1½ tablespoons olive oil

2   cloves garlic, finely minced

½   teaspoon salt

1   teaspoon freshly ground black pepper

1   tablespoon fresh lemon juice

1   teaspoon grated lemon zest

3 to 4 fresh basil leaves, minced

Put the beans in a large, microwaveable bowl with the water or chicken broth, the italian seasoning, olive oil, garlic, salt, black pepper, and ½ tablespoon of the lemon juice and ½ teaspoon of the lemon zest. Mix well. Cover with microwave-safe plastic wrap. Turn back one corner of the wrap to vent steam. Microwave on high for 2 minutes. Remove the plastic wrap and stir in the remaining lemon juice, the zest, and the basil leaves.

SERVING SIZE: 1 cup
EXCHANGE LIST VALUES: 1 vegetable, 1 fat
CARBOHYDRATE CHOICES: ½
CALORIES: 83

CALORIES FROM FAT: 50
TOTAL FAT: 6 g
SATURATED FAT: 1 g
CHOLESTEROL: 0 mg
SODIUM: 297 mg

TOTAL CARBOHYDRATE: 8 g
FIBER: 3 g
TOTAL SUGARS: 3 g
PROTEIN: 2 g

Sunflower Green Beans

MAKES 4 SERVINGS

If you have access to a farmers' market or a grocery store that sells local produce, buy fresh green beans for this recipe. You can make this dish in the microwave in less than 5 minutes.

1	pound fresh green beans, trimmed, or frozen cut green beans
2	tablespoons water or reduced-sodium chicken broth
¼	cup finely chopped yellow onion
2	cloves garlic, minced
1	tablespoon Italian seasoning
¼	teaspoon salt
1	teaspoon freshly ground black pepper
¼	teaspoon red pepper flakes
2	tablespoons dry-roasted sunflower seeds
1	tablespoon olive oil

Cut the beans into pieces about 2 inches long. If they are very small, leave the beans whole.

In a microwaveable bowl, combine the beans, water or chicken broth, onion, garlic, Italian seasoning, salt, black pepper, and red pepper flakes. Toss to combine. Cover with microwave-safe plastic wrap. Turn back one corner of the plastic wrap to vent the steam. Microwave on high for 3 to 4 minutes, or until the beans are crisp-tender. Drain.

Alternatively, place the beans in a medium saucepan; add the water or broth, onion, garlic, Italian seasoning, salt, black pepper, and red pepper flakes. Cover and bring to a boil, then decrease the heat to a simmer and cook for about 8 minutes, until the beans are crisp-tender. Drain.

Sprinkle the beans with the sunflower seeds and drizzle with the olive oil. Toss lightly to mix.

SERVING SIZE: ½ cup
EXCHANGE LIST VALUES: 1 vegetable, 1 fat
CARBOHYDRATE CHOICES: ½
CALORIES: 94

CALORIES FROM FAT: 52
TOTAL FAT: 6 g
SATURATED FAT: 1 g
CHOLESTEROL: 0 mg
SODIUM: 152 mg

TOTAL CARBOHYDRATE: 10 g
FIBER: 4 g
TOTAL SUGARS: 4 g
PROTEIN: 3 g

Mixed Greens with Okra and Bulgur

MAKES 8 SERVINGS

Hearty greens, tender young okra pods, and whole-grain bulgur make a delicious side dish, and are a powerful combination to help lower cholesterol and add fiber to your diet. Steaming the greens in a flavorful liquid is the best way to preserve their nutrients. Strong-tasting greens such as mustards are best when the salt is added at the end of cooking; otherwise, the greens will retain their bitterness. This dish freezes beautifully.

1   cup medium-grind bulgur wheat

3   tablespoons olive oil

1   large yellow onion, chopped

2   cloves garlic, minced

½   jalapeño chile, minced

1   tablespoon poultry seasoning

1   teaspoon freshly ground black pepper

1   cup reduced-sodium chicken broth

3   teaspoons no-sugar-added apple-cider vinegar

3   cups thinly sliced kale (about 1 bunch, stemmed), or 1 (16-ounce) bag frozen chopped kale

3   cups thinly sliced collard greens (about 1 bunch, stemmed), or 1 (16-ounce) bag frozen chopped collard greens

2   cups thinly sliced mustard green leaves (about 1 bunch, stemmed), or 1 (16-ounce) bag frozen chopped mustard greens

1   pound small okra pods, or 1 (10-ounce) box frozen whole okra pods

1   teaspoon salt

Over high heat, bring 2 cups of water and a teaspoon of salt to a boil. Stir in the bulgur and turn the heat to low and simmer, 20 minutes. Alternatively, place the 2 cups of water and a teaspoon of salt in a large, microwave-safe bowl and cook on high in the microwave until the water boils, about 5 minutes. Stir in the bulgur and cook on low or defrost setting for 10 to 12 minutes. Stir the cooked bulgur, cover the bowl with a lid, and allow to steam for 5 minutes. Transfer the cooked bulgur to a colander and rinse under cool water. Drain and set aside.

SERVING SIZE: 1½ cups
EXCHANGE LIST VALUES: 1 starch, 1 vegetable, 1 fat
CARBOHYDRATE CHOICES: 1
CALORIES: 157

CALORIES FROM FAT: 53
TOTAL FAT: 6 g
SATURATED FAT: 1 g
CHOLESTEROL: 0 mg
SODIUM: 385 mg

TOTAL CARBOHYDRATE: 24 g
FIBER: 7 g
TOTAL SUGARS: 2 g
PROTEIN: 5 g

In a large Dutch oven or heavy pot, heat the oil over medium-low heat. Add the onion and cook until golden, 4 to 6 minutes. Add the garlic, jalapeño, poultry seasoning, and pepper. Cook, stirring, for about 2 minutes. Pour in the broth and 2 teaspoons of the vinegar. Bring the liquid to a boil.

Add the kale, collard greens, mustard greens, and okra. Cover with a tight-fitting lid and reduce the heat to low. Cook for 10 to 15 minutes, stirring occasionally, until the greens are tender and the liquid has evaporated. Taste a piece to check for tenderness and add 3 to 4 tablespoons of water if the pot is dry before the greens are tender. Stir in the salt and bulgur and cook until heated through, about 1 minute. Drizzle with the remaining 1 teaspoon of vinegar before serving. Place leftovers in a freezer bag, press out any air, and freeze for up to 6 months.

Cooking Greens

STORE UNWASHED FRESH GREENS IN A PLASTIC BAG, REMOVING AS MUCH OF THE AIR FROM THE BAG AS POSSIBLE, FOR UP TO 5 DAYS. THE LONGER THEY ARE STORED, THE MORE BITTER THE FLAVOR BECOMES. DO NOT WASH GREENS BEFORE STORING BECAUSE EXPOSURE TO WATER ENCOURAGES SPOILAGE.

TO CLEAN FRESH GREENS, DISCARD ANY LEAVES THAT ARE WILTED, BROWN, YELLOWING, OR DAMAGED. IMMERSE THE GREENS IN A SINK FULL OF WATER AND WASH WELL TO REMOVE SAND, GRIT, AND ANY DEBRIS. LIFT OUT, DRAIN, RINSE, AND REPEAT UNTIL THE WATER IS CLEAN.

TO STEM, MAKE A V-SHAPED CUT WHERE THE STEM MEETS THE LEAF. DISCARD THE STEMS. STACK THE LEAVES AND COARSELY CHOP THEM INTO 3- TO 4-INCH RIBBONS, OR ROLL TOGETHER SEVERAL LEAVES INTO A CIGAR SHAPE AND SLICE INTO THIN RIBBONS.

Kohlrabi Cakes

MAKES 6 SERVINGS

Cruciferous vegetables include cabbage, broccoli, cauliflower, bok choy, kale, Swiss chard, Brussels sprouts, and beet and mustard greens. Kohlrabi is a relative unknown that looks like a green or purple fennel bulb and tastes like a cross between a potato and jicama. Kohlrabi can be cooked and mashed or puréed, eaten raw (sliced, julienned, grated, or diced), roasted, steamed, stir-fried like water chestnuts or bamboo shoots, or grilled. Here, they are shredded and formed into patties to panfry. Serve with unsweetened applesauce or a mixture of low-fat sour cream or Greek yogurt and chopped fresh mint.

4	kohlrabi (about 1½ pounds), trimmed and peeled (reserve leaves and chop finely)
1	teaspoon salt
3	green onions, including green parts, chopped
2	large eggs, lightly beaten
½	cup whole-wheat panko (Japanese bread crumbs)
½	teaspoon grated fresh ginger
½	teaspoon cayenne pepper or red pepper flakes
1	teaspoon freshly ground black pepper
2	tablespoons canola oil

Shred the kohlrabi using the large holes of a box grater. Sprinkle the kohlrabi with the salt and place it in a colander to drain for 30 minutes. Squeeze out any excess moisture by rolling the shredded kohlrabi in a paper towel and wringing it out.

In a large bowl, combine the shredded kohlrabi, kohlrabi leaves, green onions, eggs, panko, ginger, cayenne pepper or red pepper flakes, and black pepper. Blend well.

Heat the oil in a large nonstick skillet over medium-high heat. Form the patties by placing 2 heaping tablespoons of the kohlrabi mixture in the oil and pressing the mixture flat with a spatula. Fry in batches, until golden brown, 4 to 5 minutes per side. Using a slotted metal spatula, transfer to paper towels to drain.

SERVING SIZE: 4 patties
EXCHANGE LIST VALUES: ½ starch, 1 vegetable, 1 fat
CARBOHYDRATE CHOICES: 1
CALORIES: 122

CALORIES FROM FAT: 57
TOTAL FAT: 7 g
SATURATED FAT: 1 g
CHOLESTEROL: 62 mg
SODIUM: 249 mg

TOTAL CARBOHYDRATE: 13 g
FIBER: 5 g
TOTAL SUGARS: 3 g
PROTEIN: 5 g

Kohlrabi: Supermarket Mystery Solved!

This odd-looking vegetable is a relatively new addition to the produce section of most supermarkets. Kohlrabi is available year-round, with its peak season and sweetest flavor in spring through early summer. The purple globe is sweeter and tastier than the apple green variety. Both have a pale green, almost ivory flesh inside. While the entire vegetable is edible raw or cooked, small, young kohlrabi, 1½ to 2 inches in diameter, are ideal. The leaves of young kohlrabi can be used in the same way as kale. One cup of raw kohlrabi has only 40 calories and is high in vitamin C, potassium, and fiber.

People who consume kohlrabi and other cruciferous vegetables have been found to have a lower incidence of the risk factors for type 2 diabetes and heart disease. Some people believe kohlrabi can be effective against edema, candida, and viral conditions. Kohlrabi is a simple, nutritious way to incorporate more cruciferous vegetables into your diet.

Choose fresh-looking kohlrabi with no yellow leaves. Only large kohlrabi, over 2 inches in diameter, need to be peeled. Cut off the stems. Chop the leaves to cook along with the bulb, or use as part of a tossed salad.

Store kohlrabi in a perforated plastic bag in the refrigerator crisper for up to 1 week.

Crispy Oven-Fried Onion Rings

MAKES 6 SERVINGS

My family dearly loves fried onion rings, so I had to find a way for us to enjoy this dish in a healthier way by baking them in the oven to reduce the calories. My crispy oven-fried onion ring recipe is almost 100 calories less than the traditional battered and fried version. Use them to top your favorite casseroles, such as the Holiday Green Bean Casserole (page 211).

2	large yellow, Spanish, or Vidalia onions
½	cup all-purpose flour
1	teaspoon baking powder
1½	cups low-fat buttermilk
1	large egg
1	teaspoon Hungarian paprika
1	teaspoon ground cumin
½	teaspoon salt, plus more for sprinkling
1	teaspoon freshly ground black pepper
2	cups whole-wheat panko (Japanese bread crumbs)
½	teaspoon cayenne pepper
	Cooking oil spray

Position racks in the upper and lower thirds of the oven and preheat the oven to 450°F. Place two large, rimmed baking sheets in the oven to heat.

Cut the onions into ½-inch-thick slices and separate into rings. Place the rings in a medium bowl and cover with cold water.

Combine the flour and baking powder in a pie plate; stir to blend. Lightly beat together the buttermilk, egg, paprika, cumin, the ½ teaspoon of salt, and the black pepper in another pie plate. Combine the panko and cayenne pepper in a third shallow dish; stir to blend.

SERVING SIZE: about 8 to 10 onion rings
EXCHANGE LIST VALUES: 1½ starch, 1 vegetable
CARBOHYDRATE CHOICES: 2
CALORIES: 210

CALORIES FROM FAT: 37
TOTAL FAT: 4 g
SATURATED FAT: 1 g
CHOLESTEROL: 35 mg
SODIUM: 374 mg

TOTAL CARBOHYDRATE: 35 g
FIBER: 4 g
TOTAL SUGARS: 6 g
PROTEIN: 9 g

Remove one onion ring from the water, letting any excess drip off. Coat the ring in the flour mixture, shaking off any excess. Dip the ring in the egg mixture and let any excess drip off. Then press the ring into the bread crumbs on both sides to coat evenly. Shake off any excess. Repeat with the remaining onion rings and mixtures and place on a plate.

Carefully remove the heated baking sheets from the oven. Coat the baking sheets with cooking oil spray. Place the battered onion rings on the prepared baking sheets. Generously coat the onion rings with cooking spray.

Bake for 10 minutes. Remove the pans, turn each onion ring over, and spray with cooking oil spray. Return the pans to the oven, switching their positions. Continue baking until the rings are brown and crispy, 8 to 10 minutes more. Season with salt to taste and serve immediately.

Sensational Sunchokes

Sunchokes (also known as Jerusalem artichokes) are the nutty-flavored tubers of a perennial sunflower plant. Native Americans grew sunchokes long before the arrival of the Europeans, who called them sun roots.

Sunchokes are similar in texture to potatoes. Their taste has been compared to jicama, water chestnuts, radishes, and artichoke hearts. Sunchokes are a good source of iron, calcium, riboflavin, phosphorous, thiamine, and vitamins B_6, and C. Sunchoke flour is recommended for those who are allergic to wheat and other grains.

Sunchokes come in a range of colors from dark brown to light brown, similar to ginger. These tubers need to be refrigerated, unwashed, in a plastic bag. They will keep for up to 1 week. The skin on the sunchoke is thin, so there is no need to peel them; just wash them well. Place sunchokes in acidulated (lemon or vinegar) water after slicing.

Sautéed Sunchokes with Sage Butter Sauce

MAKES 4 SERVINGS

The sunchoke, also known as the Jerusalem artichoke, didn't originate in Jerusalem and is not an artichoke, although the flavor is similar to a cross between an artichoke and a potato. Sunchokes are delicious in soups or salads and as a side dish, whether sautéed, mashed, roasted, or puréed.

1 tablespoon whipped butter

1 pound sunchokes, cut crosswise into ¼-inch-thick rounds

1 clove garlic, minced

3 tablespoons coarsely torn fresh sage leaves

1 tablespoon Italian seasoning

½ teaspoon salt

1 teaspoon freshly ground black pepper

2 teaspoons fresh lemon juice

½ teaspoon grated lemon zest

Melt ½ tablespoon of the butter in a large nonstick skillet over medium-high heat. Add the sunchokes, garlic, 1½ tablespoons of the sage leaves, and the Italian seasoning. Sprinkle with the salt and pepper. Sauté until the sunchokes turn golden brown and soften, about 10 minutes.

Using a slotted spoon, transfer the sunchokes to a serving bowl. Add the remaining ½ tablespoon of butter and the remaining 1½ tablespoons of sage leaves to the skillet. Sauté until the sage darkens slightly and crisps, about 30 seconds. Add the lemon juice and simmer for 1 minute. Pour the lemon-sage butter over the Jerusalem artichokes, tossing to coat. Sprinkle with the lemon zest. Serve immediately.

SERVING SIZE: ½ cup
EXCHANGE LIST VALUES: 1 starch, ½ fat
CARBOHYDRATE CHOICES: 1
CALORIES: 85

CALORIES FROM FAT: 18
TOTAL FAT: 2 g
SATURATED FAT: 1 g
CHOLESTEROL: 5 mg
SODIUM: 311 mg

TOTAL CARBOHYDRATE: 16 g
FIBER: 2 g
TOTAL SUGARS: 8 g
PROTEIN: 2 g

Kale with Garlic and Lemon

MAKES 4 SERVINGS

Kale is in the same family as cabbage and comes in several varieties, including curly, ornamental, dinosaur (also known as lacinato or Tuscan kale), and Redbor, all of which differ in taste, texture, and appearance. Kale with smaller leaves will be more tender and have a milder flavor. Kale is a good source of beta-carotene, manganese, iron, potassium, lutein, zeaxanthin, calcium, and vitamins K and C.

1	tablespoon olive oil
½	yellow onion, thinly sliced
2	cloves garlic, minced
½	teaspoon red pepper flakes
½	cup reduced-sodium chicken broth or water
1	teaspoon reduced-sodium soy sauce
2	large bunches kale (about 2 pounds total), cleaned, stemmed, and chopped
1	teaspoon finely grated lemon zest
1	teaspoon fresh lemon juice
1	teaspoon freshly ground black pepper

In a large nonstick skillet or Dutch oven, heat the oil over medium heat. Add the onion and cook until translucent, about 3 minutes. Add the garlic and red pepper flakes and stir until the garlic is fragrant, about 1 minute. Add the broth or water and soy sauce, stirring to combine. Increase the heat to high and bring the sauce to a boil.

Decrease the heat to medium-low, add the kale, toss to mix, cover, and cook for 7 to 10 minutes, until the kale is tender. Stir in the lemon zest, lemon juice, and black pepper. Remove from the heat and serve.

SERVING SIZE: ¾ cup
EXCHANGE LIST VALUES: 3 vegetable, ½ fat
CARBOHYDRATE CHOICES: 1
CALORIES: 112

CALORIES FROM FAT: 41
TOTAL FAT: 5 g
SATURATED FAT: 1 g
CHOLESTEROL: 0 mg
SODIUM: 176 mg

TOTAL CARBOHYDRATE: 16 g
FIBER: 5 g
TOTAL SUGARS: 4 g
PROTEIN: 5 g

Moroccan-Style Slow-Cooked Vegetables

MAKES 8 SERVINGS

I discovered the basic spices and ingredients for this recipe when I was researching African culinary history. This dish complements meat courses beautifully, or it can be served over brown rice or quinoa as a vegetarian main dish.

2	large sweet potatoes, peeled and cut into rounds
1	pound carrots, peeled and sliced into rounds
1	pound turnips, peeled and diced
2	medium yellow onions, chopped
6	dried apricots or pitted prunes, chopped
1½	tablespoons chopped fresh parsley
1½	tablespoons chopped fresh cilantro
1	teaspoon ground turmeric
1	teaspoon ground cumin
½	teaspoon ground ginger
½	teaspoon ground cinnamon
¼	teaspoon cayenne pepper
1	(14-ounce) can reduced-sodium vegetable or chicken broth

Combine all the ingredients in a 3½- to 5-quart slow cooker and stir. Cover and cook for 4 hours on high or 6 hours on low. Alternatively, you can prepare this dish in a large, covered Dutch oven or a baking dish covered with aluminum foil; bake in a preheated 350°F oven for 1 to 1½ hours, or until the sweet potatoes and turnips are tender.

SERVING SIZE: 1 cup

EXCHANGE LIST VALUES: 1 starch, 1 vegetable

CARBOHYDRATE CHOICES: 1½

CALORIES: 105

CALORIES FROM FAT: 3

TOTAL FAT: 0 g

SATURATED FAT: 0 g

CHOLESTEROL: 0 mg

SODIUM: 199 mg

TOTAL CARBOHYDRATE: 24 g

FIBER: 5 g

TOTAL SUGARS: 9 g

PROTEIN: 3 g

Tomato, Squash, and Zucchini Gratin

MAKES 6 SERVINGS

A gratin is baked in a shallow dish (also called a gratin), with a topping of bread crumbs or cheese. The colors and flavors of the vegetables in this gratin are the perfect accompaniment to any type of meat dish. Feel free to experiment with different types of vegetables to create your own gratin.

2½ pounds (10 to 12) ripe plum tomatoes

2 pounds firm zucchini

1 pound yellow squash

1 teaspoon kosher salt

1 tablespoon Italian seasoning

1 teaspoon freshly ground black pepper

½ cup whole-wheat panko (Japanese bread crumbs)

¼ cup grated Parmesan cheese

2 tablespoons chopped fresh flat-leaf parsley

2 tablespoons olive oil

Preheat the oven to 375°F. Slice the tomatoes, zucchini, and squash into ¼-inch-thick, uniformly round slices. Place the vegetables on a plate or pan and sprinkle them with salt to remove any excess water. Let them drain for 30 to 45 minutes. Pat them dry with paper towels on both sides to remove excess moisture and salt.

Spray a 9-inch pie pan or ovenproof platter with cooking oil spray. Overlap the tomatoes, zucchini, and the yellow squash slices in a decorative pattern. Sprinkle with the Italian seasoning and pepper. Blend the panko, cheese, and parsley in a small bowl. Sprinkle the topping over the vegetables. Sprinkle the olive oil on top and bake until golden and crusty, about 20 minutes.

SERVING SIZE: 1 cup
EXCHANGE LIST VALUES: ½ starch, 3 vegetable, 1 fat
CARBOHYDRATE CHOICES: 1
CALORIES: 153

CALORIES FROM FAT: 63
TOTAL FAT: 7 g
SATURATED FAT: 1 g
CHOLESTEROL: 3 mg
SODIUM: 268 mg

TOTAL CARBOHYDRATE: 19 g
FIBER: 5 g
TOTAL SUGARS: 10 g
PROTEIN: 7 g

Herb-Roasted Vegetables

MAKES 6 SERVINGS

This is, hands down, my favorite vegetable dish. The beauty of this recipe is that almost any kind of vegetable works well cooked this way. Vegetables benefit from roasting at high heat because doing so retains most of their nutrients and brings out the natural sugars. In a pinch, I've used thawed frozen vegetables that I've drained and patted dry.

1 tablespoon balsamic vinegar

1½ tablespoons poultry seasoning

½ tablespoon Dijon mustard

¼ teaspoon agave syrup

1 teaspoon kosher salt

½ teaspoon freshly ground black pepper

2 tablespoons olive oil

2 cloves garlic, smashed

½ large red onion, thinly sliced

1 red bell pepper, seeded, deribbed, and cut into ½-inch-wide strips

2 medium sweet potatoes (about 1½ pounds total), peeled and cut crosswise into ½-inch-thick slices

1 cup baby carrots

¼ pound broccoli florets, halved

¼ pound cauliflower florets, thinly sliced

¼ pound baby okra

Preheat the oven to 450°F. Place two large, rimmed baking sheets in the oven to heat.

Whisk together the vinegar, 1 tablespoon of the poultry seasoning, the mustard, agave syrup, ½ teaspoon of the salt, and the pepper in a medium bowl. Gradually whisk in the oil.

Combine the remaining ½ tablespoon of the poultry seasoning, the garlic, onion, bell pepper, sweet potatoes, carrots, broccoli, cauliflower, okra, and the remaining ½ teaspoon of salt in a large bowl. Pour on the dressing and toss to coat.

Carefully remove the hot baking sheets from the oven. Spray the pans with cooking oil spray. Divide the vegetables between the 2 baking sheets and arrange in an even layer. Roast for 15 minutes. Stir the vegetables and spray with more cooking oil spray, then switch the pans to different racks. Continue to roast until the vegetables are tender and slightly brown around the edges, about 20 minutes. Serve immediately.

SERVING SIZE: 1½ cups
EXCHANGE LIST VALUES: 1 starch, 1 vegetable, 1 fat
CARBOHYDRATE CHOICES: 1½
CALORIES: 153

CALORIES FROM FAT: 51
TOTAL FAT: 6 g
SATURATED FAT: 1 g
CHOLESTEROL: 0 mg
SODIUM: 366 mg

TOTAL CARBOHYDRATE: 24 g
FIBER: 5 g
TOTAL SUGARS: 8 g
PROTEIN: 3 g

Sweet Finishes
and
Nighttime Nibbles

JUST BECAUSE YOU HAVE DIABETES doesn't mean you can't ever have sweets or carbohydrates. As with everything else in life, what you eat when you have diabetes is all about balance and moderation. New research has shown that eating sugar has a similar effect on blood glucose levels as other carbohydrates, such as bread, potatoes, or starchy foods.

If you have a sweet tooth, plan your meals so that you can substitute small portions of something sweet for other carbohydrates in the meals and snacks you eat throughout the day. Planning your sweets intake to maintain balance in your diet plan will keep blood glucose levels normal. So if you want to have a cookie after a meal, reduce or eliminate the carbohydrate content to compensate.

Most sweets are high in calories and lack important vitamins and minerals. When choosing sweets in your meal plan, include the necessary nutrients required for a healthy body. Foods labeled no sugar added, reduced sugar, or sugar-free, as in the case of sugar-free candies or gum containing sugar alcohols (such as isomalt, mannitol, sorbitol) all still contain carbohydrates.

The bread recipes in this chapter use sugar substitutes, whole grains, and buttermilk to reduce calories without changing the flavor. The sweets and desserts use sweeteners such as agave syrup, stevia, and Splenda brown sugar blend as part of the ingredients.

The use of low-calorie sweeteners in these recipes reduces the overall calories and sugar, and still produces delicious foods for diabetics and those who dine with them.

QUICK SWEET POTATO BREAD   231

WHOLE-WHEAT BISCUITS   232

FLOURLESS ALMOND MINI CAKES
   WITH MIXED-BERRY TOPPING   237

PUMPKIN–NUT BARS   239

CINNAMON–PECAN CAKE   243

PINEAPPLE UPSIDE-DOWN CAKE   245

BUTTERMILK CORN BREAD   246

EASY FRUIT COBBLER   248

FUDGE PUDDING CAKE   250

LIGHT BANANA PUDDING   252

HEAVENLY TIRAMISU   253

NO-BAKE COOKIES   255

CHOCOLATE-DIPPED STRAWBERRIES AND CREAM   257

PECAN–PRALINE SWEET POTATO PIE   258

Quick Sweet Potato Bread

MAKES 1 LOAF

The combination of low-fat vanilla Greek yogurt and nutrient-rich sweet potatoes adds a rich, moist texture to this delicious quick bread. Serve this for breakfast or make it into a dessert by topping it with fresh fruit, ice cream, or Creamy Whipped Topping (page 257).

1	cup whole-wheat pastry flour
½	cup all-purpose flour
½	teaspoon baking soda
½	teaspoon baking powder
½	teaspoon salt
½	teaspoon ground cinnamon
¼	teaspoon ground cloves
¼	teaspoon ground nutmeg
3	large egg whites
1½	cups Splenda no-calorie sweetener, granulated
½	cup low-fat vanilla Greek yogurt
1¼	cups drained canned or cooked sweet potato (about 1 large sweet potato), mashed lightly

Preheat the oven to 350°F. Lightly spray an 8½ by 4½-inch nonstick loaf pan with butter-flavored cooking spray. In a medium bowl, whisk together the flours, baking soda, baking powder, salt, cinnamon, cloves, and nutmeg; set aside.

In a large bowl, whisk together the egg whites, Splenda, and yogurt into a large bowl until well blended. Stir in the sweet potato. Stir the dry ingredients into the sweet potato mixture until the flour mixture is well blended. Pour the batter into the prepared loaf pan.

Bake until a toothpick inserted into the center of the loaf comes out clean, 55 to 60 minutes. Let cool in the pan on a wire rack for 10 minutes, then unmold onto the wire rack. Let cool completely, about 2 hours. Cut into 10 slices with a serrated bread knife.

SERVING SIZE: 1 (¾-inch) slice
EXCHANGE LIST VALUES: 2 starch
CARBOHYDRATE CHOICES: 2
CALORIES: 134
CALORIES FROM FAT: 10

TOTAL FAT: 1 g
SATURATED FAT: 0 g
CHOLESTEROL: 1 mg
SODIUM: 246 mg
TOTAL CARBOHYDRATE: 27 g

FIBER: 2 g
TOTAL SUGARS: 7 g
PROTEIN: 4 g

Whole-Wheat Biscuits

MAKES 16 BISCUITS

Biscuits are easy to make and, with the addition of a few ingredients such as whole-wheat flour, wheat germ, and buttermilk, can be a healthy part of a meal. Here, these ingredients add more fiber and less fat to this traditional comfort food.

1	cup whole-wheat pastry flour
¾	cup all-purpose flour, plus extra for kneading
3	tablespoons toasted wheat germ
2	teaspoons baking powder
½	teaspoon baking soda
¼	teaspoon salt
3	tablespoons whipped butter, chilled, cut into small pieces
1	cup low-fat buttermilk, chilled

Preheat the oven to 400°F. In a large bowl, whisk together the whole-wheat pastry flour, all-purpose flour, wheat germ, baking powder, baking soda, and salt until well blended. Add the butter to the flour mixture and cut it in using a pastry blender or 2 dinner knives. The finished mixture should resemble coarse crumbs. Add the buttermilk and stir until a moist dough forms. Don't overwork the dough or it will create tough biscuits. Cover the bowl with plastic wrap and refrigerate for 30 minutes or overnight.

Turn out the dough onto a generously floured work surface and, with floured hands, knead gently 6 to 8 times until smooth and manageable. Using a rolling pin, roll the dough into a rectangle ½ inch thick. To cut out biscuits, use a 2½-inch round biscuit cutter or drinking glass of the same size dipped in flour. Press down the cutter or glass firmly into the dough and bring the cutter or drinking glass straight up without twisting to allow the biscuits to rise fully. Cut close together for a minimum of scraps. Gather the scraps and roll out to make additional biscuits.

Place the biscuits about 1 inch apart on a baking sheet. Bake until the biscuits rise to twice their unbaked height and are light golden, 8 to 10 minutes. Serve hot.

SERVING SIZE: 1 biscuit	**TOTAL FAT:** 2 g	**FIBER:** 1 g
EXCHANGE LIST VALUES: 1 starch	**SATURATED FAT:** 1 g	**TOTAL SUGARS:** 1 g
CARBOHYDRATE CHOICES: 1	**CHOLESTEROL:** 5 mg	**PROTEIN:** 2 g
CALORIES: 75	**SODIUM:** 155 mg	
CALORIES FROM FAT: 18	**TOTAL CARBOHYDRATE:** 12 g	

HERB OR SPICED BISCUITS: Adding herbs or paprika transforms this quick bread. The herb biscuits are especially good served with Italian dishes. After mixing together the dry ingredients, stir in either ½ teaspoon of dried rosemary, 2 tablespoons of chopped fresh flat-leaf parsley, or ¼ cup snipped fresh chives. Or, dust 2 tablespoons of sweet paprika onto the biscuits after removing them from the oven.

SERVING SIZE: 1 biscuit
EXCHANGE LIST VALUES: 1 starch
CARBOHYDRATE CHOICES: 1
CALORIES: 77
CALORIES FROM FAT: 19

TOTAL FAT: 2 g
SATURATED FAT: 1 g
CHOLESTEROL: 6 mg
SODIUM: 156 mg
TOTAL CARBOHYDRATE: 12 g

FIBER: 2 g
TOTAL SUGARS: 1 g
PROTEIN: 3 g

CHEESE, GARLIC, AND JALAPEÑO BISCUITS: These biscuits are delicious with soups, stews, and chili. After mixing together the dry ingredients, add either ¾ cup shredded reduced-fat cheddar cheese (and ½ tablespoon garlic powder, if desired), ½ cup shredded reduced-fat cheddar cheese and ¼ cup diced jalapeño or drained canned diced green chiles, or ½ cup grated Parmesan cheese (and ½ tablespoon garlic powder, if desired).

¾ cup shredded reduced-fat cheddar cheese (and ½ tablespoons garlic powder, if desired)

SERVING SIZE: 1 biscuit
EXCHANGE LIST VALUES: 1 starch
CARBOHYDRATE CHOICES: 1
CALORIES: 84
CALORIES FROM FAT: 21

TOTAL FAT: 2 g
SATURATED FAT: 1 g
CHOLESTEROL: 6 mg
SODIUM: 187 mg
TOTAL CARBOHYDRATE: 12 g

FIBER: 1 g
TOTAL SUGARS: 1 g
PROTEIN: 4 g

Continued on page 234

½ cup shredded reduced-fat cheddar
cheese and ¼ cup diced jalapeño or
canned, diced green chiles, drained

SERVING SIZE: 1 biscuit
EXCHANGE LIST VALUES: 1 starch
CARBOHYDRATE CHOICES: 1
CALORIES: 81
CALORIES FROM FAT: 20

TOTAL FAT: 2 g
SATURATED FAT: 1 g
CHOLESTEROL: 5 mg
SODIUM: 177 mg
TOTAL CARBOHYDRATE: 12 g

FIBER: 1 g
TOTAL SUGARS: 1 g
PROTEIN: 3 g

½ cup grated Parmesan cheese (and ½
tablespoon garlic powder, if desired)

SERVING SIZE: 1 biscuit
EXCHANGE LIST VALUES: 1 starch
CARBOHYDRATE CHOICES: 1
CALORIES: 85
CALORIES FROM FAT: 24

TOTAL FAT: 3 g
SATURATED FAT: 2 g
CHOLESTEROL: 7 mg
SODIUM: 193 mg
TOTAL CARBOHYDRATE: 12 g

FIBER: 1 g
TOTAL SUGARS: 1 g
PROTEIN: 3 g

Almond Flour and Almond Meal

Almond flour and almond meal are interchangeable products made from ground almonds with a cornmeal-type consistency. Both are gluten-free, making them a low-carb substitute for wheat flour in baked goods. Almond flour is most often made with blanched almonds, while almond meal can be made with either raw or blanched almonds. To make your own almond flour or meal: Preheat the oven to 350°F. Spread 1 pound of blanched or raw almonds on a rimmed baking sheet and toast in the oven, stirring once, until fragrant, 7 to 9 minutes. Working in batches, pulse the almonds 8 to 9 times in a food processor or blender, or until finely ground. Overprocessing the almonds will turn them into almond butter. You should have about 3½ cups of almond flour or meal. Store in an airtight container in the refrigerator for up to 6 months or in the freezer for up to 6 months. Almond meal must be thawed out before using it in recipes.

Flourless Almond Mini Cakes with Mixed-Berry Topping

MAKES 16 MINI CAKES

These little cakes are good on their own, but even more delicious served with warm mixed-berry topping. The eggs are the key ingredient and must be used at room temperature. Either set out the eggs on the counter for 15 minutes beforehand, or submerge in a bowl of warm water for 5 minutes before using.

Butter-flavored cooking oil spray

4 large eggs, at room temperature, separated

½ cup agave syrup

1 teaspoon vanilla extract

½ teaspoon baking soda

½ teaspoon salt

2 cups almond flour or almond meal

TOPPING

2 cups frozen mixed berries or 2 (10-ounce) boxes frozen mixed berries

2 tablespoons agave syrup

1½ teaspoons cornstarch

Preheat the oven to 350°F. Spray one mini muffin pan with a light coating of cooking oil spray. You can also use individual ramekin baking cups, but the yield will be less.

In a large bowl, combine the 4 egg yolks, agave syrup, vanilla, baking soda, and salt in a large bowl. Using an electric mixer, beat until the ingredients are well blended. Add the almond flour or meal and beat on low speed until combined, about 2 minutes.

Place the 4 egg whites in a large, clean bowl. Use either a handheld mixer with clean beaters or the whisk attachment on a stand mixer and beat the whites on medium speed until opaque, doubled in volume with soft peaks.

SERVING SIZE: 1 mini cake plus 1 tablespoon of the topping
EXCHANGE LIST VALUES: 1½ carbohydrate, 2 fat
CARBOHYDRATE CHOICES: 1½

CALORIES: 231
CALORIES FROM FAT: 119
TOTAL FAT: 13 g
SATURATED FAT: 1 g
CHOLESTEROL: 74 mg

SODIUM: 216 mg
TOTAL CARBOHYDRATE: 25 g
FIBER: 3 g
TOTAL SUGARS: 19 g
PROTEIN: 8 g

Using a rubber spatula, gently fold the egg whites into the batter until just combined. Scrape the batter evenly into the prepared muffin cups, filling each three-quarters full. Bake, rotating halfway through, until the edges are light brown and a dime-sized soft center remains, 18 to 20 minutes. If using larger baking cups, you'll need to increase the baking time by 5 to 10 minutes. Transfer the pan to a wire rack and let cool completely, at least 15 minutes.

To make the berry topping, combine all the ingredients in a large microwaveable bowl and toss until combined. Microwave on high for 2 minutes, then stir and microwave again until slightly thickened and steaming, about 2½ minutes more.

Unmold the cakes. To serve, spoon 1 tablespoon of the warm berry topping on each cake. Extra cakes may be stored in an airtight container at room temperature for up to 7 days.

Pumpkin–Nut Bars

MAKES 12 SERVINGS

The bright orange color of pumpkin indicates that it's a good source of beta-carotene. An important antioxidant, beta-carotene is converted to vitamin A in the body, and is believed to reduce the risk of developing certain types of cancer and to offer some protection against heart disease. These bars showcase the rich flavor of pumpkin to perfection. Delicious warm from the oven and served with whipped topping or low-fat ice cream, they also can be eaten for breakfast or as a snack.

2	large egg whites
1	cup fresh or canned cooked pumpkin purée
½	cup whipped butter
2	cups old-fashioned oats
1	cup firmly packed Splenda brown sugar blend
½	cup sweetened shredded coconut, toasted (see Note)
½	cup toasted wheat germ
1	cup chopped walnuts or almonds

Preheat the oven to 350°F. Spray a 17½ by 13-inch rimmed baking sheet with butter-flavored cooking oil spray. In a large bowl, lightly beat the egg whites with a whisk. Add the pumpkin and butter and beat until smooth. In another large bowl, combine the oats, brown sugar blend, coconut, wheat germ, and walnuts. Stir the ingredients into the pumpkin mixture to form a stiff dough.

Press the dough into the prepared pan. Bake for 40 to 45 minutes, or until golden brown. While still warm, cut into 48 bars. Serve warm or let cool completely.

NOTE: To toast the coconut, spread the coconut in an even layer on a rimmed baking sheet and toast in a preheated 350°F oven for about 10 minutes, or until lightly browned, stirring every 3 minutes.

SERVING SIZE: 1 bar
EXCHANGE LIST VALUES:
    1 carbohydrate, 1 starch, 2 fat
CARBOHYDRATE CHOICES: 2
CALORIES: 275

CALORIES FROM FAT: 110
TOTAL FAT: 12 g
SATURATED FAT: 5 g
CHOLESTEROL: 13 mg
SODIUM: 64 mg

TOTAL CARBOHYDRATE: 33 g
FIBER: 4 g
TOTAL SUGARS: 19 g
PROTEIN: 6 g

Smashing Pumpkins

Current research indicates that a diet rich in foods containing beta-carotene, such as pumpkins and sweet potatoes, may offer protection against cataracts, arthritis, and high blood pressure, as well as some cancers and heart disease. While canned pumpkin purée is readily available year-round, it's worth the time to prepare homemade pumpkin purée when these vegetables are at their peak in the fall.

To select a pumpkin, look for one with 1 to 2 inches of stem left. If the stem is cut down too low, the pumpkin will quickly decay, or may be decaying at the time of purchase. Pumpkins should be heavy for their size, without blemishes and soft spots. Shape is unimportant, as a lopsided pumpkin is not necessarily a bad pumpkin. Each pound of pumpkin should yield about 1 cup of purée.

To prepare a pumpkin for cooking, carefully remove the stem with a sharp knife. Smash the pumpkin on a newspaper-covered surface, or drop the pumpkin on a hard surface covered with newspaper. Scoop out the stringy mass in the center, saving the seeds if you want to roast them. It's a messy job, but it will pay off.

Cook the pumpkin by boiling, steaming, roasting, or using the microwave, as follows:

BOILING/STEAMING: Cut the pumpkin into pieces and scrape away the stringy mass and seeds. Reserve the seeds for roasting, if desired. Place the pieces in a large pot with about 1 cup of water. Cover the pot and boil for 20 to 30 minutes, or until tender. Check for doneness by poking the pumpkin with a fork. Drain the cooked pumpkin in a colander. Reserve the liquid to use as a base for soup.

BAKING: Cut the pumpkin into pieces and scrape away the stringy mass and seeds. Reserve the seeds for roasting, if desired. Rinse under cold water. Place the pumpkin, cut side down, on a large baking sheet. Bake in a preheated 350°F oven for 1 hour, or until fork-tender.

MICROWAVING: Cut the pumpkin into pieces and scrape away the stringy mass and seeds. Reserve the seeds for roasting, if desired. Place cut side down on a microwaveable plate or tray. Microwave on high for 15 minutes. Check for doneness at 1- to 2-minute intervals until the pumpkin is fork-tender.

Allow the cooked pumpkin to cool. Remove the peel, using a small, sharp knife and your fingers, or scoop out the flesh with a spoon. Place the pumpkin flesh in a food processor, food mill, or ricer, or mash in a pot with a potato masher. Freeze and store the purée in 1-cup portions in small freezer bags for up to 1 year.

Cinnamon–Pecan Cake

MAKES 12 SERVINGS

This is one of my husband's favorite cakes. When Michael was diagnosed with diabetes, I made a few adjustments so that he could still have an occasional slice for special celebrations. The diabetic-friendly additions of the brown sugar blend, sugar substitute, and nonfat yogurt cut down on the sugar and carbs without sacrificing flavor.

Butter-flavored cooking oil spray

¼ cup firmly packed Splenda brown sugar blend

1½ teaspoons ground cinnamon

2¼ cups all-purpose flour

2 teaspoons baking powder

½ teaspoon baking soda

¾ cup Splenda no-calorie sweetener, granulated

2 large eggs, lightly beaten

2 large egg whites

½ cup canola oil

1 cup plain nonfat yogurt

1 teaspoon vanilla extract

¼ cup chopped pecans

GLAZE (OPTIONAL)

⅓ cup whipped butter

1 cup confectioners' sugar

1½ teaspoons vanilla extract

2 to 4 tablespoons hot water

Continued on page 244

SERVING SIZE: 1 (½-inch) slice

EXCHANGE LIST VALUES: 2 starch, 2 fat

CARBOHYDRATE CHOICES: 2

CALORIES: 236

CALORIES FROM FAT: 109

TOTAL FAT: 13 g

SATURATED FAT: 2 g

CHOLESTEROL: 31 mg

SODIUM: 152 mg

TOTAL CARBOHYDRATE: 26 g

FIBER: 1 g

TOTAL SUGARS: 7 g

PROTEIN: 5 g

Preheat the oven to 350°F. Spray a 10-cup Bundt pan with butter-flavored cooking oil spray and dust with flour. Shake out any excess flour.

In a small bowl, stir together the brown sugar blend and cinnamon. Set aside. In a large bowl, combine the flour, baking powder, baking soda, and Splenda in a large bowl. Stir in the eggs, egg whites, oil, yogurt, and vanilla. Stir in the chopped pecans.

Pour half of the batter into the prepared pan. Sprinkle with the brown sugar mixture and pour the remaining batter on top. Bake for 40 minutes, or until a toothpick inserted in the cake comes out clean. Remove from the oven and let cool in the pan on a wire rack for 10 minutes. Run a knife around the edges of the cake and invert it onto a plate.

To make the optional glaze, melt the butter in a small microwaveable bowl in the microwave on high for 1 minute. Add the confectioners' sugar and vanilla and stir. Add the water 1 tablespoon at a time, stirring until the glaze is the desired consistency. Drizzle the glaze over the top and down the sides of the cooled cake.

Pineapple Upside-Down Cake

MAKES 9 SERVINGS

Using Splenda brown sugar blend instead of regular brown sugar makes this Southern favorite a diabetic-friendly cake. This recipe re-creates the traditional pineapple, cherry, and brown sugar glaze for the topping that makes this cake so unique.

3   tablespoons plus 5 tablespoons whipped butter

¾   cup firmly packed Splenda brown sugar blend

4   slices canned pineapple in juice, drained

4   maraschino cherries

1¼   cups all-purpose flour

1½   teaspoons baking powder

½   teaspoon salt

¼   cup Splenda no-calorie sweetener, granulated

1   large egg

1   teaspoon vanilla extract

½   cup low-fat evaporated milk

Preheat the oven to 350°F. Place 3 tablespoons of the butter in an 8-inch square baking pan. Place the pan in the oven to melt the butter. Remove the pan from the oven and stir in the Splenda brown sugar blend. Place the pineapple slices on the sugar mixture, centering the slices closely so all the pieces are touching. Place a cherry in the center of each pineapple slice. Set aside.

In a medium bowl, whisk together the flour, baking powder, and salt. Set aside. In another medium bowl, using an electric mixer on medium speed, beat the remaining 5 tablespoons of butter and the Splenda until blended, about 1 minute. Add the egg and vanilla and beat until smooth, about 30 seconds. The batter will be thin. Beat the flour mixture into the batter in thirds, alternating with the milk, until all the ingredients have been incorporated, beating until smooth, about 2 minutes.

Spoon the batter on top of the pineapple mixture and spread evenly. Bake until golden brown and a toothpick inserted in the center comes out clean, 25 to 35 minutes. Unmold by sliding a thin knife around the edge of the cake. Invert onto a cake plate. Serve warm or at room temperature.

SERVING SIZE: 1 (2½-inch) square
EXCHANGE LIST VALUES:
     1 carbohydrate, 1 starch, 1 fat
CARBOHYDRATE CHOICES: 2
CALORIES: 246

CALORIES FROM FAT: 71
TOTAL FAT: 8 g
SATURATED FAT: 5 g
CHOLESTEROL: 41 mg
SODIUM: 280 mg

TOTAL CARBOHYDRATE: 36 g
FIBER: 1 g
TOTAL SUGARS: 22 g
PROTEIN: 3 g

Buttermilk Corn Bread

MAKES 1 8-INCH SQUARE PAN

Low-fat buttermilk is a traditional addition to Southern-style corn bread. Today, buttermilk is made by adding a special type of bacteria to nonfat or low-fat milk. The bacterium thickens the milk and gives it a tangy taste. Buttermilk adds tenderness and flavor to baked goods. You can make a buttermilk substitute by adding 1 tablespoon of vinegar or lemon juice to 1 cup of milk, then mixing it well and letting it stand for 5 minutes.

1	cup yellow cornmeal
1	cup all-purpose flour or whole-wheat pastry flour
¼	cup stevia granulated sweetener
1	teaspoon baking powder
1	cup low-fat buttermilk
1	large egg, lightly beaten
¼	cup whipped butter

Preheat the oven to 350°F. Spray an 8-inch square baking dish or 8-inch cast iron skillet with butter-flavored cooking spray. Combine the cornmeal, flour, stevia, and baking powder in a medium bowl and stir with a whisk to blend.

Combine the buttermilk and egg in a small bowl. Beat lightly to blend. Gradually add the buttermilk and egg to the dry ingredients. Stir in the butter until blended. Allow the batter to rest for 15 to 30 minutes. Pour into the prepared baking dish and bake for 20 to 25 minutes, or until golden brown. Remove from the oven and let cool. Cut into 10 squares.

SERVING SIZE: 1 (2½-inch) square
EXCHANGE LIST VALUES: 2 starch
CARBOHYDRATE CHOICES: 2
CALORIES: 134
CALORIES FROM FAT: 10

TOTAL FAT: 1 g
SATURATED FAT: 0 g
CHOLESTEROL: 1 mg
SODIUM: 246 mg
TOTAL CARBOHYDRATE: 27 g

FIBER: 2 g
TOTAL SUGARS: 7 g
PROTEIN: 4 g

Easy Fruit Cobbler

MAKES 8 SERVINGS

My granddaughter, Anysa, is an apprentice pastry chef, or as we like to call her, a Diva-in-training. She learned to make a fresh peach and blueberry version of this fabulous cobbler on her first day at work. I've made the recipe lighter, with more choices of fruit. The trick to my cobbler is to bake the fruit filling without the topping first. This makes it the perfect recipe for a spur-of-the-moment dessert using frozen fruits. The hot filling cooks the biscuit topping from the bottom as the hot oven browns it on the top. Best of all, this recipe uses ingredients you should already have on hand.

3	cups fresh blueberries, blackberries, or strawberries, or 2 cups individually quick-frozen (IQF) berries
3	cups sliced fresh peaches, or 2 cups individually quick-frozen (IQF) peaches
⅓	cup stevia granulated sweetener
2	tablespoons fresh lemon juice
1	tablespoon cornstarch
½	teaspoon vanilla extract
½	teaspoon ground cinnamon
¼	teaspoon ground nutmeg

BISCUIT TOPPING

½	cup all-purpose flour
½	cup whole-wheat pastry flour
3	tablespoons cornmeal
¼	cup plus 2 tablespoons stevia granulated sweetener
1	teaspoon baking powder
¼	teaspoon baking soda
¼	teaspoon salt
⅓	cup low-fat buttermilk
3	tablespoons whipped butter
½	teaspoon vanilla extract
⅛	teaspoon ground cinnamon
⅛	teaspoon ground nutmeg

SERVING SIZE: ⅛ of cobbler
EXCHANGE LIST VALUES: 2 starch, 1 fruit, ½ fat
CARBOHYDRATE CHOICES: 2
CALORIES: 169

CALORIES FROM FAT: 35
TOTAL FAT: 4 g
SATURATED FAT: 2 g
CHOLESTEROL: 8 mg
SODIUM: 199 mg

TOTAL CARBOHYDRATE: 32 g
FIBER: 4 g
TOTAL SUGARS: 13 g
PROTEIN: 3 g

Put an oven rack in the center of the oven. Preheat the oven to 400°F. Spray a 9-inch deep-dish pie pan with butter-flavored cooking oil spray.

In a large bowl, mix together the fruit, stevia, lemon juice, cornstarch, vanilla, cinnamon, and nutmeg until well combined. Place the fruit filling in the prepared pie pan. Place the pie pan on a rimmed baking sheet to catch any liquid. Bake until the fruit releases its liquid and is hot and bubbling around the edges, 20 to 30 minutes for fresh fruit, 50 to 60 minutes for frozen.

Meanwhile, make the topping: In a large bowl, whisk together the all-purpose flour, pastry flour, cornmeal, the ¼ cup of stevia, the baking powder, baking soda, and salt. Set aside. In a small bowl, mix together the buttermilk, butter, and vanilla. Set aside.

Remove the hot filling from the oven. Stir the buttermilk mixture into the flour mixture until just combined. Scoop one-quarter portions of dough ½ inch apart on the hot filling.

In a small bowl, stir together the remaining 2 tablespoons of stevia, the cinnamon, and nutmeg. Sprinkle the spice mixture over the dough. Place the cobbler in the oven and bake until the biscuits are brown and the filling is hot and bubbling, 15 to 20 minutes. Remove from the oven and let cool for 15 minutes before serving.

Fudge Pudding Cake

MAKES 12 SERVINGS

Combining unsweetened cocoa with coffee enhances the chocolate flavor of this moist, fudgy cake. The mocha sauce collects in the bottom of the cooked cake and becomes partially absorbed as the cake cools, leaving a puddinglike layer on the bottom.

¼	cup pecan halves
1	cup all-purpose flour
⅓	cup Splenda no-calorie sweetener, granulated
¼	cup plus 3 tablespoons unsweetened cocoa powder
2	teaspoons baking powder
½	teaspoon salt
½	cup nonfat milk
1	large egg, lightly beaten
2	tablespoons canola oil
1	teaspoon vanilla extract
¾	cup firmly packed Splenda brown sugar blend
1⅓	cups hot, strong coffee

Preheat the oven to 375°F. Lightly coat an 8-inch square baking dish with butter-flavored cooking spray.

Place the nuts on a rimmed baking sheet and bake, stirring once, until fragrant, about 6 minutes. Pour into a bowl to cool.

In a large bowl, combine the flour, Splenda, the ¼ cup of cocoa, the baking powder, and salt and stir with a whisk to blend. In a glass measuring cup, combine the milk, egg, canola oil, and vanilla. Make a well in the center of the dry ingredients and gradually stir in the milk mixture until combined. Stir in the pecans. Spoon the batter into the prepared pan and spread evenly. Dissolve the brown sugar blend in the coffee and spoon it over the batter.

Bake until the cake is almost set, 25 minutes. Remove from the oven and let stand for 10 minutes. Dust with the remaining 3 tablespoons of cocoa powder. Serve hot or warm.

SERVING SIZE: ¹/₁₂ of cake
EXCHANGE LIST VALUES:
    1 carbohydrate, ½ starch, ½ fat
CARBOHYDRATE CHOICES: 1½
CALORIES: 159

CALORIES FROM FAT: 42
TOTAL FAT: 5 g
SATURATED FAT: 0 g
CHOLESTEROL: 16 mg
SODIUM: 175 mg

TOTAL CARBOHYDRATE: 23 g
FIBER: 1 g
TOTAL SUGARS: 13 g
PROTEIN: 3 g

Light Banana Pudding

MAKES 10 SERVINGS

Banana pudding is a cool and creamy way to finish off a wonderful meal. This lighter version of the classic dish uses nuts and crushed vanilla wafers as a crust for a delicious low-fat pudding.

25	reduced-fat vanilla wafers, finely crushed (about 1 cup)
½	cup finely chopped walnuts, almonds, or pecans
¼	cup whipped butter, melted
1	package (8-ounce) low-fat cream cheese (such as Neufchâtel), softened
½	cup confectioners' sugar
1½	cups Creamy Whipped Topping (page 257)
3	medium to large bananas, peeled and sliced
2	(1-ounce) packages fat-free and sugar-free vanilla instant pudding
½	teaspoon banana, almond, or vanilla extract
2	(14-ounce) cans low-fat evaporated milk, chilled

In a medium bowl, mix together the cookie crumbs, nuts, and butter until blended. Reserve 2 tablespoons of the crumb mixture for a topping. Press the remaining crumb mixture into the bottom of a 13 by 9-inch dish. Refrigerate to set the crust for at least 30 minutes.

Whisk the cream cheese and confectioners' sugar in a medium bowl until blended. Stir in 1 cup of the whipped topping and spread the mixture over the crust. Top with the bananas.

Whisk the pudding mixes, extract, and evaporated milk for 2 minutes; spread over the bananas. Top with the remaining ½ cup of whipped topping and sprinkle with the reserved crumb mixture. Cover with plastic wrap and refrigerate for 3 hours before serving.

SERVING SIZE: 4 inch by 4 inch square
EXCHANGE LIST VALUES:
   2 carbohydrate, 2 fat
CARBOHYDRATE CHOICES: 2
CALORIES: 260

CALORIES FROM FAT: 97
TOTAL FAT: 11 g
SATURATED FAT: 5 g
CHOLESTEROL: 31 mg
SODIUM: 397 mg

TOTAL CARBOHYDRATE: 33 g
FIBER: 1 g
TOTAL SUGARS: 23 g
PROTEIN: 9 g

Heavenly Tiramisu

MAKES 6 SERVINGS

This smaller, lighter version of tiramisu contains all of the "heaven in your mouth" flavors of the Italian recipe. You can make espresso from an instant powder for this dessert with great results.

½   cup nonfat ricotta cheese

2   tablespoons confectioners' sugar

½   teaspoon vanilla extract

½   teaspoon rum extract

⅛   teaspoon ground cinnamon

12 (about 1¾ ounces) ladyfingers

4   tablespoons brewed espresso
    or strong coffee

3   tablespoons unsweetened cocoa powder

2   teaspoons stevia granulated sweetener

In a medium bowl, combine the ricotta, confectioners' sugar, vanilla and rum extracts, and cinnamon and stir until well blended.

Place 6 ladyfingers in a 9 by 5-inch loaf pan. Drizzle with 2 tablespoons of the espresso or coffee. Spread the ricotta mixture over the ladyfingers. Place another layer of ladyfingers over the ricotta mixture and drizzle with the remaining 2 tablespoons of espresso or coffee.

In a small bowl, mix together the cocoa powder and stevia. Using a fine-mesh sieve, dust the tiramisu with the cocoa powder mixture. Refrigerate until set, about 30 minutes.

SERVING SIZE: ⅙ of dessert
EXCHANGE LIST VALUES:
1 carbohydrate, ½ fat
CARBOHYDRATE CHOICES: 1
CALORIES: 118

CALORIES FROM FAT: 20
TOTAL FAT: 2 g
SATURATED FAT: 1 g
CHOLESTEROL: 52 mg
SODIUM: 52 mg

TOTAL CARBOHYDRATE: 19 g
FIBER: 1 g
TOTAL SUGARS: 9 g
PROTEIN: 4 g

No-Bake Cookies

MAKES 1 DOZEN COOKIES

These tasty, nutritious cookies contain agave syrup and unsweetened applesauce instead of sugar and butter. The simple recipe is easy for children to make and can be used to create several different types of cookies. Add your favorite ingredients to make your own unique cookies.

½   cup no-sugar-added peanut butter

½   cup agave syrup

¼   cup unsweetened applesauce

1½ cups nonfat dry milk

½   teaspoon salt

Mix together all the ingredients in a large bowl until smooth. Shape into golf ball–size pieces, then flatten. Store in an airtight container in the refrigerator for up to 3 days.

Continued on page 256

SERVING SIZE: 1 cookie
EXCHANGE LIST VALUES:
    1 carbohydrate, 1 fat
CARBOHYDRATE CHOICES: 1
CALORIES: 136

CALORIES FROM FAT: 51
TOTAL FAT: 6 g
SATURATED FAT: 1 g
CHOLESTEROL: 1 mg
SODIUM: 194 mg

TOTAL CARBOHYDRATE: 18 g
FIBER: 1 g
TOTAL SUGARS: 17 g
PROTEIN: 5 g

OAT AND RAISIN COOKIES: Add 2 cups of old-fashioned oats, 1½ cups of raisins, 1 teaspoon of vanilla extract, and ½ teaspoon of ground cinnamon to the no-bake cookie dough and stir until blended; proceed with the recipe. Makes 3 dozen cookies.

SERVING SIZE: 1 cookie
EXCHANGE LIST VALUES:
  1 carbohydrate
CARBOHYDRATE CHOICES: 1
CALORIES: 80

CALORIES FROM FAT: 20
TOTAL FAT: 2 g
SATURATED FAT: 0 g
CHOLESTEROL: 0 mg
SODIUM: 65 mg

TOTAL CARBOHYDRATE: 14 g
FIBER: 1 g
TOTAL SUGARS: 9 g
PROTEIN: 3 g

CRUNCHY COOKIES: Stir 4 cups of crispy rice cereal into the no-bake cookie dough until blended; proceed with the recipe. Makes 3 dozen cookies.

SERVING SIZE: 1 cookie
EXCHANGE LIST VALUES:
  ½ carbohydrate
CARBOHYDRATE CHOICES: ½
CALORIES: 57

CALORIES FROM FAT: 17
TOTAL FAT: 2 g
SATURATED FAT: 0 g
CHOLESTEROL: 0 mg
SODIUM: 81 mg

TOTAL CARBOHYDRATE: 9 g
FIBER: 0 g
TOTAL SUGARS: 6 g
PROTEIN: 2 g

COCOA–PEANUT CLUSTERS: Stir ¼ cup unsweetened cocoa powder, 2 cups roasted peanuts, and 1 teaspoon vanilla extract into the no-bake cookie dough until blended; proceed with the recipe. Makes 3 dozen cookies.

SERVING SIZE: 1 cookie
EXCHANGE LIST VALUES:
  ½ carbohydrate, 1 fat
CARBOHYDRATE CHOICES: ½
CALORIES: 95

CALORIES FROM FAT: 54
TOTAL FAT: 6 g
SATURATED FAT: 1 g
CHOLESTEROL: 0 mg
SODIUM: 65 mg

TOTAL CARBOHYDRATE: 8 g
FIBER: 1 g
TOTAL SUGARS: 6 g
PROTEIN: 4 g

Chocolate-Dipped Strawberries and Cream

MAKES 6 SERVINGS

This twist on strawberries and cream is sweet, simple, and elegant. The creamy whipped topping can be used in place of high-calorie whipped cream in other recipes and can be flavored with a variety of extracts.

3   ounces unsweetened dark chocolate, chopped

1½   ounces semisweet chocolate, chopped

2   cups large strawberries with stems (about 12), washed and dried very well

CREAMY WHIPPED TOPPING

1   cup low-fat Greek-style yogurt

¼   cup agave syrup

¼   cup chopped toasted almonds, for garnish

Place the dark and semisweet chocolates in a medium stainless-steel bowl. Fill a medium saucepan with a couple inches of water and bring to a simmer over medium heat. Turn off the heat and set the bowl of chocolate over the water to melt. Stir until smooth. Alternatively, melt the chocolate in a microwave at half power for 1 minute; stir and then heat for another minute or until melted. Remove the chocolate from the heat.

Line a baking sheet with waxed paper or parchment paper. Holding a strawberry by the stem, dip the fruit into the chocolate, lift, and twist slightly, letting any excess chocolate fall back into the bowl. Set the strawberry on the lined pan. Repeat with the remaining strawberries. Set the strawberries aside until the chocolate sets, about 30 minutes.

To make the topping, whisk together the yogurt and agave syrup in a small bowl until creamy and fluffy. Store in an airtight container in the refrigerator for up to 2 weeks.

Place 3 tablespoons of the topping in the center of each of 6 small saucers. Place 2 strawberries in the center of the topping. Sprinkle with the almonds and serve immediately.

SERVING SIZE: 2 strawberries and 3 tablespoons topping
EXCHANGE LIST VALUES: 2 carbohydrate, 2 fat
CARBOHYDRATE CHOICES: 2

CALORIES: 214
CALORIES FROM FAT: 87
TOTAL FAT: 10 g
SATURATED FAT: 5 g
CHOLESTEROL: 3 mg

SODIUM: 18 mg
TOTAL CARBOHYDRATE: 29 g
FIBER: 1 g
TOTAL SUGARS: 25 g
PROTEIN: 6 g

Pecan–Praline Sweet Potato Pie

MAKES 1 9-INCH PIE

I've found that oven-roasted sweet potatoes greatly enhance the flavor of this pie. When baking sweet potatoes for a savory meal, prepare an extra-large one or two medium ones for this recipe. To bake a sweet potato, preheat the oven to 400°F and bake for 45 to 60 minutes, or until tender. Or, cook whole sweet potatoes in the microwave with the smaller ends pointed toward each other on high for 12 to 15 minutes, or until tender. Let cool, scoop out the flesh, and mash. Use now or freeze mashed flesh for up to 6 months.

SWEET POTATO PIE FILLING

1½ cups mashed cooked sweet potatoes (1 large or 2 medium sweet potatoes), or 1 (15-ounce) can no-sugar-added sweet potatoes, drained and mashed

⅓ cup nonfat evaporated skim milk

¼ cup firmly packed Splenda brown sugar blend

1 tablespoon whipped butter, melted

½ teaspoon vanilla extract

¼ teaspoon salt

½ teaspoon ground cinnamon

¼ teaspoon ground allspice

¼ teaspoon ground nutmeg

1 Light Pie Crust (recipe follows)

PECAN–PRALINE TOPPING

1 large egg

⅓ cup firmly packed Splenda brown sugar blend

¼ cup agave syrup

1 tablespoon whipped butter, melted

¼ teaspoon vanilla extract

⅔ cup chopped pecans

Continued on page 260

SERVING SIZE: ¹⁄₁₀ of pie	**CALORIES FROM FAT:** 106	**TOTAL CARBOHYDRATE:** 38 g
EXCHANGE LIST VALUES:	**TOTAL FAT:** 12 g	**FIBER:** 3 g
1½ carbohydrate, 1 starch, 2 fat	**SATURATED FAT:** 3 g	**TOTAL SUGARS:** 22 g
CARBOHYDRATE CHOICES: 2½	**CHOLESTEROL:** 23 mg	**PROTEIN:** 4 g
CALORIES: 282	**SODIUM:** 216 mg	

Adjust an oven rack on the bottom shelf. Preheat the oven to 350°F.

To make the filling, combine all the ingredients in a medium bowl and stir until combined. Spread the filling evenly into the pie crust.

To make the pecan topping, whisk the egg and brown sugar blend together in a medium bowl until blended. Add the agave syrup, butter, and vanilla and mix well. Stir in the pecans. Spread the pecan topping evenly over the sweet potato filling.

Bake for 45 to 55 minutes, or until a knife inserted near the center comes out clean. Remove from the oven and let cool completely on a wire rack. Refrigerate for at least 3 hours before serving.

VARIATIONS: Use 1½ cups pumpkin purée (see Smashing Pumpkins, page 240), or leave off the pecan–praline layer.

Light Pie Crust

MAKES TWO 9-INCH PIE CRUSTS

This recipe cuts down on the calories found in prepared crusts by using healthier ingredients such as whole-wheat pastry flour and stevia. The pie crusts can be frozen for up to 6 months.

1   cup all-purpose flour, plus
    more for sprinkling

1   teaspoon apple cider vinegar

½   cup ice water, plus more as needed

1   cup whole-wheat pastry flour

3   tablespoons stevia granulated sweetener

1   teaspoon salt

7   tablespoons butter-flavored or plain
    nonhydrogenated vegetable shortening

In a small bowl, whisk together ¼ cup of the all-purpose flour, the vinegar, and ice water. In a large bowl, combine the remaining ¾ cup of flour, the whole-wheat flour, stevia, and salt. Cut in the shortening, using a pastry cutter or 2 dinner knives, until the mixture resembles coarse cornmeal. Gradually stir in the vinegar mixture 3 tablespoons at a time, mixing gently until just blended. Add more water as needed until the dough forms a sticky ball and no excess flour remains in the bottom of the bowl.

On a lightly floured work surface, divide the dough in half. Press the halves into disks with the palm of your hand. Cover in plastic wrap and refrigerate for 1 hour. This allows the dough to become less resistant to rolling and for the shortening to become firmer, making the dough easier to handle.

SERVING SIZE: ¹⁄₁₀ of 1 crust
EXCHANGE LIST VALUES: ½ starch, ½ fat
CARBOHYDRATE CHOICES: ½
CALORIES: 85

CALORIES FROM FAT: 40
TOTAL FAT: 4 g
SATURATED FAT: 1 g
CHOLESTEROL: 0 mg
SODIUM: 117 mg

TOTAL CARBOHYDRATE: 10 g
FIBER: 1 g
TOTAL SUGARS: 0 g
PROTEIN: 1 g

Lightly spray a 9-inch pie pan with butter-flavored cooking spray. Remove one disk of dough from the refrigerator. Roll the dough out on a lightly floured work surface into an 11- or 12-inch round, turning the dough and sprinkling the work surface with additional flour as needed to keep it from sticking.

Roll the dough onto the rolling pin to transfer to the pie pan. Unroll the pie dough, starting at one side of the pie pan. Fit into the prepared pan. Tuck the excess pastry under and press the edges lightly with a fork, or pinch to crimp, as desired.

Baking Pie Crust

Some pie recipes direct that the pie crust be partially or fully baked before filling. Here are some tips for baking a pie crust:

PARTIALLY BAKED CRUST: For a filling that requires further baking, preheat the oven to 400°F. Prick the sides and bottom of the crust with a fork. If using the crust for fruit pies, lightly dust the bottom of the crust with 2 teaspoons of flour to prevent crust from becoming soggy. Place a piece of aluminum foil or parchment paper the size of the pie plate inside the crust. (You can use the bottom of the pie plate, draw around it, cut out a circle, and place it on the bottom of the pie crust.) Place dried beans or metal pie weights on the foil or paper in the bottom of the crust. This helps the crust to retain its shape. Bake 5 minutes, then carefully remove the foil or paper and weights. Let the crust cool and proceed with the recipe as directed.

FULLY BAKED PIE CRUST: For a recipe (such as a cream filling) requiring a pie crust that is already baked, place a piece of aluminum foil or parchment paper the size of the pie plate inside the crust. (You can draw around the pie plate, cut out a circle, and place it in the crust.) Place dried beans or metal pie weights in the foil or paper to help the crust retain its shape.

Bake for 5 minutes and then carefully remove the foil or parchment and weights. Bake 3 to 5 minutes, or until the fluted edge is golden brown. Let cool completely, then fill as directed.

Photo Credits

p. ii (left to right): great-niece Dezarae; oldest sister, Sandra; Angela and her husband, Michael; and granddaughter Anysa

p. xii: Angela and Michael

p. 7: Dezarae

p. 78 (left to right): Michael, daughter Deanna, and her husband, Patric

p. 89: Michael and Anysa

p. 121: youngest sister, Marcia

p. 123: nephew Evan

p. 131: mother, Angeline, and father, Howard

p. 205: Dezarae and grandmother Sandra

p. 238: Howard and Angela

p. 249: Niece Kendra and her daughter Dezarae

p. 264 (back row, left to right): Howard (brother), Marcia, Sandra, Anysa, Deanna, Patric, Michael, Angela, and Kendra

(front row, left to right): Evan, Howard (father), Angeline (mother), and Dezarae

Metric Conversions and Equivalents

METRIC CONVERSION FORMULAS

TO CONVERT	MULTIPLY
Ounces to grams	Ounces by 28.35
Pounds to kilograms	Pounds by .454
Teaspoons to milliliters	Teaspoons by 4.93
Tablespoons to milliliters	Tablespoons by 14.79
Fluid ounces to milliliters	Fluid ounces by 29.57
Cups to milliliters	Cups by 236.59
Cups to liters	Cups by .236
Pints to liters	Pints by .473
Quarts to liters	Quarts by .946
Gallons to liters	Gallons by 3.785
Inches to centimeters	Inches by 2.54

APPROXIMATE METRIC EQUIVALENTS

WEIGHT

¼ ounce	7 grams
½ ounce	14 grams
¾ ounce	21 grams
1 ounce	28 grams
1¼ ounces	35 grams
1½ ounces	42.5 grams
1²/₃ ounces	45 grams
2 ounces	57 grams
3 ounces	85 grams
4 ounces (¼ pound)	113 grams
5 ounces	142 grams
6 ounces	170 grams
7 ounces	198 grams
8 ounces (½ pound)	227 grams
16 ounces (1 pound)	454 grams
35.25 ounces (2.2 pounds)	1 kilogram

VOLUME

¼ teaspoon	1 milliliter
½ teaspoon	2.5 milliliters
¾ teaspoon	4 milliliters
1 teaspoon	5 milliliters
1¼ teaspoons	6 milliliters
1½ teaspoons	7.5 milliliters
1¾ teaspoons	8.5 milliliters
2 teaspoons	10 milliliters
1 tablespoon (½ fluid ounce)	15 milliliters
2 tablespoons (1 fluid ounce)	30 milliliters
¼ cup	60 milliliters
⅓ cup	80 milliliters
½ cup (4 fluid ounces)	120 milliliters
⅔ cup	160 milliliters
¾ cup	180 milliliters
1 cup (8 fluid ounces)	240 milliliters
1¼ cups	300 milliliters
1½ cups (12 fluid ounces)	360 milliliters
1²/₃ cups	400 milliliters
2 cups (1 pint)	460 milliliters
3 cups	700 milliliters
4 cups (1 quart)	0.95 liter
1 quart plus ¼ cup	1 liter
4 quarts (1 gallon)	3.8 liters

LENGTH

¹/₈ inch	3 millimeters
¼ inch	6 millimeters
½ inch	1¼ centimeters
1 inch	2½ centimeters
2 inches	5 centimeters
2½ inches	6 centimeters
4 inches	10 centimeters
5 inches	13 centimeters
6 inches	15¼ centimeters
12 inches (1 foot)	30 centimeters

COMMON INGREDIENTS AND THEIR APPROXIMATE EQUIVALENTS

1 cup uncooked white rice = 185 grams

1 cup all-purpose flour = 140 grams

1 stick butter (4 ounces • ½ cup • 8 tablespoons) = 110 grams

1 cup butter (8 ounces • 2 sticks • 16 tablespoons) = 220 grams

1 cup brown sugar, firmly packed = 225 grams

1 cup granulated sugar = 200 grams

OVEN TEMPERATURES

To convert Fahrenheit to Celsius, subtract 32 from Fahrenheit, multiply the result by 5, then divide by 9.

DESCRIPTION	FAHRENHEIT	CELSIUS	BRITISH GAS MARK
Very cool	200°	95°	0
Very cool	225°	110°	¼
Very cool	250°	120°	½
Cool	275°	135°	1
Cool	300°	150°	2
Warm	325°	165°	3
Moderate	350°	175°	4
Moderately hot	375°	190°	5
Fairly hot	400°	200°	6
Hot	425°	220°	7
Very hot	450°	230°	8
Very hot	475°	245°	9

Information compiled from a variety of sources, including *Recipes into Type* by Joan Whitman and Dolores Simon (Newton, MA: Biscuit Books, 2000); *The New Food Lover's Companion* by Sharon Tyler Herbst (Hauppauge, NY: Barron's, 1995); and *Rosemary Brown's Big Kitchen Instruction Book* (Kansas City, MO: Andrews McMeel, 1998).

Index

A

After-School Berry Smoothie, 55
almonds
  Deluxe Slow-Cooker Oatmeal, 43
  Flourless Almond Mini Cakes with Mixed-
    Berry Topping, 237–38
  in freezer, xv
  as garnish, 257
  homemade almond butter, 235
  homemade almond flour and almond
    meal, 235
  Light Banana Pudding, 252
  nutritional content, 69
  Pumpkin–Nut Bars, 239
  as Quick Snack Fix, 67
  quinoa served with, 187
  Sweet Balsamic-Glazed Almonds, 69
amaranth
  Cinnamon Multigrain Breakfast Cereal, 44
  nutritional content, 45
American Dietetic Association, 15
anthocyanins, 132
antioxidants
  beans, 199
  eggplant, 132
  fruit smoothies, 21
  mushrooms, 136
  pumpkin, 239
  watermelon, 91
appetite control, breakfast and, 15
apples
  Apple Cider Glaze, 30
  Apple–Cinnamon Syrup, 39
  Apple–Pecan Pork Chops, 135
  Apple-Stuffed Waffle Sandwiches, 39
  Carolina Coleslaw, 74
  Chicken and Apples with Lemon Balsamic
    Sauce, 143
  Cinnamon–Apple Chips, 56
  Deluxe Slow-Cooker Oatmeal, 43
  Instant Oatmeal, 37
  as Quick Snack Fix, 65
Asian-style dishes
  Asian-Style Asparagus with Walnuts, 196
  Asian-Style Chicken Wraps, 153
  Asian-Style Salmon and Cabbage Salad
    with Ginger–Soy Dressing, 82
  Ginger Beef Stir-Fry With Soba Noodles,
    126–27
  Stir-Fried Cherry Chicken with Diva-Style
    Sweet and Sour Sauce, 150
asparagus
  Asian-Style Asparagus with Walnuts, 196
  Creamy Veggie Rice, 200
  Microwave Asparagus with Lemon
    Butter, 193
  nutritional content, choosing, preparation
    of, 194
athletes, eating patterns of, 71

B

bacon
  Canadian Bacon, 27, 30
  Microwave Breakfast Bowl, 34
  Baked Catfish with Green Onion and Butter
    Sauce, 162–63
bananas
  Frozen Yogurt-Dipped Banana Pops, 60
  Light Banana Pudding, 252
  Barbecue Burgers, 93
barley, 44
basil, fresh, 98, 109, 144, 209, 210, 214
beans. See also black-eyed peas; garbanzo
  beans; green beans
  Crunchy Chili Beans, 53
  Fiesta Tacos, 188
  Hot From-Texas Hummus, 8
  nutritional content, 199
  Power Smoothie, 22
  Quick Black Bean Breakfast Tacos, 36
  Smoky Red Beans and Rice, 198
  Soul Food Spread, 50
  Three-Bean Soup, 107
  Turkey Enchiladas, 160
beef
  Beef Fajitas, 124
  Beefy Mini Meat Loaves, 116
  Chili–Cheese Dip, 7
  French Dip Sandwiches, 125
  Garlic Flank Steak, 120–21
  Ginger Beef Stir-Fry With Soba Noodles,
    126–27
  lean deli meats, 57
  Roast Beef Sliders with Spicy Walnut
    Mustard, 97
  Texas-Style Beef Stew, 122
berries. See also fruit
  After-School Berry Smoothie, 55
  Berry Topping, 237
  Chocolate-Dipped Strawberries and
    Cream, 257
  Flourless Almond Mini Cakes with Mixed-
    Berry Topping, 237–38
  French Tortilla Toast, 46
  Fruity Tofu Smoothie, 23
  Power Smoothie, 22
  as Quick Snack Fix, 53
beverages. See drinks
Biscuit Topping, 248
black-eyed peas
  Black-Eyed Pea Cakes, 197
  Southern Salad, 75
blood sugar
  breakfast impacting, 15
  garbanzo beans and, 53
  snacks impacting, 49
Blue Cheese Dressing, 9
breads
  Buttermilk Bran Muffins, 40

Buttermilk Corn Bread, 246
Cheese, Garlic, and Jalapeño Biscuits,
  233–34
Herb or Spiced Biscuits, 233
Quick Sweet Potato Bread, 231
reading labels on, 71
Whole-Wheat Biscuits, 232
breakfast
  appetite control, breakfast and, 15
  Apple Cider Glaze for Canadian Bacon, 30
  Apple–Cinnamon Syrup, 39
  Apple-Stuffed Waffle Sandwiches, 39
  Buttermilk Bran Muffins, 40
  Canadian Bacon, 27
  Cinnamon Multigrain Breakfast Cereal, 44
  Deluxe Slow-Cooker Oatmeal, 43
  Farmer's Market Veggie Juice, 17
  French Tortilla Toast, 46
  Fruit Basket Butter, 48
  Fruity Tofu Smoothie, 23
  Green Tea Cider Refresher, 19
  Healthy Breakfast Sausage, 32
  Hot Pepper Glaze for Canadian Bacon, 30
  importance of, 15
  Instant Oatmeal, 37
  Mexican Hot Chocolate, 19
  Microwave Breakfast Bowl, 34
  Microwave Breakfast Sandwich, 35
  Mini Cheese Quiches, 42
  Mini Oatmeal Pancakes with Fruit Basket
    Butter, 47–48
  Mocha Morning Smoothie, 24
  Peach Tea Smoothie, 25
  Peanut Butter Breakfast Bars, 33
  Power Smoothie, 22
  Quick Black Bean Breakfast Tacos, 36
  quinoa for, 186–87
  Spinach and Tomato Crustless Quiche, 41
  Turkey Chorizo, 31
broccoli
  Broccoli and Carrots with Orange–Mustard
    Sauce, 202
  Cheesy Broccoli and Noodles, 203
  Pasta, Broccoli, and Lentil Salad with Greek
    Dressing, 80
Broiled Pimiento Cheese and Roasted Tomato
  Sandwiches, 98
Brussels sprouts, 191, 192
Buffalo-Style Stuffed Eggs, 63
bulgur wheat
  Cinnamon Multigrain Breakfast Cereal, 44
  Mixed Greens with Okra and Bulgur, 216–17
  Shrimp and Bulgur Risotto, 169
buttermilk
  Buttermilk Bran Muffins, 40
  Buttermilk Corn Bread, 246
  Buttermilk Pecan-Crusted Tilapia, 180

C

cabbage
  Asian-Style Salmon and Cabbage Salad
    with Ginger-Soy Dressing, 82
  Carolina Coleslaw, 74
  Chinese Cabbage Soup, 108
  Microwave Egg Foo Yung Cabbage
    Wrap, 103
Cajun Popcorn, 67
cakes
  Cinnamon-Pecan Cake, 243
  Flourless Almond Mini Cakes with Mixed-
    Berry Topping, 237-38
  Fudge Pudding Cake, 250
  Heavenly Tiramisu, 253
  Pineapple Upside-Down Cake, 245
calcium, 50
calories, 50
Calypso Coconut Shrimp Salad with Island
  Vinaigrette, 84
Canadian Bacon, 27, 30
Carolina Coleslaw, 74
cheese
  Blue Cheese Dressing, 9
  Broiled Pimiento Cheese and Roasted To-
    mato Sandwiches, 98
  Cheese, Garlic, and Jalapeño Biscuits,
    233-34
  Cheesy Broccoli and Noodles, 203
  Chili-Cheese Dip, 7
  Creamy Veggie Rice, 200
  Fiesta Tacos, 188
  Mini Cheese Quiches, 42
  Mini Muffulettas, 94
  Pumpkin and Tortellini Soup with Feta
    Cheese Croutons, 105
  Quick Black Bean Breakfast Tacos, 36
  Three-Cheese Dip, 6
  Veggie Lasagne, 184
cherries, 150-51
chicken
  Asian-Style Chicken Wraps, 153
  Barbecue Burgers, 93
  Chicken and Apples with Lemon Balsamic
    Sauce, 143
  Chicken Lollipops, 148
  Creole Chicken Stew, 110
  Crispy Roasted Chicken, 140
  Jerk Chicken Salad with Tropical Fruit
    Dressing, 77-79
  nutritional content, 145
  Open-Faced Chicken Salad Sandwiches, 100
  Peppercorn Chicken, 146
  Quick Curried Chicken, 139
  rotisserie, 138
  Southern Salad, 75
  Spaghetti and Chicken Meatballs, 144
  Stir-Fried Cherry Chicken with Diva-Style
    Sweet and Sour Sauce, 150
children, breakfast importance for, 15
Chili-Cheese Dip, 7

chocolate
  Chocolate Popcorn, 65
  Chocolate-Dipped Strawberries and
    Cream, 257
  Cocoa-Peanut Clusters, 256
  diabetic choices for, 49
  Heavenly Tiramisu, 253
  Mexican Hot Chocolate, 19
cholesterol-low foods, 15, 20, 24, 91
  amaranth, 45
  black-eyed peas, 75
  cabbage, 108
  cherries, 150-51
  Fire-Roasted Tomato and Kale Soup, 109
  garbanzo beans, 53
  Ginger Beef Stir-Fry With Soba Noodles,
    126-27
  Mixed Greens with Okra and Bulgur, 216-17
  Oven-Fried Trout with Papaya Sauce,
    171-72
  Spicy Vinaigrette, 11
Cinnamon Multigrain Breakfast Cereal, 44
Cinnamon-Apple Chips, 56
Cinnamon-Pecan Cake, 243
Cinnamon-Spiced Walnuts, 70
cobbler, 248
Cocoa-Peanut Clusters, 256
coconut, sweetened, toasting technique, 239
complex carbohydrates, 50
condiments. See also dressings
  Orange-Mustard Sauce, 202
  prepackaged vs. homemade, 71
  Spicy Walnut Mustard, 96, 97
cookies
  Cocoa-Peanut Clusters, 256
  Crunchy Cookies, 256
  No-Bake Cookies, 255
  Oat and Raisin Cookies, 256
corn, 169, 188
cornmeal, 167
couscous, 209-10
crab, 58-59
Cracker Snack Mix, 64
Cream Sauce, 212
Creamy Mushroom Sauce, 213
Creamy Veggie Rice, 200
Creamy Whipped Topping
  for Chocolate-Dipped Strawberries and
    Cream, 257
  for Light Banana Pudding, 252
Creole Chicken Stew, 110
Crispy Oven-Fried Onion Rings, 220
Crispy Roasted Chicken, 140
croutons, Feta Cheese Croutons, 106
Crunchy Chili Beans, 53
Crunchy Cookies, 256
Crunchy Fish Sticks, 167
Crunchy Kohlrabi Sticks, 57

D

dairy products, healthy choices for, 50. See
  also buttermilk; cheese; yogurt,
Deluxe Slow-Cooker Oatmeal, 43

dinner
  Apple-Pecan Pork Chops, 135
  Asian-Style Chicken Wraps, 153
  Baked Catfish with Green Onion and Butter
    Sauce, 162-63
  Beef Fajitas, 124
  Beefy Mini Meat Loaves, 116
  Buttermilk Pecan-Crusted Tilapia, 180
  Chicken and Apples with Lemon Balsamic
    Sauce, 143
  Chicken Lollipops, 148
  Crispy Roasted Chicken, 140
  Crunchy Fish Sticks, 167
  at the dinner table, 113
  Diva-licious Potpie, 182
  Fast Turkey Patties with Maple-Rosemary
    Sauce, 156-57
  Fiesta Tacos, 188
  Five-Spice Fish, 168
  French Dip Sandwiches, 125
  Garlic Flank Steak, 120-21
  Greek-Style Lamb-Stuffed Eggplant, 130
  Italian-Style Microwave Salmon, 173
  Jamaican-Style Fish en Papillote, 178
  Lamb and Sweet Potato Casserole, 134
  Microwave Meat-Stuffed Bell Peppers, 117
  Orange Pepper Shrimp and Texmati Rice,
    175-76
  Oven-Fried Trout with Papaya Sauce,
    171-72
  Peppercorn Chicken, 146
  Pork and Mushroom Stroganoff, 136
  Quick Creole Cod, 166
  Quick Curried Chicken, 139
  Salmon Cakes with Dill Sauce, 177
  Salsa Verde Pork, 137
  Shrimp and Bulgur Risotto, 169
  Spaghetti and Chicken Meatballs, 144
  Stir-Fried Cherry Chicken with Diva-Style
    Sweet and Sour Sauce, 150
  Texas-Style Beef Stew, 122
  Turkey Enchiladas, 160
  Turkey Sausage and Peppers Pasta, 154
  Veggie Lasagne, 184
dips. See also French Dip Sandwiches
  Chili-Cheese Dip, 7
  Hot From-Texas Hummus, 8
  Soul Food Spread, 50
  Spicy Pita Chips with, 5
  Three-Cheese Dip, 6
Diva-licious Potpie, 182
Diva-Style Sweet and Sour Sauce, 150
dressings. See also Southern-Style Dressing
  (side dish)
  Blue Cheese Dressing, 9
  Ginger-Soy Dressing, 83
  Greek Dressing, 81
  Honey-Mustard Dressing, 89
  Island Vinaigrette, 85
  Italian Garlic and Herb Salad Dressing, 10
  Lite Dressing, 73
  Mediterranean-Style Dressing, 92
  Pear and Walnut Salad, 86
  Spicy Vinaigrette, 11
  Tropical Fruit Dressing, 79

dried fruits, 225
drinks
    After-School Berry Smoothie, 55
    Farmer's Market Veggie Juice, 17
    Fruity Tofu Smoothie, 23
    Green Tea Cider Refresher, 19
    Mocha Morning Smoothie, 24
    Peach Tea Smoothie, 25
    Power Smoothie, 22

E
Easy Fruit Cobbler, 248
Egg Foo Yung Cabbage Wrap, 103
eggplant
    antioxidants in, 132
    Greek-Style Lamb-Stuffed Eggplant, 130
    Grilled Eggplant and Peppers, 206
    nutritional content and preparation of, 207
    selection, storage, and preparation of, 133
eggs
    Buffalo-Style Stuffed Eggs, 63
    Hard-Cooked Eggs, 62, 63
    Microwave Breakfast Bowl, 34
    Microwave Breakfast Sandwich, 35
    Microwave Egg Foo Yung Cabbage
        Wrap, 103
    Mini Cheese Quiches, 42
    Spinach and Tomato Crustless Quiche, 41
enchiladas, 160–61

F
family dinner table, 113
Farmer's Market Veggie Juice, 17
Fast Turkey Patties with Maple–Rosemary
    Sauce, 156–57
Fiesta Tacos, 188
figs, 77–79
Fire-Roasted Tomato and Kale Soup, 109
fish. See also shrimp
    Asian-Style Salmon and Cabbage Salad
        with Ginger–Soy Dressing, 82
    Baked Catfish with Green Onion and Butter
        Sauce, 162–63
    Buttermilk Pecan-Crusted Tilapia, 180
    Crunchy Fish Sticks, 167
    Five-Spice Fish, 168
    Italian-Style Microwave Salmon, 173
    Jamaican-Style Fish en Papillote, 178
    nutritional content, storage, and preparation
        of, 164–65
    Oven-Fried Trout with Papaya Sauce,
        171–72
    Quick Creole Cod, 166
    rainbow trout, 170
    Salmon Cakes with Dill Sauce, 177
    sardines, 59, 73, 101
    Seafood Burgers, 95
    Tuna–Sunchoke Salad Niçoise with Honey–
        Mustard Dressing, 88–89
Flourless Almond Mini Cakes with Mixed-
    Berry Topping, 237–38
freezer
    make-ahead meals from, 158–59
    stocking of, xv

French Dip Sandwiches, 125
French Tortilla Toast, 46
fruit. See also apples; berries
    After-School Berry Smoothie, 55
    antioxidants in, 21
    cherries as "superfruit," 151
    dried, 225
    Easy Fruit Cobbler, 248
    Frozen Yogurt-Dipped Banana Pops, 60
    Fruit Basket Butter, 48
    Fruity Tofu Smoothie, 23
    Light Banana Pudding, 252
    in Moroccan-Style Slow-Cooked
        Vegetables, 225
    Papaya Sauce, 171–72
    Peach Tea Smoothie, 25
    pomegranate, 79
    refrigerator stocked with, xiii
    scaling down meat and increasing, 213
    in smoothies, 21
    Tropical Fruit Dressing, 79
Fudge Pudding Cake, 250

G
garbanzo beans
    blood sugar and, 53
    Crunchy Chili Beans, 53
    Hot From-Texas Hummus, 8
    pantry stocked with, x
    Two-Chick Salad with Mediterranean-Style
        Dressing, 92
Garlic Flank Steak, 120–21
Ginger Beef Stir-Fry With Soba Noodles,
    126–7
Ginger–Soy Dressing, 83
glazes
    Apple Cider Glaze, 30
    Hot Pepper Glaze, 30
    Sweet Balsamic-Glazed Almonds, 69
glucose levels, snacks and energizers for,
    49–50
Greek Dressing, 81
Greek-Style Lamb-Stuffed Eggplant, 130
green beans
    Holiday Green Bean Casserole, 211–12
    Microwave Lemon and Garlic Green
        Beans, 214
    nutritional content, 213
    Sunflower Green Beans, 215
    Tuna–Sunchoke Salad Niçoise with Honey–
        Mustard Dressing, 88–89
Green Onion and Butter Sauce, 163
Green Tea Cider Refresher, 19
greens
    cleaning, storage, and preparation, 217
    Fire-Roasted Tomato and Kale Soup, 109
    Kale with Garlic and Lemon, 224
    Mixed Greens with Okra and Bulgur, 216–17
Grilled Eggplant and Peppers, 206

H
ham, 94
Hard-Cooked Eggs, 62, 63
Hashed Brussels Sprouts, 191

Healthy Breakfast Sausage, 32
Heavenly Tiramisu, 253
Herb or Spiced Biscuits, 233
Herb-Roasted Vegetables, 228
Holiday Green Bean Casserole, 211–12
Honey–Mustard Dressing, 89
Hot From-Texas Hummus, 8
Hot Pepper Glaze, 30

I
Instant Oatmeal, 37
Island Vinaigrette, 85
Italian Garlic and Herb Salad Dressing, 10
Italian-Style Microwave Salmon, 173

J
Jamaican-Style Fish en Papillote, 178
Jerk Chicken Salad with Tropical Fruit
    Dressing, 77–79
junk food, homemade snacks vs., 49–50

K
Kale with Garlic and Lemon, 224
Kickin' Barbecue Sauce, 12
The Kitchen Diva's Seasoning Mix, 13
kitchen guide
    freezer, xv
    pantry, x–xi
    refrigerator, xii–xiii
    spices, xiv
kohlrabi
    Crunchy Kohlrabi Sticks, 57
    Kohlrabi Cakes, 218
    nutritional content, choosing, and storage
        of, 219

L
lamb
    Greek-Style Lamb-Stuffed Eggplant, 130
    Lamb and Sweet Potato Casserole, 134
    Spiced Lamb Shanks, 129
Lemon and Herb Cauliflower Couscous,
    209–10
lentils, 80
Light Banana Pudding, 252
Light Pie Crust, 261–62
Lite Dressing, 73
lunch
    Asian-Style Salmon and Cabbage Salad
        with Ginger–Soy Dressing, 82
    Barbecue Burgers, 93
    Broiled Pimiento Cheese and Roasted
        Tomato Sandwiches, 98
    Calypso Coconut Shrimp Salad with Island
        Vinaigrette, 84
    Carolina Coleslaw, 74
    Chinese Cabbage Soup, 108
    Creole Chicken Stew, 110
    Fire-Roasted Tomato and Kale Soup, 109
    Jerk Chicken Salad with Tropical Fruit
        Dressing, 77
    Microwave Egg Foo Yung Cabbage
        Wrap, 103
    Microwave Veggie Tortilla Wraps, 102
    Mini Muffulettas, 94

lunch *(continued)*
  Open-Faced Chicken Salad Sandwiches, 100
  as part of diabetic meal plan, 71
  Pasta, Broccoli, and Lentil Salad with Greek
    Dressing, 80
  Pear and Walnut Salad, 86
  Pumpkin and Tortellini Soup with Feta
    Cheese Croutons, 105
  Roast Beef Sliders with Spicy Walnut
    Mustard, 97
  Sardine Toasts, 101
  Seafood Burgers, 95
  Slim Caesar with Lite Dressing, 73
  Slow-Cooker Curry Stew, 112
  Southern Salad, 75
  Sweet and Sour Watermelon and Cucumber
    Salad, 91
  Three-Bean Soup, 107
  Tuna-Sunchoke Salad Niçoise with Honey-
    Mustard Dressing, 88–89
  Two-Chick Salad with Mediterranean-Style
    Dressing, 92

M

Maple–Rosemary Sauce, 157
marinade
  Beef Fajitas, 124
  Crunchy Kohlrabi Sticks, 57
  Garlic Flank Steak, 120–21
  Ginger Beef Stir-Fry With Soba Noodles,
    126–27
  Ginger–Soy Dressing, 83
  Jerk Chicken Salad with Tropical Fruit
    Dressing, 77–79
  Orange Pepper Shrimp and Texmati Rice,
    175–76
  Spiced Lamb Shanks, 129
  Spicy Vinaigrette, 11
meat. *See* beef; chicken; fish; lamb; pork
Meatless Monday, 181
Mediterranean-Style Dressing, 92
Mexican Hot Chocolate, 19
  Creamy Whipped Topping for, 257
microwave
  benefits of, 118–19
  Italian-Style Microwave Salmon, 173
  Microwave Asparagus with Lemon Butter,
    193
  Microwave Breakfast Bowl, 34
  Microwave Breakfast Sandwich, 35
  Microwave Egg Foo Yung Cabbage
    Wrap, 103
  Microwave Lemon and Garlic Green
    Beans, 214
  Microwave Meat-Stuffed Bell Peppers, 117
  Microwave Veggie Tortilla Wraps, 102
  pumpkin cooking by, 240–41
midmorning snacks. *See* snacks and energizers;
    Quick Snack Fix
millet, 44
Mini Cheese Quiches, 42
Mini Muffulettas, 94

Mini Oatmeal Pancakes with Fruit Basket
  Butter, 47–48
Mixed Greens with Okra and Bulgur, 216–17
Mocha Morning Smoothie, 24
Moroccan-Style Slow-Cooked Vegetables, 225
mushrooms
  antioxidants, 136
  Creamy Mushroom Sauce, 213
  Pork and Mushroom Stroganoff, 136

N

No-Bake Cookies, 255
nori seaweed wrap, 58–59
nut butters
  homemade almond butter, 235
No-Bake Cookies, 255
  Peanut Butter Breakfast Bars, 33
  as Quick Snack Fix, 67
nuts. *See also* almonds; peanuts; pecans;
    walnuts
  in freezer, xv
  in Fudge Pudding Cake, 250
  homemade almond flour and almond
    meal, 235
  Instant Oatmeal with, 37
  in Light Banana Pudding, 252
  pantry stocked with, xi
  as Quick Snack Fix, 67
  toasting technique, 86

O

oats
  Deluxe Slow-Cooker Oatmeal, 43
  Instant Oatmeal, 37
  Mini Oatmeal Pancakes with Fruit Basket
    Butter, 47–48
  Oat and Raisin Cookies, 256
okra, 110
  Herb-Roasted Vegetables, 228
  Mixed Greens with Okra and Bulgur, 216–17
  Open-Faced Chicken Salad Sandwiches, 100
Orange Pepper Shrimp and Texmati Rice,
  175–76
Orange–Mustard Sauce, 202
Oven-Fried Trout with Papaya Sauce, 171–72

P

Papaya Sauce, 172
parsley, 8, 52, 63, 81, 85, 89, 101, 109, 126–27,
  136, 144, 225
  Fast Turkey Patties with Maple–Rosemary
    Sauce, 156–57
  Herb or Spiced Biscuits, 233
  Parsley–Walnut Pesto, 3
  Roasted Tomatoes Stuffed with Lemon and
    Herb Cauliflower Couscous, 209–10
pasta
  Cheesy Broccoli and Noodles, 203
  Pasta, Broccoli, and Lentil Salad with Greek
    Dressing, 80
  Spaghetti and Chicken Meatballs, 144
  Turkey Sausage and Peppers Pasta, 154
  Veggie Lasagne, 184
Peach Tea Smoothie, 25

peanut butter
  No-Bake Cookies, 255
  Peanut Butter Breakfast Bars, 33
  as Quick Snack Fix, 67
peanuts
  Cocoa–Peanut Clusters, 256
  Slow-Cooker Curry Stew, 112
Pear and Walnut Salad, 86
Pecan–Praline Sweet Potato Pie, 258
pecans
  Apple–Pecan Pork Chops, 135
  Buttermilk Pecan-Crusted Tilapia, 180
  Cinnamon–Pecan Cake, 243
  in freezer, xv
  Fudge Pudding Cake, 250
  Instant Oatmeal, 37
  Light Banana Pudding, 252
  pantry stocked with, xi
Pecan–Praline Sweet Potato Pie, 258
Peppercorn Chicken, 146
peppercorns, varieties of, 147
pie
  baking of crust, 263
  Light Pie Crust, 261–62
  Pecan–Praline Sweet Potato Pie, 258
pineapple
  Calypso Coconut Shrimp Salad with Island
    Vinaigrette, 84
  celery with ricotta and pineapple, 59
  Jerk Chicken Salad with Tropical Fruit
    Dressing, 77–79
  Pineapple Upside-Down Cake, 245
pomegranate, 79
popcorn
  Cajun Popcorn, 67
  Chocolate Popcorn, 65
  as snack, 49
pork
  Apple–Pecan Pork Chops, 135
  Barbecue Burgers, 93
  Canadian Bacon, 27, 30
  Healthy Breakfast Sausage, 32
  lean deli meats, 57
  Pork and Mushroom Stroganoff, 136
  Salsa Verde Pork, 137
potatoes
  Creole Chicken Stew, 110
  Diva-licious Potpie, 182
  Herb-Roasted Vegetables, 228
  Lamb and Sweet Potato Casserole, 134
  Moroccan-Style Slow-Cooked
    Vegetables, 225
  Salmon Cakes with Dill Sauce, 177
  Slow-Cooker Curry Stew, 112
Power Smoothie, 22
protein. *See also* specific meat
  amaranth, 44
  hard-cooked eggs, 62, 63
  lean deli meats, 57
  quinoa, 186–87
  sardines, salmon, tuna, or imitation
    crabmeat, 59
  in snacks and energizers, 50
  Soul Food Spread, 50
  vegetarian meals, 181
  whole grains with dairy, 70

pudding
Fudge Pudding Cake, 250
Light Banana Pudding, 252
pumpkin
nutritional content, choosing, and
preparation of, 240–41
Pumpkin and Tortellini Soup with Feta
Cheese Croutons, 105
Pumpkin–Nut Bars, 239
Taco-Spiced Pumpkin Seeds, 68

Q

Quick Black Bean Breakfast Tacos, 36
Quick Creole Cod, 166
Quick Curried Chicken, 139
Quick Snack Fix, 53
baby carrots, 59
celery with ricotta and pineapple, 59
frozen blueberries or grapes, 53
Frozen Yogurt–Dipped Banana Pops, 60
hard-cooked eggs, 62, 63
lean deli meats, 57
nuts, seeds, and nut butters, 67
ricotta on raisin bagel with apple or pear, 65
rye crackers with salsa and cheese, 70
sardines, salmon, tuna, or imitation
crabmeat, 59
tangerines, raisins, or diced peaches, 55
whole grains with dairy, 70
Quick Sweet Potato Bread, 231
quinoa
Fiesta Tacos, 188
nutritional value, 186–87

R

rainbow trout, 170
rice
Cinnamon Multigrain Breakfast Cereal, 44
Creamy Veggie Rice, 200
Creole Chicken Stew, 110
Fiesta Tacos, 188
Microwave Meat-Stuffed Bell Peppers, 117
Orange Pepper Shrimp and Texmati Rice,
175–76
Smoky Red Beans and Rice, 198
Texmati, 176
Roast Beef Sliders with Spicy Walnut
Mustard, 97
Roasted Brussels Sprouts, 192
Roasted Tomatoes Stuffed with Lemon and
Herb Cauliflower Couscous, 209–10

S

Sage Butter Sauce, 223
salads
Asian-Style Salmon and Cabbage Salad
with Ginger-Soy Dressing, 82
Feta Cheese Croutons for, 106
Jerk Chicken Salad with Tropical Fruit
Dressing, 77
Pasta, Broccoli, and Lentil Salad with Greek
Dressing, 80
Pear and Walnut Salad, 86
Slim Caesar with Lite Dressing, 73

Southern Salad, 75
Sweet and Sour Watermelon and Cucumber
Salad, 91
Tuna–Sunchoke Salad Niçoise with Honey–
Mustard Dressing, 88–89
Two-Chick Salad with Mediterranean-Style
Dressing, 92
salmon, 59
Asian-Style Salmon and Cabbage Salad
with Ginger-Soy Dressing, 82
Italian-Style Microwave Salmon, 173
Salmon Cakes with Dill Sauce, 177
Salsa Verde Pork, 137
sandwiches
Apple-Stuffed Waffle Sandwiches, 39
Barbecue Burgers, 93
Broiled Pimiento Cheese and Roasted To-
mato Sandwiches, 98
French Dip Sandwiches, 125
Microwave Breakfast Sandwich, 35
Mini Muffulettas, 94
Open-Faced Chicken Salad Sandwiches, 100
Roast Beef Sliders with Spicy Walnut
Mustard, 97
Sardine Toasts, 101
Seafood Burgers, 95
sardines, 59
Sardine Toasts, 101
Slim Caesar with Lite Dressing, 73
sauces
Chicken and Apples with Lemon Balsamic
Sauce, 143
Cream Sauce, 212
Creamy Celery Sauce, 213
Creamy Mushroom Sauce, 213
Enchilada Sauce, 161
Green Onion and Butter Sauce, 163
Kickin' Barbecue Sauce, 12
Maple-Rosemary Sauce, 157
Orange–Mustard Sauce, 202
Papaya Sauce, 172
Parsley–Walnut Pesto, 3
Sage Butter Sauce, 223
Salmon Cakes with Dill Sauce, 177
Stir-Fried Cherry Chicken with Diva-Style
Sweet and Sour Sauce, 150
Sautéed Sunchokes with Sage Butter
Sauce, 223
Seafood Burgers, 95
seaweed wrap, 58–59
serving size, 50
shrimp
Calypso Coconut Shrimp Salad with Island
Vinaigrette, 84
Orange Pepper Shrimp and Texmati Rice,
175–76
Shrimp and Bulgur Risotto, 169
side dishes
Asian-Style Asparagus with Walnuts, 196
Black-Eyed Pea Cakes, 197
Broccoli and Carrots with Orange–Mustard
Sauce, 202
Cheesy Broccoli and Noodles, 203
Creamy Veggie Rice, 200

Crispy Oven-Fried Onion Rings, 220
Grilled Eggplant and Peppers, 206
Hashed Brussels Sprouts, 191
Herb-Roasted Vegetables, 228
Holiday Green Bean Casserole, 211–12
Kale with Garlic and Lemon, 224
Kohlrabi Cakes, 218
Microwave Asparagus with Lemon
Butter, 193
Microwave Lemon and Garlic Green
Beans, 214
Mixed Greens with Okra and Bulgur, 216–17
Moroccan-Style Slow-Cooked
Vegetables, 225
Roasted Brussels Sprouts, 192
Roasted Tomatoes Stuffed with Lemon and
Herb Cauliflower Couscole, 209–10
Sautéed Sunchokes with Sage Butter
Sauce, 223
Smoky Red Beans and Rice, 198
Southern-Style Dressing, 204
Sunflower Green Beans, 215
Tomato, Squash, and Zucchini Gratin, 226
vegetables as, 189
Slim Caesar with Lite Dressing, 73
Slow-Cooker Curry Stew, 112
Smoky Red Beans and Rice, 198
smoothies
After-School Berry Smoothie, 55
freezing leftover, 50
fruit smoothies, 21
Fruity Tofu Smoothie, 23
Mocha Morning Smoothie, 24
Peach Tea Smoothie, 25
Power Smoothie, 22
snacks and energizers. See also Quick
Snack Fix
After-School Berry Smoothie, 55
Buffalo-Style Stuffed Eggs, 63
Cajun Popcorn, 67
Chocolate Popcorn, 65
Cinnamon–Apple Chips, 56
Cinnamon-Spiced Walnuts, 70
Cracker Snack Mix, 64
Crunchy Chili Beans, 53
Crunchy Kohlrabi Sticks, 57
glucose levels and, 49–50
Hard-Cooked Eggs, 62, 63
Hot From-Texas Hummus, 8
Soul Food Spread, 50
Spicy Pita Chips, 5
Sushi-Style Crab Roll, 58–59
Sweet Balsamic-Glazed Almonds, 69
Taco-Spiced Pumpkin Seeds, 68
soba noodles, 126–27
sorbet, 50
Soul Food Spread, 50
soups
Chinese Cabbage Soup, 108
Creole Chicken Stew, 110
Feta Cheese Croutons for, 106
Fire-Roasted Tomato and Kale Soup, 109
Pumpkin and Tortellini Soup with Feta
Cheese Croutons, 105

soups *(continued)*
   Slow-Cooker Curry Stew, 112
   Texas-Style Beef Stew, 122
   Three-Bean Soup, 107
Southern Salad, 75
Southern-Style Dressing (side dish), 204
soy milk
   Deluxe Slow-Cooker Oatmeal, 43
   Mini Cheese Quiches, 42
   Mini Oatmeal Pancakes with Fruit Basket
     Butter, 47–48
   Mocha Morning Smoothie, 24
Soyrizo, 184
Spaghetti and Chicken Meatballs, 144
Spencer, Percy, 118
spice mixes
   The Kitchen Diva's Seasoning Mix, 13
   No-Salt Spice Mix, 14
   Spiced Lamb Shanks, 129
   Spicy Pita Chips, 5
   Spicy Vinaigrette, 11
   Spicy Walnut Mustard, 97
spinach
   antioxidants, 132
   Southern Salad, 75
   Spinach and Tomato Crustless Quiche, 41
split peas, 112
Stir-Fried Cherry Chicken with Diva-Style
   Sweet and Sour Sauce, 150
sugars, reading labels to avoid, 50
sunchokes
   nutritional content and preparation of, 222
   Sautéed Sunchokes with Sage Butter
     Sauce, 223
   Tuna–Sunchoke Salad Niçoise with Honey–
     Mustard Dressing, 88–89
Sunflower Green Beans, 215
Sweet and Sour Sauce, 150
Sweet and Sour Watermelon and Cucumber
   Salad, 91
Sweet Balsamic-Glazed Almonds, 69
sweet finishes
   almond flour and almond meal, 235
   in balance and moderation, 229
   Buttermilk Corn Bread, 246
   Cheese, Garlic, and Jalapeño Biscuits,
     233–34
   Chocolate-Dipped Strawberries and
     Cream, 257
   Cinnamon–Pecan Cake, 243
   Cocoa-Peanut Clusters, 256
   Creamy Whipped Topping, 257
   Crunchy Cookies, 256
   Easy Fruit Cobbler, 248
   Flourless Almond Mini Cakes with Mixed-
     Berry Topping, 237–38

   Fudge Pudding Cake, 250
   Heavenly Tiramisu, 253
   Herb or Spiced Biscuits, 233
   Light Banana Pudding, 252
   Light Pie Crust, 261–62
   No-Bake Cookies, 255
   Oat and Raisin Cookies, 256
   Pecan-Praline Topping, 258
   Pineapple Upside-Down Cake, 245
   Pumpkin–Nut Bars, 239
   Quick Sweet Potato Bread, 231
   Sweet Potato Pie Filling, 258
   Whole-Wheat Biscuits, 232
sweet potatoes
   antioxidants, 132
   Lamb and Sweet Potato Casserole, 134
   Pecan–Praline Sweet Potato Pie, 258
   Quick Sweet Potato Bread, 231
syrup
   Apple–Cinnamon Syrup, 39

T
Taco-Spiced Pumpkin Seeds, 68
tagine, 138
Texas-Style Beef Stew, 122
Texmati Rice, 176
thecaloriecounter.com, 50
Three-Bean Soup, 107
Three-Cheese Dip, 6
tofu
   Broiled Pimiento Cheese and Roasted To-
     mato Sandwiches, 98
   Fruity Tofu Smoothie, 23
   Slim Caesar with Lite Dressing, 73
tomatillos, 137
tomatoes
   Broiled Pimiento Cheese and Roasted To-
     mato Sandwiches, 98
   Fire-Roasted Tomato and Kale Soup, 109
   Roasted Tomatoes Stuffed with Lemon and
     Herb Cauliflower Couscous, 209–10
   Spinach and Tomato Crustless Quiche, 41
   Tomato, Squash, and Zucchini Gratin, 226
tortilla, 46, 102
trail mix, homemade, 49
Tropical Fruit Dressing, 79
Tuna–Sunchoke Salad Niçoise with Honey–
   Mustard Dressing, 88–89
turkey
   Barbecue Burgers, 93
   Chili-Cheese Dip, 7
   Fast Turkey Patties with Maple–Rosemary
     Sauce, 156–57
   Healthy Breakfast Sausage, 32
   lean deli meats, 57
   Microwave Breakfast Bowl, 34

   Mini Cheese Quiches, 42
   Slow-Cooker Curry Stew, 112
   Smoky Red Beans and Rice, 198
   Turkey Chorizo, 31
   Turkey Enchiladas, 160
   Turkey Sausage and Peppers Pasta, 154
Two-Chick Salad with Mediterranean-Style
   Dressing, 92

V
vegetarian meals, 181
Veggie Lasagne, 184
vinaigrettes. *See also* dressings.

W
walnuts
   Asian-Style Asparagus with Walnuts, 196
   Cinnamon-Spiced Walnuts, 70
   in freezer, xv
   Parsley–Walnut Pesto, 3
   Pear and Walnut Salad, 86
   Roast Beef Sliders with Spicy Walnut
     Mustard, 97
watermelon
   choosing and storing of, 90
   Sweet and Sour Watermelon and Cucumber
     Salad, 91
whole grain
   amaranth, 44, 45
   on bread label, 71
   buckwheat (soba) noodles, 126–27
   bulgur wheat, 44, 144, 169, 177, 216–17
   Cinnamon Multigrain Breakfast Cereal, 44
   couscous, 209–10
   Cracker Snack Mix, 64
   French Tortilla Toast, 46
   millet, 44
   oats, 37, 43, 47–48, 256
   as Quick Snack Fix, 70
   quinoa, 186–87
   rice, 44, 110, 117, 175–76, 188, 198, 200
   in snacks and energizers, 50
   Whole-Wheat Biscuits, 232

Y
yellow squash
   Farmer's Market Veggie Juice, 17
   Tomato, Squash, and Zucchini Gratin, 226
yogurt
   low- or non-fat, 211–12
   low-fat Greek, 231
   soy, 55

Z
zucchini
   Tomato, Squash, and Zucchini Gratin, 226